ONE WOMAN WALKS EUROPE

Praise for Ursula's previous book

'A remarkable story of self-discovery through physical connection with the landscape, & of one woman's admirable bravery & bravado.' **Mslexia**

'A wonderful achievement, a remarkable story.' **Connie Fisher**

'Hilarious tales, often with a sweet but moral undertow.' **Morning Star**

'A rare combination of an epic tale of an extraordinary adventure and a delicately woven study of the kindness of random strangers. Hugely enjoyable.' **Clare Balding**

'Ursula Martin's candid account of her epic adventure tells an inspiring tale of fortitude, determination & generosity that leaves the reader breathless with admiration.' **Kate Humble**

'A remarkable story both of self-discovery through physical connection with the landscape and of one woman's admirable bravery and bravado.' ***The Bookseller***

'Brave, fierce, honest and deeply moving... a remarkable, arresting debut.' ***Justin Marozzi***

CONTENTS

Journey Roots	1
Journey Beginning	7
Getting There	9
Ukraine	15
Romania	61
Bulgaria	102
Serbia	121
Kosovo	145
Serbia	153
Hitch-hiking back to the UK	160
Visiting Tom in Albania	168
Serbia	174
Montenegro	181
Bosnia and Herzegovina	192
Entering the EU	220
Croatia and Slovenia	223
Italy	235
Fleeing	258
First Lockdown	268
France	275
Pyrenees Traverse	294
Second Lockdown	318
Entering Spain	323
Spain: The Arrival and the First Ending	342
Turning for Home	359
The Final Stretch	369
Journey End	374

To all the people I have been unable to name or thank, in addition to the ones who get a mention.

These steps have been supported by the energy, efforts and good wishes of thousands of people.

Compassion and community is the only way we're going to get through this.

JOURNEY ROOTS

I've walked 9,000 miles now, in two major journeys.

During a single decade I spent more than four years on foot.

'Why?' is usually the first question I get asked. 'How many pairs of boots?' and 'How do you charge your phone?' often come shortly after that.

It can feel insulting, as people look me up and down, their faces twisted in incomprehension, gaze running critically over my sweat-stained dishevelment, from the mad wisps escaping my ponytail down to my filthy boots. 'What are you doing to yourself?' I read in their eyes. 'How can this possibly be worth the effort?'

It's the hardest question to answer; if someone doesn't already understand why months spent coaxing your body to walk thousands of miles, completely alone, crossing the wilds on your own strength, would be totally worth it, then how do you find the words to convince them?

People only see the huge challenge of living for months at a time with all my possessions on my back, post-cancer, raising charity money, walking intense journeys of thousands of miles. They don't understand how I can be capable of it, how I could even conceive of such a thing.

My huge journeys didn't come out of nowhere, they have always been part of a progression. Don't start with a marathon, start with one small step, take a single action towards a distant goal, you can't judge how far that movement will take you.

I don't enjoy feeling misunderstood – it's a familiar unpleasantness, my long-held ache of being an odd one out, the weird kid. So when people ask why, it's easiest to say, 'Because I felt like it,' without attempting to shift the buried stone that is their lack of understanding.

I get tired of trying to convince people who don't understand the reward for all this effort. Of course it's worth it, it's the greatest experience I've ever had.

Everyone has dreams, don't they? To ride a horse across an open plain. To learn the trapeze. 'What if I was a rally driver?' we say to ourselves, and then carry on with the washing up. Most people see life in terms of qualifications, career, relationships, children, financial commitments; which wind up being a series of distractions from dreams.

I've always been one for the 'what if...?' What if we climbed that derelict crane on the way home from the pub? What if I bought a fire engine in an online auction? What if we glued shut the locks of every shop in town as a protest against capitalism? What if we hung some sheets off the rugby posts and showed a film out on the rec?

I'm not so good at keeping my nose to the grindstone of a steady job, but I do come up with some brilliant flights of fancy.

Where most people's 'what ifs?' dissolve back into the bong water of their stoner years, somehow I kept doing mine.

What if I walked the length of that river in Spain?

What if I kayaked the length of the Danube?

What if I walked to hospital?

These were my adult urges and I followed my nose and did them, allowing myself to become more spontaneous, masochistically testing myself and discovering my strength, showing myself who I was in a way I'd never been able to discover in the eyes of others.

Kayak east, walk west. That was my original idea, back in 2011.

I'd been travelling a couple of years by then, bumming around in Spain, working small survival jobs to save money for the next escape. I had kayaked the length of the Danube in a whirlwind of day drinking and beach picnics, experiencing an ill-advised affair with a controlling Serb and a near drowning, all as the kilometre markers counted down from 2,500 to 0. Everyone else went home at the river mouth, but the Serb and I continued to kayak south along the Black Sea coast and the journey finished with a mind-bending twenty-two-hour final stretch from Mangalia, Romania down to Varna, Bulgaria. We tied the kayaks behind a friendly yacht to ride the waves as aquatic hitch-hikers, then, from the safety of the boat, watched them submerge into a choppy moonlit sea as we rounded Cape Kaliakra. After hours of fighting to save my belongings from the seabed, I stepped onto the harbourside barefoot, all my shoes lost to the water.

Once I mustered the guts to send the Serb packing, I found a housesit in a remote Bulgarian village at the end of a back road on the autumnal brown Ludogorie plateau, planning to walk home to Wales the following spring.

But that walk never happened. I chopped a winter's worth of wood, hitch-hiked home for a supposedly brief Christmas visit, and then life lurched in a new direction with a diagnosis of ovarian cancer. Sleeping off New Year's Eve 2012 on a friend's sofa, I mentioned a strange feeling in my belly, wondering out loud about my sudden inability to bend or sit comfortably. The friend advised a doctor's visit and, fresh from the athletic peak of months spent outdoors kayaking thousands of kilometres, I thought I'd tick off a quick check-up before disappearing back to more adventures in Eastern Europe. But one GP referral led to another, then scans led to blood tests led to consultants, and six weeks later I underwent major abdominal surgery to remove an ovarian tumour. All my adventures, the travelling, hitch-hiking, kayaking, had meant total freedom to me, and I reeled in the life-limiting aftermath of a sudden cancer diagnosis, major surgery, and the vulnerability of facing a serious illness while staying on a friend's sofa.

The only fixed commitment in my life became a sequence of

hospital check-up appointments, a schedule of blood tests and scans stretching a full five years into the future, longer than I had ever been able to imagine my fragmented life before. The appointments were both security against the return of malignancy and a restrictive net, keeping my hitherto free life oscillating from a fixed point in time and space in a way it hadn't for years. To recover, I moved to Machynlleth and I walked. It was the simplest, most accessible way to recover my health. Eventually, six months post-diagnosis, I decided to follow the River Severn from the source near my home down to Bristol where I had my hospital appointments. Wild camping as I walked, this 400-mile journey down the Severn and up the Wye made me feel normal again. I still could get out there and challenge myself, even after cancer's attack on my body and mind. That first walk to hospital led, a year later, to a 3,700 mile walk across Wales, between cancer check-ups, a story told in my first book, *One Woman Walks Wales*.

After a whirlwind few years, where my only life plan was to respond to the challenge directly in front of me, I faced a sudden absence of direction as I came to the end of the Welsh journey.

Walking across Europe felt like the simplest thing to do next. It gave me a fully-formed plan to throw myself into, without my truly stopping to question what I was taking on.

Quite often, because I'm not always a very happy person and I express that in my writing, people think I have walked all those miles to seek or escape something; it's a simplistic reduction of such a complex journey. I had a pretty awful time when I was a child. There was violence in my home and then there was neglect, both emotional and physical. I spent most of my childhood being afraid and anxious, or frantically trying to pretend I was fine. I felt isolated from every child around me who seemed to be happy and functional, who didn't have their own overshadowing horror of a derelict, non-functional home life. As I grew up into a traumatised adult, with an internal void where any adequately loved child's sense of self would be, I had no idea who I was and made painful, bad decisions – of man, of education, of job. I dropped out of school and wound up at age 25 with two A levels gained through evening classes, and low level work experience in social care and office admin.

I don't feel it's the presence of these awful things that drove me to walk thousands of miles, it's the space they left in my life.

The artist Andy Goldsworthy goes for a solitary walk most days and makes what he calls 'interventions' with the land, creating art from sticks, leaves, stones or ice. He plays with nature, forming shapes from organic materials that are both completely natural and could never exist without him.

The works that make me pause the longest are when he creates absences, deliberate voids. He will pick long shafts of dry grass that can stand straight, piercing the strong stems with thorns to make a screen that hangs in the air, balanced against the ground, a tree trunk or a low hanging branch, vulnerable to the breeze. The centre of the screen is left deliberately empty; where the pieces end, there forms a circular hole. Negative space. Absence, that is also potential.

My walking journeys weren't a long-imagined choice, but as I grew from unresolved childhood trauma into an adulthood that was too messed up to fill successfully with the creation of babies or a career or healthy romantic relationships, the absence of those time-consuming, long-term commitments left a gap where potential shimmered and sparks of my creative imagination could breathe ideas into being.

This is inevitably a trauma story, because it's about what drives me as much as what I achieved; but it's not the story of that trauma, nor is it about how the journey healed me. Not every life gets lived as neatly as that.

This is just the story of a woman who walked across Europe.

Key:
— Walking Route
····· Diversion to meet Jan in Greece

Kyiv

UKRAINE

SLOVAKIA

HUNGARY

HOVERLA

MOLDOVA

APUSENI MOUNTAINS

THE CARPATHIANS

ROMANIA

SERBIA

REPUBLIC OF KOSOVO

BULGARIA

NORTH MACEDONIA

ALBANIA GREECE

TURKEY

JOURNEY BEGINNING

One by one I took the keys off my keyring and handed them to other people. No more house or office. No work, no vehicle, nothing left with me but what I could carry. I bought an apple in the veg shop, hugged the last person I saw with a frantic goodbye, and heaved my rucksack into the boot of my lift from Llanidloes, pulsating with nerves.

I was off to hitch-hike to Kyiv.

In 2012, when I kayaked east down the Danube, I had intended to cross the Black Sea to the Crimean Peninsula and explore Ukraine on foot, before cancer and the Welsh walk elbowed that dream aside. By 2018 when I managed to return, Crimea was no longer accessible.

In 2014, Ukrainian President Viktor Yanukovych had moved away from political alignment with the EU and re-established closer relations with Russia.

The Ukrainian people protested violently, Yanukovych was booted out, and in response Russia annexed Crimea, a crucial access point for their navy. After the indigenous inhabitants, the Crimean Tatars, were deported to Uzbekistan, mostly in 1944, and replaced with ethnic Russians, the peninsula was pro-Russian. A stage-managed referendum was hastily arranged, asking for a return to the Russian Federation.

A month later Donbas joined the dissent. The coal-producing region of eastern Ukraine is heavily industrialised, traditionally Russian-speaking, and with a high proportion of ethnic Russians (almost 40%). Seemingly organic local protests quickly turned into Russian-backed separatist action. Ukraine lost control of parts of its eastern provinces. Tentative ceasefire agreements remained barely respected.

This was the Ukraine I was walking into in September 2018, living with a constant threat from the north and suffering four years of fighting in the east. Thousands of lives had been lost, but life continued across the country. I couldn't enter Ukraine through a disputed border so the planned Crimean route was off the table and instead I started in Kyiv.

I was planning to walk from one edge of Europe to the other; starting in a country divided over joining the EU and finishing in a country divided over leaving it.

GETTING THERE

I have a hundred stories about hitch-hiking: the people who went out of their way for me, the lifts in unusual vehicles, the intimate stories I've heard of love, revenge, bereavement. The reaching out of my arm sends a questing thread into the air, waiting to be picked up and entwined with someone else's for a while, each car an unspooling of the line of someone's life. The in-between time of driving with a stranger becomes a liminal space that invites honesty, with no defining relationship boundaries and nothing to pass the time except the sharing of stories.

My funny hitching stories make for great party anecdotes: the guy in the Porsche who told me his secrets of war in Iraq and turned out to be an armed robber; the time I thumbed across Germany with a kayak. The deeper emotions of hitch-hiking don't get mentioned. The unfettered freedom of it, or how it feels to wait. As I stand by the side of a grey road, wild pulses of exhaust air blowing past me, there is a release of tension. I settle into the fact that I can no longer control how long it's going to take me to get somewhere, or who is going to stop and how far they are going. The worry drops away; all the frenzied preparations to get to the point of beginning are over and now I am simply doing it. I let go of time and expectation, abandon myself to circumstance and allow chance to take the lead. My urgency shrinks. I shrink, becoming a small thing under a wide-open sky, buffeted by the rushing wind of passing cars, standing where a slip road snakes towards connection with the roaring smash of fast motorway traffic.

The usual unusual hitch-hiking interactions took me from the ferry exit at Hook of Holland, through forty-eight hours thumbing my way to southern Poland. I met a polyamorous Dutch pharmacist, a placid man en route to collect his mother's ashes, and a Polish lorry driver heading to Russia with a load of bootleg whisky. I spent a wild night crossing Germany with Polish Marius, racing home for a treasured weekend with his children.

He drove nonstop for ten hours until 4am, by which time I had attempted to sleep in every conceivable position on the front seat. Then, when he finally parked up in front of his first delivery address, I was evicted into the back of the van to curl around the plastic wrapped pallets while he stretched across the front seat. Three hours later, he knocked on the side of the van. 'The factory is opening, time to get up and make the delivery.' I felt insane with tiredness; he was a force.

Fifty-five hours after leaving Wales, I stood dazed on the side of a long straight road somewhere in south-east Poland. Along came a battered red VW van with a Ukrainian plate, chugging slowly. The first Ukrainian vehicle I'd seen and, like a magic spell, as I raised my arm it slowed to a stop. A large-framed man with a thick, snuffly moustache levered himself out to heave my pack into the back, where it nestled amongst a surprising number of tyres. This was Vasyl, making his way home for two weeks of downtime after a three-month shift driving lorries across the EU. He shared food with me – bread, sausage, cucumber, tomato – and stopped to pick up another set of tyres in a village along the way. I gladly surrendered to these hours of slow, certain travel rather than risk waiting for a faster car.

Vasyl worried about taking me across the border.

'Do you have passport? Visa?'

I assured him there would be no problem. I could get a visa at the border.

'But for me, they will ask questions about why an English person is in the car.' This felt like a hangover from communist control but I didn't want to challenge him.

'Ok, then I will get out when you tell me and cross the border on foot, find another car on the other side.'

We nodded. It was set.

Bleary with the broken sleep of three adrenaline-fuelled days on the road, I bundled up my jacket to lean against my cold window as Vasyl smoked incessantly out of the other.

The glowing yellow moon rose in front of us as the van puttered away and I faded in and out of sleep, heater blaring burning air against my knees. Vasyl rubbed his eyes repeatedly and eventually, close to midnight, pulled over in a dark lay-by, 30km from the border.

'Pausa. I sleep.'

I couldn't get out there. The border was too far to walk in the dark and I knew I'd never get another lift at this time of night. 'Do you want me to get in the back?'

He made non-committal noises, leaned back to sleep sitting up, then abruptly folded over towards me, slumping his head onto my thigh. As I waited a beat to see if this was sexual, I realised he was already snoring. My surprised hand came down to rest on his shoulder and I leaned to doze against the window, smiling at the unexpected tableau.

He woke after an hour, stretched and yawned, and we continued towards the border. I tried to keep alert so I could get out at the final Polish village but it passed in a long blink and suddenly we were approaching the bright lights and long traffic queue of the Ukrainian border. I waited for Vasyl to say something as we inched forward, and eventually grabbed the phone we were using for translation.

'Do you want me to get out?'

'You can stay.'

He'd slept on my knee; there was trust between us now. We looked each other in the eye and nodded.

The queue was long and slow-moving, people getting out of their cars to walk and smoke, bright lights in the distance, bus passengers disembarking, and bodies in grey clothing milling around. Passports were handed over, taken away into a Polish building, brought back, the traffic queue passed over the river border to Ukrainian land inch by inch. Vasyl couldn't turn his van off, the battery wouldn't charge to restart it, so we idled, even when he stopped to sleep.

Finally we got out to be inspected at the Ukrainian blacked-out window; my reflection squinted at the deeper shadow of the big, bald man whose sausage fingers were holding my documents. Stamp. It was done – I was in. After so many months of planning and dreaming, I had actually made it to Ukraine.

We drove ahead along pitch-black roads without streetlights. The roads were immediately worse, the buildings shabbier. I had wanted to stay awake to see the sunrise as we headed east but could feel myself fading back towards sleep and Vasyl obviously felt the same. A faint dawn light tinged the trees dull green as he pulled over in the first town, derelict apartment buildings on either side of the road. I slapped my thigh in invitation and we both laughed as he curled over onto me, nestling his head onto my thigh, the engine purring as we slept.

The remaining 200 miles into the centre of the country took us a further five hours to drive. Even on the single-lane main highway the tarmac was cracked and pitted, creating a two-tier driving system where faster vehicles swerved in and out around slower cars and the bumpy, potholed road edges. I watched eagerly out of the window. What was this new country? It was the furthest east I'd ever travelled. Poland had been full of new houses, the country transformed in the last fifteen years of EU membership, but here there were much older wooden cabins, sometimes carefully tended, sometimes bushy with trailing greenery. I was surprised to see people walking along the road edge where I wouldn't expect them in the UK, old men shuffling with bundles of plastic bags, or women squatting beside trays of foraged fungus, patiently attempting roadside mushroom sales.

Vasyl showed me photos of the vehicles he'd rebuilt: bikes, cars and even a glider. He had a passion for boats. 'My father was captain of a boat in the Danube Delta. I was born on the water.'

He asked if he could get work as a boat mechanic in the UK, thinking that it was part of the Schengen Agreement, and I told him no. 'We sit separate on our island and think we are kings.'

'But the king is naked,' he said through the phone translation, and I shot him a sharp smile of agreement.

Once we reached Zhytomyr, Vasyl dropped me where the road split, him to turn south for Vinnytsia and me facing north-east for Kyiv, now only 200km away. I offered him a hand to shake, unsure of how a hug would be regarded, and he opened his arms to engulf me. My first Ukrainian interaction.

He left me at a great spot: the gas station at the beginning of the main highway towards Kyiv. It was a wide-open road, small clouds scudding in the blue sky. There was a huge metal arch crossing all six lanes, carrying the logo of the gas station, and I felt small and serene under this gigantic structure. Since the ferry, I'd slept four or five hours a night: in the back of a van, in a tent on the edge of a service station, and up against a van window with a man on my leg. Dazed and happy, no longer clinging to control, this journey was flowing and, following the whims of the road, I would make it all the way to Kyiv.

After maybe twenty minutes a jeep pulled in. Shades, baseball cap, takeaway coffee. 'We can speak English,' he said. 'I live in the USA.' Ivan was back for his annual visit, my age, pockmarked cheeks and blond hair, very money focused, a little abrasive, and talked more than he listened. Here was a man who was fifteen when

Ukraine left the Soviet Union and, in the economic free-for-all that followed, had learnt to take full part in the race for new riches: land ownership, house building, bragging about paying pocket change to local village drunks for their daily labour.

As we approached the capital city, the road dipped down and rose up again, allowing an incredible view of a broad avenue stretching a mile ahead, skyscrapers bristling in the distance. Here was Kyiv, the city I'd been aiming towards for so long.

This kind man took me on a tour of his city. We whirled past Saint Sophia's Cathedral, the tall motherland statue, looming dark embassies and government buildings, the jeep wheels rattling on ancient cobbles. Ivan drove a loop over the wide, quiet Dnieper river to the suburbs and back again, showing me river beaches and summer amusements. He gestured to a patch of high-rise apartments: 'Here used to be summer houses. We would come here to drink and swim in the river. Then they sold all, once the land became precious.' Ivan was constantly throwing out information about who owned what: stories of corruption; the riches pulled out of ex-president Yanukovych's house when he lost power; arson to gain building plots; stories of his friends growing up, the scrapes, the lucky escapes. He talked about political corruption: Akhmetov, the billionaire businessman with links to organised crime; the 'Chocolate King' oligarch, President Poroshenko's refusal to give up ownership of his businesses, despite promising to do so pre-election.

Ivan had played his small part in the 2013 revolution of the Euromaidan, as one of thousands gathered in Maidan Square in Kyiv to protest the government reversal of a move towards EU membership.

It was breathtaking, to be driven around this huge city and treated to a big soup bowl of politics, revolution and corruption stories, swirling around like the river current as we crossed bridges.

UKRAINE

The hostel was the same as that in any major European city – Wi-Fi on tap, pay extra for a towel, burgers and breakfast pancakes on an English-language menu. A bunch of fellow travellers, uniformly fifteen years younger than me, slumped on sofas staring at their phones, bonding in the smoking area, stumbling into our shared rooms at 4am and shagging in the bunkbeds. I felt very separate from their shenanigans, clumping around in unfashionable walking boots, eyes fixed on a solitary horizon, thinking about maps. I walked the streets a little and hung out in a restaurant near the hostel – Puzata Hata – pointed out by Ivan as doing real Ukrainian food but which turned out to be a chain, school dinner style, where you pull dishes off stainless steel shelves, without navigating a waiter or a menu.

I wasn't interested in the city, or any city really. I only wanted to take a few days there to rest and source maps. I was planning a south-westerly route towards the Romanian border and wanted to navigate by map and compass, as I had done in Wales. I'd been able to buy the touristic mountain areas online but needed the rest of the country. Andrew, an English contact working for the British Council, helped me find a map shop to fill in the gaps.

I had ninety days to walk 400 miles across agricultural central Ukraine before my visa ran out, more than enough time. Ninety days and a completely unforeseeable variety of experiences to fill them. Here was where the unknown started. I was about to slip sideways out of view, into the shadows of the trees.

I stuck to tarmac for the couple of days it took to reach the edge of the city, walking out to the end of the subway system and using it to skip back to my hostel at night while I still had the chance of a cheap bed. This was what it meant to me to walk every step: if I deviated from the route to find a bed or take time off, I'd always return to where I had stopped walking before continuing on. On the last day of Kyiv, I said a final goodbye to Andrew at the Podil metro station, rode the rattling train to the end of the network and faced the final scattered suburbs that blurred into forest.

Central Kyiv had been a city of flowing fabric, well-tailored dresses and smart suits, but people became noticeably less well dressed as I left my fashionable central district; the click of high heels and billowing long skirts downgraded to thick padded jackets and shuffling trainers.

The Bentleys and Mercedes had faded from the picture too. Here I passed rotten Ladas and nondescript Peugeots and Renaults – rusting family vehicles.

This was the spontaneity I was searching for: to walk out of Kyiv without knowing what lay ahead. It was terrifying and exciting but I was here to allow the unknown. This was the core of my journey style; to open myself to possibility, trusting that I had the character and skills to deal with whatever came.

Finally at the edge of the houses, I turned away from the road into pine forest, beginning a few hundred miles of flat land all the way to the Carpathian Mountains.

For months I had been declaring I was going to walk across Europe but this was where it became reality.

I'd brought myself to this point, telling everyone about it, making all the motions of preparation, and now here I was, plunging in, soft pines all around me, standing at a fork in the yellow path of sandy soil, my breath caught in my chest. To move myself forward through the momentary paralysis, I gave myself directions:

Check your map, make a compass bearing, and hold it up to the two options.
Take a deep breath.
Trust yourself; all your strengths and all your choices.
And begin.

This was a wholesome wood, a picnic wood close to town. The trees were widely spaced, light trickling through them to a sandy floor covered in criss-crossing tracks. I could easily follow the compass in the right direction and emerged from the forest into hot, bright sun and immense fields, miles of earth with green shoots of winter wheat emerging, undivided by hedge or fence. Picking around the edges of the turned earth, I found a yellow track that crossed the centre and headed south into a sharp horizon line of dusty sky and ploughed ground. There were no visible boundaries around farmland here; private land ownership was less than 25 years old in Ukraine, and the strict permissions and restrictions of UK land access were absent. Without official footpaths it seemed I could walk where I wanted.

An hour through fields and I came to pine forest again, another plantation, human-made. To my right, a twisted apple tree nestled amidst the shadowing pines. I stood with the tree for a few breaths, acknowledged it, small and mottled and surviving. I asked the forest to see me as I passed, to be benevolent. This felt like my first days in an unknown land – I needed to feel it, come to learn how I would live with it and travel on it.

Deep amongst the trees, after a few hours of walking, I came to a clearing where three men crouched around a fire. There was a moment of shock as we stared at each other, then my preservation instincts kicked in and I muttered a greeting, breaking eye contact to look ahead, keeping my stride purposeful. All the warnings about 'wild, dangerous' Ukraine, all the worry pressed upon me, all the messages I've absorbed throughout my life about the dangers of being a woman travelling alone were guiding me in that moment. 'Don't talk to strange men, beware of the forest, Ukraine is dangerous, there's a war happening there.' The men didn't call after me, just watched silently as I crossed the edge of the clearing. Once out of their sight, the track split into two. I wanted the village of Koshchiivka but wasn't sure which path to take. A thought flashed: *You could go and ask those men.*

It was completely against what I'm indoctrinated to do. 'Be hidden, don't draw attention to yourself, avoid danger, avoid unnecessary interactions.'

But it felt right. I turned around and walked back to where the three men crouched on the ground, watching me approach.

It was a birthday celebration. Nikolai was 52, big blue eyes beaming over a scar the width of his cheek, pinpoint suture marks still visible. Viktor and Ruslav had come with him to the forest to grill meat and get gently, irrevocably drunk.

It took a whirling of arms and many repetitions of words for us to exchange the simplest of facts, but I was invited to sit at a rickety table littered with plastic plates of gherkins and rice salad; cigarette packets, knives and dirty shot glasses scattered like Slavic seasoning. They poured me shots, slid dripping chunks of meat off thick metal skewers, tore bread with grimy fingers, and we took a few toasts.

Not long after I'd said goodbye, with handshakes all round, a loud roaring rose behind me and I turned to see Nikolai chasing after me on the most incredibly ancient motorbike and sidecar to ask if I wanted a lift. 'No, I must only walk,' I managed to explain, and he gently kissed my cheek before leaving.

On my first night of wild camping I made an extra effort to stay hidden, pushing deep into the centre of a copse of young pine trees clustered at field edge, their low branches knitted tightly together with an open space at the heart just big enough for my tent to snuggle into. An ancient Lada chugged past on the nearby track, bouncing and creaking on the rutted surface, with the occupants looking straight ahead, not noticing me. I sat there for a while, relaxing down from the alertness of walking; nobody would see me here, there was nobody here to see me. This was a familiar rhythm, walking all day then creeping and nosing like a small animal to find a place to sleep, before packing up and shouldering my burden the next morning to do it all again. I'd done this for months on end in my own country, I could do it here. As the realisation sank into me, I let out a breath and sagged with relief, feeling safe and happy. This was possible, even comfortable. I could do this.

The only maps I'd been able to buy in Kyiv were at a 1:250,000 ratio, meaning that each paper centimetre represented a vast 2.5km of ground. They showed no fine details like footpaths, or contour lines, just green blobs for forest and white for agriculture. Fortunately the first 100 miles or so would be dead flat. Black lines marked back roads, which were twin-line grooves in the earth; sometimes well worn by car and sometimes overgrown and branch-covered. The bigger tarmacked roads were potholed and cracked; I hardly saw any cars on them.

I had never had such a loose connection to my precise location. With minimal clues on the horizon to orientate myself and no phone reception to pinpoint me as a glowing blob on a scrollable map, I had to walk by following my compass bearing, keeping steadfast and fixed ahead.

This journey was too big for me to pin down in daily targets. I had to stay vague about how far I'd walk each day or where I'd sleep.

Keeping my targets vague had another motive: it allowed me to fail.

In talking about the journey before I left, I'd pulled the figure of two years out of the air, a long enough number to show that this was a serious undertaking. Faster, younger, fitter walkers could probably do it much more quickly, but I had to consider my physicality. I was 38, overweight and had a tendency to be really hard on myself. If I didn't set strict targets then I couldn't force myself into injury trying to meet them, or brutally berate myself when I didn't.

I'd already walked one journey of thousands of miles and knew that the success of this challenge was rooted in my mental strength, the ability to drive myself forward through pain and exhaustion while balancing the downtime necessary to avoid breaking myself altogether.

There at the beginning of the journey, I could relax into the idyllic days, before the inevitable pain set in. I was heading from Kyiv to Romania in as much of a straight line as I could manage, sticking to the quieter rural backwaters and avoiding the suburbs and cities with their harsh tarmac underfoot and lack of free sleeping options.

Walking from village to village, small dots on the map became similar clusters of houses huddled together between miles of forest and field; there were no scattered dwellings built out alone. I found tiny, shabby, wooden cottages with earthen yards where washing flapped, chicken and geese pecked and dogs on short chains would usually feel provoked to bark at me voraciously. Tiny old women stumped along the street, bent bodies wrapped in layers of insulating clothing, headscarves tied tight under their chins. Street fashion here was flower print cotton underneath lumpy knits, wrinkled layers of thick socks, feet in clogs or crocs. They were always interested in me and what I was doing but interactions in those early days were mostly a spatter of conversation from them, gold teeth glinting, and me in a nervous sweat, trying desperately to pick out a word I understood.

On a back road, houses hidden behind battered wooden fences containing flowers and drooping apple trees, there was a well. I dropped the bucket down, marvelling at the smooth unwinding of the metal-bound wooden spindle, waiting for the *sploosh* when bucket hits water and the sudden heaviness as the water swells into it. I leaned over to see it far down in the depths, a tiny circle of reflection dimmed by my body's looming, and wound the well-worn crank handle to bring the pail swaying to the sunlight.

Bending to grasp the swinging bucket gave the sensation of memory – one century old? Two? In a movement that felt part of my generational history, I heaved the bucket onto the stone lip and took a draught of cold, clear water. I plucked a soft red apple from the tree across the road, sat back against the wall and rested for a while, legs stretched out into the dirt, an occasional chicken scratching and bobbing nearby. I slept in an empty field, where the impenetrable, head high corn crop turned to cleared earth, with yellow peas scattered on the ground and a fuzz of cut stalks snapping under my feet. The sun set far away over the flat land, yellow gold filling the clear white sky, and I basked in the warmth until it disappeared, then wrapped up for the cold. I would often leave the outer covering of my tent off, just the inner mesh between me and the darkening sky above, feeling part of the world rather than shut inside a tiny plastic cave. I was toasty all night, and woke to find a thin frost on my sleeping bag. Frozen beads of condensation covered the tent mesh, like crystals on a wedding dress.

My maps marked each hotel with a big red 'H' but they were so sparse outside the cities that I thought there surely must be more.

To my amazement, when I asked for a hotel in a town of 5,000 people I was told there wasn't one and had to catch a minibus packed full of silent passengers, rattling twenty minutes south to the nearest 'H' for my day off. Lesson learnt.

My rest breaks, usually one a week, were essential. I'd take off the clothes I'd worn day and night for six days, and put on my other set. Socks were the only clothing I changed daily. I packed three pairs and washed them wherever I could, in springs and streams.

Kozyatyn was a confusing town where I couldn't seem to find the centre. Instead, I walked long streets of high-rise apartment blocks, with small cabin shops squirrelled away between them, until I found a market selling socks, phone cases and homegrown veg. There were tables with milk in reused pop bottles. At the quiet end, old women sat behind small amounts of vegetables placed on squares of fabric laid carefully on the ground – a bag of apples, a cup of white beans, a jar of preserved cabbage; augmenting their insufficient pensions with these distressingly inadequate market sales.

I hadn't felt dirty, even after a week without a shower, but as I stood in the hotel corridor, wallpaper peeling away from unfinished plasterwork at the door frames, the air thick with hairspray from the salon two doors down, I noticed my greasy hair in the smoke-brown mirror and realised I was absolutely filthy. The water coming from the shower-head stank like a rubbish dump, but thankfully the smell didn't stick to my skin.

The step counter remained at three that day as I rested in polyester bedding, gaudy pink-and-green flower print, watching fuzzy music videos on the old TV. Dry the tent, air the sleeping kit, wash my clothes in the sink, darn my leggings, stretch my body and prepare myself to go out there and repeat the same again for another week – the same frost, the same autumn colours, shabby villages, wide flat fields, deep quiet forests.

***

Central Ukraine was passing in a hazy blur of pleasant walking.

I could walk all day in the quiet of the fields; the close cropped grass, the rustling of dry corn stalks.

I could lie in my tent at night, safely hidden, listening to a horse and cart clinking and clopping past me, watching the glow of a cigarette pulse on and off.

Cows were driven past as I was packing up the tent one frosty morning and I felt the wave of heat radiating from their round bellies. One scooped up the too-hard pear I'd discarded the previous night with a quick lick of her giant tongue, barely pausing her stride.

Walking through the first village of the day, while the mist hung low over the fields, bright sun in waiting, I watched a flurry of chickens and geese fan out from a garden gate as they were gently shooed out onto the road to pick and scratch. Red squirrels ran light along fence tops. A dog pattered along the dirt road, intent on its own mysterious mission.

Leaving the village, I plunged again and again into the fields, plants growing above my head or flat land to the horizon, no views, corn leaves rustling in the breeze, harvester lorries roaring back and forth, turning down a line of uncut sunflowers to where a cloud of dust-marked men at work. As I walked though fields of leafy kale, I would pluck single stems, chewing them into my mouth like a rabbit. Ladybirds flew past, sometimes perching on me, the warm tree, their transparent wings slipping back under the shell like a barely glimpsed petticoat edge.

Walking through the fields was totally immersive; just me and the animals, no people or houses for hours at a time.

I reached a line of trees between two great spreads of brown, ploughed earth, and stopped for lunch, tucked in against the wind as it whirled small tornados of dust across the field. Passing crows angled sharply and I heard the thrumming swish of the wind against their twisting wings. I sat there so still and for so long that eventually a mouse came flickering in and out of the undergrowth nearby.

Walking through a couple of days of deep forest, dogs came lolloping towards me, a buoyancy of bodies, rippling and swaying. Every head rose up to stare as they saw me, paws poised; they each stopped a moment then turned and pattered into the forest to my left, fluid and completely silent. They were Alsatian-looking. I stood still and peered into the trees but there was nothing to see and no sound; they'd disappeared, quick as blinking. I walked on, imagining it was a hunting pack, waiting for the human to come pacing along behind ... but no human ever appeared.

Later that week I chatted to a woman outside her shop as I munched through a handful of freshly purchased biscuits.

'Be careful of wolves.'

'There are wolves here?'

'Yes, my brother saw a pack of them, twenty-two, running across the road.'

'Are they dangerous to me?'

'No,' she smiled, arm around her daughter just home from school. *'Udachi.'* Everyone had been saying this, and now I knew it meant good luck.

I lay in the tent that night, picturing the wolves running through the forest, the pack scattering and merging, splashing and swaying like a flash flood, snapping up mice like cocktail sausages.

I felt like an animal, just like them, blurring into the environment, passing by without trace, living in total concord with my needs, sleeping with the dark and moving with the light.

This was the adventure I was looking for, walking ahead into the unknown and allowing experiences to come to me, plunging into uncertainty and swimming in it, revelling in such an unbounded experience.

One day a farmer and his wife passed me on their tractor, her becroced foot dangling perilously close to the wheel, and we had the usual short conversation where I told them I was a tourist and that I was walking. Ten minutes later the man hailed me as I walked past their house. Igor was his name. I sat with him in the yard and mugs of sugary instant coffee were passed out to us as we talked. Then came a plate of cheese. 'It was made here.' He gestured to a corner of the yard where, behind a few sheets hanging haphazardly, there seemed to be nothing but piles of plastic boxes. I must have looked incredulous because Igor told me, through the phone translation, of how they wanted a better dairy but there were no government grants or loans to help them build anything.

Two small children were flitting in and out of the house, staring at me, transfixed by this strange conversation.

'Do you receive any government money at all?'

'None.'

I struggled to comprehend a farm without government help, where a family must make their own money or they will have nothing. Igor kept fourteen cows and five pigs and lived on the money he made from their milk and meat. Forget the lack of a handwash basin or temperature records; the EHO officer who used to strike such fear into the food businesses of Llanidloes would faint dead away at cheese being made on a trestle table in the corner of an open-fronted concrete barn and taken into the main room of the house to mature. It was really good cheese, dry and white and crumbly. Natasha showed me the different stages of the process, the leaven she used, the brine it soaked in. She was plump and glowing with a chubby, round-eyed smile, where Igor was slight, darker and drawn.

Igor took me to the barn 2 miles away where they kept the cows. On the way I asked him if he was satisfied with life. He highlighted the unfairness of his situation; saying that the 'deputies' all have their own farms which take money from the state. They can improve their stock by buying cows from abroad and Igor cannot – blatant unfair competition. Following the dissolution of the collective farms of the USSR, land was returned to the rural people, to either be utilised by them for subsistence farming or leased to large agribusinesses. An immediate moratorium on land sales in 2001, supposedly temporary, prevented Ukrainian land passing into foreign ownership, an emotive issue for a country freshly independent of Soviet control, but also meant that farmers were unable to use land as collateral for loans to improve their businesses.

'In Ukraine, life is hard and there is no choice.'

No choice. The same thing that Vasyl said to me as we drove into Ukraine in his little red van. 'You can visit all these countries and I can only drive through them, only allowed to cross the border when I am driving lorries.'

This is the plain fact of my UK privilege, that I live in a fairyland of disposable consumer goods and leisure time, that I have multiple opportunities to change my circumstances, waving my passport to skip across borders. Igor and Natasha were the same age as me and I felt like a child in comparison. They had everything I didn't – four children, a house, land, a business, skills at building and creating and maintaining a life. I felt like the fool, prancing and playing with my existence, replete with disposable riches and freedom of leisure time.

We talked a lot that night. They invited me to stay with them in their basic home, built by Igor fourteen years ago, unpainted walls with dollops of grey cement squeezing out between concrete blocks. There were three rooms; a kitchen, then a second room with a table and a double bed where Igor and Natasha slept, and the family ate, piling the pyramid of maturing cheeses temporarily in the kitchen and dragging the table to the bed for extra seating. The third room contained four single beds, where I could sleep alongside the children, Valya, 15, Oleg, 12 and Katya, 7. Natasha had been cooking while we visited the cows and brought out a huge plate of meat; ribs and liver and all the joints tumbled together. It was hare, shot by Igor, followed by a mounded plate of mashed potato, then gherkins, mustard, mushrooms and fried dumplings. We drank home-distilled schnapps, and the children had a redcurrant drink, poured from a huge glass jar that still had the fruit floating in there. Everything had been grown, made, hunted, foraged, pickled here on the farm.

'I might have German roots,' said Igor. 'My grandmother was taken to Germany as a war prisoner and she gave birth to my father there.'

Nazi soldiers forcibly moved more than a million Ukrainians to Germany to use as slave labour during WWII, as well as killing over a million Ukrainian Jews. They don't know where his grandmother was sent or what happened there; the translation was unclear but he told me records were impossible to access in a hidden Soviet system. His grandmother is dead now so they have no way of finding out. Igor's story forms a small piece of the tumbled history of Ukraine, a country which has been torn and divided over and over, always pulling at its ragged edges to form a semblance of centre.

I was yawning by 11pm, way past my usual bedtime, a hiker used to sleeping with the sunset. As I went to the bedroom, Igor and

Natasha whirled outside to do the final chores. 'I work so that my children might have a better life than me,' said Igor.

The next morning Natasha went to do the milking and Igor took the children to school. The car wouldn't start so they had to push it out of the muddy yard, the children running from the boot to jump in as it rolled forward, obviously a well practised manoeuvre. I packed up, chatting to Valya, who had a day off from college where she studied milk technology, aiming to help her parents. Igor came back as I finished breakfast and invited me to stay for longer but I couldn't; there was walking to be done and I wasn't tired yet. I stood up and offered my hand. He shook it and put his other hand on his heart. We smiled.

I'd left Kyiv in late September and was walking through harvest season, in a bounty of apples and walnuts. Trees bulged with hanging fruit, flinging forth their prayers for future survival. There were people collecting food everywhere I went, preserving jars on sale in every village shop. In towns they rifled through pavement drifts of fallen leaves to pocket hidden walnuts. Mushroom hunters came to the forests, pulling grimy plastic tubs from their car boots. It seemed like every house had rattling stalks of drying corn bundled against the walls, alongside tobacco leaves dangling on nails, corn cobs hanging like yellow tails.

Gargantuan combine harvesters thundered past me on the roads, ten in a row, ready to chew up hectares of yellow peas. In the smaller fields, near the villages, I saw women sitting in pairs, topping and tailing piles of swede from the black earth. The things people did changed as I walked across the country. This is the fortnight where corn is harvested. This is the fortnight where we burn the stubble. First the pumpkins were piled in corners, bright orange flashes in the yellow-brown yardscapes of chicken-trampled earth. After a while, I began to see them being split, hefted open with spades, seeds scooped out for sale and shells discarded for chicken feed, lying on the ground like collapsed balloons.

I rested for a while at a war memorial, dates for WWII beginning 1941, eating salami and crackers. I sat there for so long I went into a daze, lulled by the wind rustling the trees. It was strong today, maybe rain was coming. There was a cow chained to a stake in the grass and three brown geese drinking from a muddy puddle. I heard a clumping and jingling, and into view came a man driving a horse and cart. The wooden cart was laden with pumpkins, orange, green and yellow, mottled orbs glowing bright in the clear sunny day. The cart dipped as they turned the corner and a pumpkin rolled from the higgledy pile, hollow thuds on the short grass echoing across the silent street, followed by a long, rolling trill as the man stopped the horse. It stood quietly as he heaved the pumpkin up, then climbed on and geed the horse on its slow, patient walk. The ducks waddled back to the puddle in his wake, swaying like the cart.

The land was starting to ripple, just faintly, and my view became slightly more than a stretch of flat land to the horizon.

Each tiny village had a shop; this wasn't a car-based culture where people drive to the supermarket once a week. Car journeys were rare, with most cars being in an advanced state of decay and the ragged roads damaging rather than aiding journeys. Some 50% of the village cars I saw were Ladas; occasionally their distinctly boxy beauty was made fashionable, resprayed and done up, but mostly they were the old faithfuls that had seen decades in the same family. Judging by the noise and smoke some of these vehicles produced as they passed, I don't think Ukraine has MOTs.

The village shops were small emporia, shelves piled high with a few pieces of everything: bootlaces and gloves near to preserving jars and toothpaste, rubber shoes, washing powder, baking soda, brooms. There was usually a display of loose sweets, and biscuits sold by weight. A bag of dried fish stood on the counter next to the chocolate. Piles of water bottles, sacks of cabbages and onions made a maze on the floor. There weren't many fruits and vegetables, but I could usually find bananas and oranges. A woman behind the counter waited patiently while I stared at everything, trying to decipher the unusual packaging and Cyrillic lettering. Sometimes they added up using a battered wooden abacus, casually flicking a few beads across to tell me the total, but more often it was an electric calculator.

People would come and go as I made my culinary detective work. Maybe a man asked for forty fags and a shot of spirits or a boy came in for a single cigarette and left without paying. After miming a little, I could usually get an instant coffee in a plastic cup and a few penn'orth of biscuits to eat outside at a rickety table and chairs under a blotchy, tattered awning.

The frequency of shops was useful as I was trying to avoid carrying too much weight so would buy small portions of food most days. Instant mashed potato worked well, add salami for protein, then mix in tomato puree, salt, fresh tomato and cucumber and you have a pretty delicious meal. I bought the occasional avocado or tin of tuna. Sachets of porridge were sold individually, so I could pour water straight into the packet and eat with a spoon. I ate a banana every day, satsumas for snacks, plus nuts, halva, whatever came to hand.

It was a minimal and repetitive diet but hunger helped me keep interested.

The exertion of walking meant that occasional gut problems hit me harder. I would skim the edges of dehydration, sipping enough to keep my mouth from caking dry, gulping two litres the next day, flirting with the headache that came so quickly.

A walk like this is a balance of energy versus pain. Small problems easily had big effects. Muscles tense from exertion? I wouldn't slide into deep sleep. Not enough sleep? I would be tired and achy all day. Not enough to drink? Move immediately from dry mouth to blinding headaches. Not enough to eat? Tired and listless, no motivation. The onset of negative reactions began sooner in this endurance situation, where I was pushing myself towards my limits.

After four weeks of walking my energy began to dip. I was zonked out in the tent at night, staring into space, mind empty. I had to keep looking after myself even as my body contorted under the strain and my brain dissolved in a mist of exhaustion.

Days off became important chances to stretch out solidified muscles, from neck to toes, and get restorative nutrition, both difficult to achieve in a cramped tent. Sitting on the bed in my hotel room, I would carefully chop and mix a sequence of salads in my tiny food bowl. Tear apart cooked chicken with my fingers. Stretch. Red cabbage, carrots, onion, mayo, parsley, lemon juice. Stretch. Feta cheese, onion, tomato, cucumber, parsley, lemon juice, avocado. Stretch. Salty crisps. Stretch. Soft juicy fruit, blueberries or strawberries, mixed into sharp yoghurt. Stretch and snooze. Write a blog, and so the day passed.

People were wonderfully friendly – they would stop, with smiling eyes, and enquire who I possibly could be and what I was doing here. I learnt to understand the questions people were asking. 'Where are you from?' 'Walking?' 'Alone?' 'Why?' They'd look me up and down, the brightly coloured clothing, the huge bag, the double walking poles and I'd say the word 'tourist' prompting an 'ooooh'. 'Where are you from, Poland or Russia?' would usually be the next question, and when I replied, 'Anglia,' the 'oooooh' would turn from understanding to shock. 'Anglia?' They could never quite believe it.

I would stumble out a Ukrainian explanation of my journey and they looked amazed and wished me well. People would often give me food, apples and walnuts or packets of biscuits, or just wish me '*Udachi*' – 'good luck'.

After an encounter outside a village shop, the proprietor rang her English-speaking friend, a teacher, and I was invited home for homemade pickled gherkins, cherry wine and an omelette made with eggs and cream from their animals. I left with yet another bulging bag of fruit and walnuts and an invitation to go and visit the school.

The following day I was welcomed at the school door with a ceremonial loaf of bread and students chanting a hastily memorised speech, before a tour of the bustling secondary school, all linoleum and single glazed windows.

In the main hall, I was unexpectedly faced with two hundred waiting children and expected to give a talk about Wales, which I stammered my way through. I was taken for a canteen lunch, where the headmaster sneaked a bottle of cherry liqueur out of his office, pouring us several toasts while the female English teachers exchanged disapproving looks. 'My teaching job is a hobby,' said one, ironically. Chronically underpaid, her annual teaching salary only covered her winter fuel bills.

The most shocking part of the day was not the sparse equipment, low salaries, or tatty classrooms, but the display of war propaganda in the foyer; guns, missiles, photos of dead soldiers lining the walls while children chattered past.

The fighting was 500 miles away from this agricultural landscape and, lacking the language to question those I met, existed mostly in the abstract for me.

I met a soldier; a tall man in dusty camouflage clothing and a peaked cap standing in the centre of the stony road, staring at me with a quizzical smile, the tourist where there weren't any. We started to walk together and talked a little, as much as I was able. He told me he was fighting in the east and was back in his home village on leave. He stumbled as he walked and I realised this man was deeply drunk. He turned his shoulder and pressed his back against my body, miming his rifle to shoot away from me, telling me he fought to protect other people. His torso leaning against mine, to place his body in the line of fire, made me suddenly tearful. Ukrainian people were dying to protect their ideals, their land, their sense of a country.

On a different day, at the village's edge, I came towards a man standing at the end of an avenue of tall trees. He was wheeling a barrow of logs through his front gate but had paused on seeing me. I felt nervous about this unknown silhouette. *'De voda?'* ('Where is the water?') I tried in my best broken Ukrainian and to my surprise he answered in English good enough for a conversation, an incredible rarity in these rural places.

'Come inside. Would you like a coffee?'

I hesitated a second. He was slow and kindly like a gentle grandad, but I needed to make sure that we wouldn't be alone in there.

He said, 'My wife will make it.'

Phew, he sensed the reason for my hesitation. His dog was friendly and didn't bark, a good sign.

We entered the dim conservatory, lined by lace curtains, filled by a long wooden table and benches, where a huge bunch of flowers trickled single petals onto the embroidered tablecloth.

This was their dacha, the summer house, where they stayed from May to October. Pavel was a computer programmer in the capital, and a retired army officer.

His wife busied herself making food and Pavel shuttled a series of dishes out to the table: beetroot salad, egg salad, fried onion and greens, salami, fried fish and potatoes, bread, soup, a bunch of tiny delights to choose from. I was taken to wash my hands, with apologies for not having indoor plumbing.

'We have in Kyiv, of course.'

'You are risky girl,' said Pavel when he learned what I was doing. 'I am retired army general. I was in Moscow. And now I am called up again in reserve.'

As he fell silent, I became aware of a deep stirring within him, his hands clasped on the table, eyes lowered to the space between us.

Once he fought with Russia, now he fights against them. The Russian-backed separatist movement had been attacking in the east of the country for four years now, thousands of people had died, multiple ceasefire agreements never seeming to stick.

There were so many questions I was too nervous to ask. 'Do you think that Ukraine can ever be free of Russia? How did it feel to be part of the USSR? Do you feel bereft of international help?' I wanted to hear so much more: of where he was in 1991 as the USSR dissolved, or in 2013 during the Euromaidan protests.

But I was bringing up the heartbreak of an unequal war; Ukraine clinging to the eastern territory that was being ripped away from them by a stronger hand, peeling fingers back one by one. To live with almost permanent underdog status, apart from the legendary Cossack era; split between Poland and Russia for many years. The maintenance of a Ukrainian national identity is the sweeping together of scattered fragments from underneath centuries of lost autonomy, and is all the more dearly guarded for it. They know what it is to lose, they know what it is to be taken over, and any Russian interference on their land reignites these same old pains.

My awkwardness trumped any latent journalistic instinct and I felt too shy to probe further.

A neighbour interrupted, come to call on Pavel's mother for their afternoon cards session; she had brought a couple of precious pears from her tree and I was given one, a hard knobbly rock to weight my pack as it ripened.

The two women were jolly and bustling, chattering with the loudness of deaf ears, and the conversation moved away from war and onto hunting – my opportunity lost.

In Kamianets-Podilskyi I met Tatyana, who hosted me in return for the chance to practise her English. I bunked up on the sofa of the family's spare room, in an old-fashioned apartment block, exposed pipes in concrete stairwells, flaking paint on cracked walls.

We mostly talked about economic migration; their young family had gone abroad to work illegally for a few summers, to Portugal for fruit picking and to Norway to work as hospital porters, hoping to come home with enough money for the deposit to buy a newer flat. Inherited from a grandparent, theirs was old-fashioned, badly insulated, and the communal heating bills were too high. But last time they came home, Tatyana with an injured back from heavy lifting at the hospital, the house prices had risen and now they were priced out of the new builds.

Tatyana, in her mid-30s, remembered times of no food, of making a sack of flour last for weeks with very little else to eat. After suffering years of desperate poverty here, they thought it was preferable to go and work illegally in the EU, but going abroad changed her mind. 'I thought it was better to accept the low status of being illegal hidden workers than to stay poor here, but I broke my body being a slave for rich countries and with nothing to show for it.' Now they'd turned to creating a life here, in whatever way they could.

Husband Valera went to fight in Donbas when the war first broke out. 'They wouldn't even equip him.' She mimed holding out a begging hand to show how they went to friends and family collecting funds for his uniform. 'They don't want to fight each other anyway. They send text messages across the front lines to warn when there will be an attack.'

Her husband was tall and quiet. He did sit-ups in the room where I slept and there was a collection of weights in the corner. I got a feeling of him staying primed.

'When I go to work, he will only watch our son as long as nobody finds out. His friends would laugh at him if they knew.' Tatyana chopped into a white cabbage and began vigorously grating.

'Does he have a job?'

'No, only I do.'

'Does he cook?'

'No, that is my job too.'

I felt a lot of anger in her, rightly so. She was still struggling to make a good life despite all the ways the world was set against her; high food prices, low wages, lack of freedom to work abroad, toxic masculinity, capitalist monopolies, global inequality, systemic corruption and bribery.

'I can only think about today and tomorrow, not about the future.'

And so she grated the cabbage, studied English online, dressed up in traditional costumes to guide tourists around the castle in a choice of three languages, home schooled her son and hoped that one day life would get easier.

Once I left the town, the land was flat and wide open, no trees, nowhere to hide, so after a day of walking, I decided to bed down in a stand of tobacco plants. The leaves were harvested from the bottom up and taken home to dry, leaving smaller leaves sprouting on top of bare stalks, tiny purple flowers swaying up high, a very alien plant to me. I lay under the leaves, hoping I was sufficiently hidden as tractors roared past on their way home, headlights rippling through the gaps, flickering and flashing. Outside of the brief human interactions, most of my time was spent alone with the land, a deep immersion in solitary walking. Each day spent completely outside passed in a smooth flow from walking to camping to sleeping, a gentle graduation like the sunset.

Next morning a storm gathered ahead. Where the sky behind was stippled with sun-gilded white cloud over a bright blue morning, ahead of me loomed a dark grey mass, filling the sky. White wisps of rain feathered the air and this bad time was coming inescapably towards me. With nowhere to run to, no shelter to keep me safe, without qualm I knew I would face this wind and rain. I was part of the land, to be equally lashed and wetted.

As much as I loved the acceptance of the storm, doggedly walking onwards into the rain, I didn't enjoy the damp aftermath and went to a hotel that night to dry off. The isolation of walking through a country more different to any I'd been before, existing almost entirely in a language I didn't speak, and with the only internet access to contact home being when I reached hotel rooms, was much harder than I'd anticipated. Out in the natural world I was completely in tune with my surroundings, experiencing constant stimulation, the daily physical grind of walking utterly fulfilling, but when I shut the door on nature and faced the detached human world of anonymous beds in blank hotel rooms, life felt empty in comparison. I was surprised to realise I was lonely, something I'd never experienced before despite many years of solitary travelling and living. Lying in bed the next morning, I asked my lover for a photograph, reaching out for connection. I'd spent the two years before I left Wales struggling in a relationship with M, who kept me at arm's length but wouldn't let me go. One of the most prickly, emotionally withdrawn, difficult men I'd ever loved. We were supposed to be casual, it was supposed to end when I left, but the texts had kept trickling. That day, though, when I needed support, he rebuffed me, told me I was demanding. It triggered a deep wail of grief within me.

I felt like I was always battering at the closed doors of emotionally unavailable men, repeating the pattern of parental rejection over and over again, dooming myself to a constant state of unmet need.

I'd stopped talking to my mother just before I left for Kyiv, tired of her lack of contact, her inability to show care towards me or create a loving, supportive relationship.

It was the first time, in all our years of arguments and hurt, that I'd drawn a line and explicitly not spoken to her. I had deliberately separated myself from my mother and she wasn't trying to contact me. That day, alone and in need, I felt all the anguish of that gap between us, a deep and powerful helplessness, as if I was a baby struggling for survival, the emotions bigger than my body could encompass.

The two burdens combined: my historic pain over the lack of loving parents and my sadness about the lack of a loving partner. I felt overwhelmingly weak as I left the hotel to start walking; sobbed and sobbed all day, solitary and grief stricken, trudging by the side of roads as cars swept past, feeling a hollow space in my body as it squeezed out tears.

As I walked and cried, in the depths of despair, I parsed through it, the movement of my body allowing unacknowledged thoughts to bubble up to the surface.

When my father was diagnosed with terminal cancer, some of my immediate emotional response was grief for the loss of a father I didn't have, the ideal of a father who loved and cared for me. Facing the death of an inadequate father included losing the hope that I would ever have a better one.

All my life I'd been struggling with an unsupportive mother but I was always focusing on what she wasn't, on what I needed her to be. In the same way as my father, during this deliberate pause in communication with her, I realised that part of what I felt was the loss of the archetypal mother, the lack of a nurturing caregiver, of never receiving unconditional love. Once I let go of the belief that she would ever change, I could grieve for what I needed and never got.

Small moments of peace came by a riverbank as I brought myself into the present moment, remembered that I was there with the trickling water and swaying reeds. But mostly it was a lost day, walking and wailing, stumbling along tracks without seeing them.

I was deep in the countryside by late afternoon, calmer and quieter, wandering between villages on worn-down strips of dirt through grassy expanses of unfenced fields.

At a crossroads, a chapel caught my eye, a small shabby wooden building, no more than a shed, with a rusty cross at the corner. The door was held closed with a bent nail and inside, filling the whole end wall with a profusion of pinned pictures, fake flowers, dried leaves, icons, ribbons and thin metal crosses and candlesticks, was a glorious altar – a dusty still life, washing peace over the road junction.

Creeping inside to take a photograph, I saw a figure coming towards me in the distance and, unsure if I should be in there, peeked out to see if he was looking at me, wondering if I'd be chastised. The man beckoned me out, signalling that I should walk with him. Sasha was young, mid 20s, dark attractive eyes and a shaved head.

His English was pretty bad and we haphazardly stumbled through an explanation of my journey, using fingers wiggling to denote walking. 'I am carpenter,' he said, and I wondered what incident had caused the fine straight scar under his right eye. Facial scarring was common in Ukraine; I'd guess at a combination of a lack of access to hospitals in rural areas, higher alcohol usage in the working day, and a macho culture that disregards health and safety procedures.

He was stuttering and pausing, hampered by his lack of language. 'You have nice smile.' He threw up his hands in frustration, and we grinned at how impossible this was.

I was utterly innocent of the direction this conversation was taking until he pointed to the long grasses. 'Sex. We have sex.' I was stunned. He'd beckoned me out of the chapel in a 'not here' kind of way, which I'd thought was because I shouldn't be in the building. Was it really because he thought I was enticing him in for a shag?

It was tempting. I could kiss the man offering himself to me, we could go into the field and lie down for a short while. I could absorb his desire, let him want me, fill me to a delightful aching.

An enticing prospect while I was feeling low and alone, but that day had been so completely tortured that I knew this temporary easing would be completely inadequate.

I took a deep breath, thankful that he was being so gentle, and decided to try and express some of the mental writhing I'd been gnashing over all day.

'I don't want sex. I want love. I want to love someone and be loved in return.' I don't think I'd ever said that out loud before.

'We can do that.'

I looked at him quizzically, not even needing to refute this impossible fantasy.

'We write, by phone...' He tailed off, shrugging. We smiled. This was over, and neatly managed too. He gave me a kiss on the cheek and headed back along the track, obviously having detoured from his route home to pursue this amorous mission.

I walked off the road, down through the valley and found myself a flat patch of grass to sleep. Almost at the point of darkness, a man came over the low rise of the hill, followed by a single line of sheep, no dog in sight. The intense emotional purge of the day had left me feeling hollow, shell-shocked, and the placid sheep walking in single file felt like a blissful dream. The shepherd was a very relaxed man who didn't mind my unexpected presence. The permission to sleep in his field didn't need to be spoken and we chatted briefly before he excused himself to do evening chores.

The interaction with Sasha had come along at the exact moment for me to talk through my feelings. Refusing his advances let me restore my agency after I'd spent the day feeling rejected and helpless. It was the first time I'd been propositioned in two months. Both he and the calm, comforting shepherd felt like mystical apparitions. The sex and the safe haven – two alternative manifestations of masculinity for me to compare my feelings with.

In the morning, sitting under a tree eating cold-water oats, I waved to the shepherd as he returned to lead his sheep away; the most well-behaved flock I have ever seen following in a line behind him, up the hill and out of sight.

Ukraine was a fairytale in many ways: the calm shepherd, the peaceful countryside, the generous villagers, the glowing autumn colours. The simplicity of small-scale rural agriculture manifested growth and harvest in a seasonal ebb and flow. There was a balance here; people felt calm, even if poverty and war meant they were not content.

It had been an idyllic beginning to the walk: flat land, friendly people, and warm, gentle weather, no colder than mild frosts at night. But it was the 2nd of November and I was aiming for the Carpathian Mountains; this lucky break wasn't going to last forever.

The looming fear of snowy camping in Romania added a sense of urgency to my steps. I was anticipating winter, anticipating mountains, thinking further ahead than my body could travel. But this challenge was too big to finish before the cold came. Spring was a full four months away, and unless I escaped to a hotel, tucking myself in there with a pile of food and warm blankets like a hibernating bear, there was no avoiding walking through winter.

Entering the Carpathian foothills, climbing at 1,000m, I came out of the forest and found myself walking crabwise on sheer hillside straight towards a smallholding. The sharp slope down from the forest was too steep to climb above it and I couldn't waste the energy needed to drop a polite distance below the house when there was so much mountain still to climb. I'd have to walk directly past the front door of this remote cabin, a dark building of weather-aged wooden planks, with a verandah running the length of the front and wet washing hanging in the eaves. Hens pecked in an enclosure on the slope below, fenced in behind high wire to protect against predators.

There was a woman in front of the house, head down, and I called to her from a respectful distance. She beckoned me over and, after a short conversation about where I was going, asked me if I'd like a coffee. We climbed the wooden steps up into the house, arched chainsaw trails weaving over each plank. A chained dog bellowed from a hidey-hole below, just within reach to nip at me as I ascended. The house was built into the steep slope of the hillside, the front elevated on thick wooden legs. The storage underneath was crammed with cardboard boxes and tarpaulin-wrapped bundles, rusty tools hanging on nails, broken buckets and torn plastic, the detritus of farm living. It was dim inside, tiny windows on one side of a room crammed with dark, worn wooden furniture. A sallow silent boy of about seven flitted about, crawling under tables. An older one, about twenty, came in to advise on how to use the phone translation before leaving again. This was a poor house, where the kitchen and the bedroom are the same room, four beds crammed together as a way to hoard warmth in the winter.

Maria told me she was 42, that she had five sons and one daughter who all lived at home, except for the daughter who had married at 16. She moved slowly and surely as the boy watched me from the floor; first boiling coffee on the wood-stove, then spreading bread with butter, putting a plate of cheap processed cheese and pink meat at my elbow, and finally sitting comfortably close on my other side so we could pass the phone between us, our plump legs pressed together like teenagers on a garden wall talking about boys.

I told her that I was 38, we smiled at the similar age, and that I had no children and no man. That I was walking across Europe and that it was an adventure. 'A painful adventure?' she joked and I laughed.

'Yes! Yes! Painful legs!'

She asked why no children and because I liked her and wanted to be funny, I pointed to my groin and said the word, 'Kaput.'

Technically I can still have children but it's not simple to explain my medical history to a stranger: that I only have part of a single ovary left inside my body, that at the time of walking it had grown a cyst that was being monitored to check it wasn't a return of cancer. Then there was the fact that I hadn't met a man who wanted to give me children. I spent the key childbearing years of my early thirties either having cancer, recovering from it or walking thousands of miles, and even if all that hadn't happened, I'm not actually certain that I want to have children, or that I'm capable of being a decent parent, or even that we should continue populating the earth with so many humans anyway. So I just point at my groin and say, 'Kaput,' and even though it's kind of a lie, it's enough of the truth that I don't feel guilty telling it.

'Where is your man?' I asked. She had the feel of a single mother about her, a self-contained woman, used to living with little.

'He's out on the hill. He's a bad man.' And she flicked her throat like the Russians do, to indicate being drunk.

'Why do Ukrainian men drink so much?' I was trying to joke but she laughed sadly, told me he's no good.

I tuned in to her sadness, the unloved feeling in her body. I looked over at the unusual profusion of bruises on the boy and got a sudden urge to ask,

'Is there violence in this house?'

'Yes, from him.'

I sat in silence for a while, absorbing the sorrow of this situation, and noticed that she was deleting the record of our conversation from the phone, leaving no replies to be read later. I rubbed her arm to show I understood.

We talked about what she could do and I asked if she could leave.

'This is my house. My parents both died of cancer and my brother is starving of poverty. I throw him out and he comes back. I go to the police and they do nothing.' Alcoholism is too common a story here. Violence in the home is not a priority.

'He is jealous.'

'Of you?'

'Yes.' She tapped the side of her head and flicked her throat again to tell me that when someone drinks, the sense leaves their head; that when abuse happens everything becomes twisted, the world inverts, and the person who is supposed to love and protect you becomes the one who does you the greatest harm.

I wanted to cry but tears would only show my weakness in the face of her problems.

'You are stuck.'

'Yes.'

We talked for an hour back and forth. I ate her bread and cheese and two small chocolates. She gave me a bag of dried mushrooms and some herbal tea mix, both foraged from the mountain.

I couldn't give this woman a safety net; the government should provide one. I couldn't give her the mental strength to overcome her husband. I couldn't give her a supportive community, a women's aid charity, a police force that would take domestic violence seriously, or courts that would pursue prosecutions. All I could do was give her some money; a secret piece of power that her husband didn't know about. I wanted to make Maria's life better and in that moment it was the only way I could.

So I shoved a bundle of hryvnia into her hand, about 25 quid. Enough for twenty pairs of crappy slip-on shoes or ninety loaves of bread. Maybe enough for her to feed seven people for a month.

As Maria walked me to the top of the pass, we handed the phone between us, talking and reading.

'I got married at 16 and now here I am with a failed life, a bad marriage and nothing to show for it but a bunch of kids. I envy a woman who can live without a man.'

She showed me photos of her daughter's wedding, the day her 16-year-old girl married a man of 40. I asked if that was OK and she twisted her face to say 'not really'.

'Is it a good marriage?'

'For now, so far.'

'Your experience has made you a cynic.'

'Maybe.'

'Maybe mine has too and that's why I have no man.'

We laughed again. I looked at the picture of her daughter's wedding day; her fresh skin, her slender hips, so many fantasies of what life might become and no experience with which to armour herself.

Maria waved over a man who was heading downhill carrying a shovel, for him to show me the way to the road. There was no place for an outpouring of emotion but we hugged and kissed. '*Udachi*' – 'Good luck,' I told her, and turned away, knowing that if the terrible loneliness I was experiencing on this journey came alongside the freedom to live the life I wanted, the ability to reach towards my full power and potential, then I still chose it every time.

I took a day off in Verkhovyna, the final town before the big mountains. The road towards the Carpathians wound slowly into the hills, gradually climbing away from the flat valley town. It followed the river, slopes of pine on either side, before entering a gorge where it became compacted mud, wet and messy where a landslide had raked across the road, twisted roots and rocks leaving a rash of chaos either side of a thin cleared strip for cars to pass.

A dog had been following me for a while, happily sniffing and pattering along in my flow. He changed here, looking intensely up into the trees, pausing and staring, paying attention, and I wondered about the hidden animals he might sense – bears and boar, squirrels and lynx. We walked upwards, the river smaller now, white water over boulders, twisting and winding with the road into the final village before the mountain, where the dog disappeared.

I passed the final shop, a shawl-wrapped old woman on a stool outside, heaving herself up as a customer approached; I passed the final church, where the final hours of sunshine cut down in visible rays between the mountain peaks to gleam on the gilded domes. Cows paced, nonchalant, along the road, neck bells clanging in their sway. A man, not so friendly, paused his log chopping to sit down and ask me for a cigarette. I told him where I was going and he asked if I was scared to go alone.

'Scared of what?'

'Bears.' He looked at me with cold eyes.

'Are there bears here?'

'Of course.'

'How many?'

'You only need one.'

It was the end of the afternoon light, sun descending to leave a pale pastel blue that would soon begin darkening.

As I reached the point where the route turned away from the track and began to climb, for the first time since Kyiv, I had to be precise about my location, and checked the map repeatedly, the contours, the shape of the river as it twisted and turned.

The track crossed the river and led sharply upwards but first was a flat area where I decided to camp.

The next morning was clammy with frosty edges and I stared blearily at the misty water, munching on an unpleasantly cold breakfast banana. The track ahead was a wet and muddy climb. I'd heard logging lorries roaring across the river in the dark, headlights raking across my tent.

The sun was shining again, as it had done for almost my entire time in Ukraine and the mist lifted to leave easy walking in warm sun.

On the other side of the mountain range was primeval forest in a biosphere reserve, relatively undisturbed for many decades. Here the land was more open, patches of cleared fields around log cabins at lower levels, parts of forest chopped for logging; small metal barcodes hammered into the end of each trunk in an attempt to control illegal forest clearance. The logging lorries roared past me at the edge of a plain leading to the steep mountains beyond, returning to their day's work. Watching these battered vehicles judder ahead, twisted metal edges showing years of hard labour, chunky tyres almost the height of me, thick chains looped and piled on bumpers, rattling and dangling, I felt at the frontier of something. This was where men came to fight with the land, not a tamed place to pluck fruit with bare fingers. A few minutes behind the lorries came a man leading a horse, the aide to the motorised winches on the front of the vehicles.

Once I'd passed the cleared area, where the men stood and smoked, the track shrank down to a path between trees and I walked into dappled shade and the deep quiet of the pine forest, the earth insulated by a thick layer of dropped needles. In a patch of mud I saw a clearly distinguishable bear print; the wide heel pad and spiked claws at the end of the toes. Maria had told me a bear was nearby as we walked away from her house, and I'd heard something large hurrying away from me a few days earlier, but this was the first proof that was anything more than rustling in the bushes; indisputably, there were bears here and I was walking alone in their territory.

As I carried on uphill, stepping over bulging tree roots, weaving left and right along the grooves worn by lines of water that trickle off the mountain, I began to talk to myself, making noise to say hello to the bears, to warn them that I was there. My thoughts ran out loud: where my foot was going next, where the nearest water source might be, that there might be none higher up the mountain and I should make sure I was fully hydrated. I was starting to tense into hyper alertness, watching over my shoulder, listening for noises.

Something scuffled in the trees ahead and I froze, until I saw a red squirrel regarding me from a safe perch. We stared for a moment, equally motionless, until it broke the tableau and scuttled away, jumping between outstretched branches. In its rustle of escape I noticed how silent the forest was and realised that I would hear a bear loud and clear – perhaps I should try to be a little less scared.

I stopped for breakfast at a small stream, a trickle really, surrounded by moss. Sunlight shone on the water. It was the last stream marked on the map, and at first my mind was full of pictures of disturbing the bear drinking at the stream or coming along the path to find me there. Eventually, however, busy finding a way to wedge my water bottle into the flow, waiting for enough slowly collecting water to soak my porridge, eating my fruit, stretching my calves, sitting in the sunlight to eat, I forgot all about bears and enjoyed the simple sensations of an outdoor breakfast.

Up on the crest of another river valley, the trees thinned out until I looked down at a vast basin, a waterfall crashing thinly in white, aerated water down the vertical cliff ahead, far away. Hills undulated away to the left, thickly forested. I needed to climb up to the right of the basin, on the edge before it turned vertical. The air felt tangible up here – it had sound. The sparse light, cold and thin where it trickled past the mountain blockade, felt lost in the width of the basin. The vastness of this place manifested in a singing to me, a vibrating of light and air that was simultaneously too high and too low for me to hear anything more than a faint sensation. It was the quietest of roars, the gentlest of booms. This was not a place where humans stay – we only pass through.

I went to the stream and filled up my tummy with water, definitely the final chance before the peak. It was warm down on the sun-baked grass and I sat for a while, drying the tent from the previous night's frost. The rest of the mountain stretched ahead of me; just a long slow plod to the ridge, stopping often to admire the view (and catch my breath). I was above everything, looking back over rippling foothills to the dark blue faraway horizon of the flatter lands away to the north. I'd been smiling to myself all day as I walked through this beauty, so glad to be here in this wild place.

I camped up before sunset, about 4.30pm, and sat happy and insulated to watch the sky darken and the ridges of a dozen hills delineate themselves between low valley mists. Getting out of the tent in the full depth of night, I was stunned by the thick profusion of stars, plentiful and bright, hanging so close to me. I even caught the soaring explosive line of a shooting star right in my eyeline. I had never seen them so clearly in the crispness of a cold night and stood entranced, looking from one constellation to another, feeling that I saw them with prehistoric clarity.

I hadn't really thought about bears for hours, even though there was scat all over the mountain, bulging with undigested red berries. My subconscious didn't forget though and I woke at 5am from a nightmare where my whole hometown linked together to defend itself against two giant bears. The tent rattled, startling me in my half-sleep into thinking that something was outside. A breeze had started, making the edges of the frozen fabric crunch and rustle like a plastic bag. It was time to get up. Cold it might be, but I wanted to use all the daylight to get over the highest point and as far as I could towards the other side. There was a gilt edge lining the ridge, showing the beginning of the morning, final stars still glinting in the blackness above.

The sky began to glow pink as I packed away. I was so happy to be here, experiencing the beauty of the day's beginning, tinges of light turning the mountain yellow brown. I walked towards the mountain peak, turning to blow a kiss and say thank you to the land that held me. There were six rounded peaks to clamber over before I reached Hoverla and I walked for half an hour before seeing the light hit the first one, my breakfast target. The sunrise illuminated the peak in cheerful rosy pink and I cheered, climbing towards the light. The rocks and grass were frost-rimed and I placed my feet carefully, paying attention all the time. Any slip or fall here could be a bad accident, so far away from any people or help. I'd seen just one group of walkers the previous day, six young men bouncing energetically over the wiry tufts that formed the vegetation up here, climbing across the frozen snow patches that nestled in the dips on the northern side, where the sun didn't hit. I understood the words *sama* and *strashno*, which meant they'd asked me the usual questions: 'Are you alone? Are you scared?' They'd shaken their heads in amazement when I told them I wasn't scared.

Alone and afraid, that's all people ever seem to think about when faced with the facts of my journey. It doesn't give much of a confidence boost, when people keep questioning your decisions.

Why wasn't I scared? I was starting not to know, when so many people told me I should be. I had everything I needed to survive up there: good equipment, insulation, waterproofing, food, water, first aid kit, the knowledge of what to do in an emergency. I had come to this expertise through practice.

I have a calm head when I need to think quickly, to assess the risks and take appropriate action. I have honed this skill through testing myself over years in all the hitch-hiking, all the travelling, all the times I've thrown myself into uncertainty.

I have the ability to be alone for long periods of time, happy in my own company. When I go somewhere alone, it's never as frightening as the anticipation of sitting inside, wondering what might happen on a future adventure. Maybe it's other people's problem that they can't imagine climbing a mountain alone.

I did do it, alone and unafraid. I climbed Hoverla, the highest mountain in Ukraine at just over 2,000m. It was 11.30am by the time I reached the peak, steadily breathing in and out in the bright blue air, my early morning excitement replaced by serenity. The top was a surprise – no people but several crosses and monuments adorning the flat summit, Ukrainian flags wrapped wherever possible, names scrawled on every surface, coins jammed into cracks.

This was the Chornohora Massif, in the centre of a national park. The lower slopes were coated with thick primeval pine forest, 'home to viable populations of lynx, bears and wolves,' said the information boards.

I had planned to descend slowly, camping in the forest that night, but my fear of bears crept and crept until I realised that I didn't want to camp at all and decided to make a big push down to Hoverla village, far below in the valley bottom where a 'H' for hotel glowed on my map.

The road wound back and forth, looping through the thick forest, and I sped downwards, focused on marching as fast as I could. My feet began to ache and I stopped to stretch them, squatted down for a wee and looked around me at the beautiful trees. Break the spell of forward momentum and there's the opportunity for appreciation. I'd been trying so hard not to strain myself all the way from Kyiv, and yet here I was rushing down a mountain, scared of bears.

My subconscious buzzed a bear alarm at every dark log and my shoulders twitched with the urge to turn around, flinching at every rustle. I thought of Pa in *Little House in the Big Woods*, how he went out hunting one day and on his way home late into the night, saw a bear in a moonlit clearing, reared up on hind legs. He waited and waited for the bear to move but it just stayed there, motionless in the stark light and shadow. Eventually he picked up a huge stick and advanced to attack, only to see it was the same dead tree he'd passed that morning, transformed by his fear.

As the light left the sky I was down by a river, water rushing white and dampness in the air, picking my way through the muddy sludge left by logging lorries.

Hoverla village was a long thin settlement following the riverbank; a single line of houses either side of the road. The land changed once we were out of the national park: fields opened up, misty in the river air, with wooden fences. I could have camped there but after hours of fast walking I was caught up in my own momentum, and unable to change focus, fixed on the comfort of a hotel bed. In the village streets I met a woman getting out of a car and stopped to ask her where the hotel was, but she gave a deeply disappointing response.

'There's no hotel here.'

My least favourite wild camping situation: standing in the middle of a settlement on a cold, dark evening with nowhere to sleep.

Blurred by exhaustion after a swift 18 miles down the mountain, I couldn't think clearly and turned to the first open patch of land I found, setting the tent up in the icy dark. I collapsed into a brief, exhausted unconsciousness but when I woke it was still only 9pm and I could hear people walking nearby, the rake of vehicle lights passing the fence. Camping like this in the village centre made me nervous. I didn't want to be seen at night.

As I sat alert, I heard a woman's voice near the tent. I steeled myself and poked my head out to talk to the dark silhouette above me. 'I'm sorry, I couldn't find the hotel.'

The woman gestured down at my tent, saying the word 'cold'.

'Yeah, it's cold.' I nodded.

She was short with a rounded pot belly, messy cropped hair and missing teeth. As she gestured again I realised she was inviting me inside.

So inside we went, uprooting the tent and dragging it up to the house while a dog barked in the background. We hurried into the warm room, a kitchen, living room and bedroom all-in-one, with carpets hanging on the wall for insulation. At the front of the house were two more unheated bedrooms. The stove was a squat piece of brickwork built out of the wall, with a few doors at the front and a large metal cooking plate with several saucepans on it, some crusted with an unidentifiable brown mush. The woman bustled while I sat dazed at the table; she built up the fire, pushed some saucepans further back, brought others to the front, set about changing the bed clothes. She scattered some leftovers on the floor in front of the stove for the cat, a solemn grey tom.

It was really difficult for us to communicate until the teenage daughter arrived with a smartphone; tapping at it with glitter-painted nails, so different to the older woman's work-worn hands. I resigned myself to being the unknown weirdo for the night. I mean, I definitely was that anyway, just for pitching a tent in their village on a frosty November evening, but now I was the weirdo who was incapable of clear conversation. The woman served me *holubtsi* – rice and slivers of meat wrapped in neat cabbage leaf rolls with some crusty fried crackling. She ladled lumpy kefir from a bucket, tangy and delicious.

When I asked her name, she didn't understand and looked for her daughter, who was out of the room, but I pointed to myself and said, 'Ja Ursula,' then pointed at her.

'Luda,' she said, and we finally smiled at each other.

The next morning Luda was up at 6am, bringing another bucket of brown mash out from the storeroom to ladle into the crusty pan, adding a dollop of kefir and a glug of water to loosen it, telling me it was pig food. She peeled potatoes and set them on to cook before tying a scarf over her head and putting on a housecoat in order to head outside. I peeked out to see a valley white with frost, woodsmoke rising from chimneys and the sunrise throwing pink light onto the forested hills. While Luda was gone, I did my stretches; the TV mumbled adverts and the potatoes bubbled.

Luda brought a bucket of milk into the house, frothy and warm. She offered me a mug and poured it through a strainer. The milk was utterly delicious, thick with cream, as if I was drinking hot chocolate, the first time I'd ever tasted it fresh from the cow. The cat meowed and wound itself against Luda's ankles, waiting for its own portion to be poured into a tiny Tupperware at the base of the stove.

The potatoes were for soup and Luda went into the storeroom, coming back with a bowlful of salted red cabbage. She gave me a pinch to taste then rinsed the rest of it, taking water from a bucket that sat with a mug on the lid, and pouring the wastewater into a second bucket. Everything so neat and contained, as it had to be when living without a sink.

'You are very kind,' I typed into the phone. Luda smiled in acknowledgement, and another piece of the barrier between us broke down. She brought out a bottle of clear liquid and asked me if I wanted some. '*Domashno,*' (homemade) she said. We worked out together that she fermented sugar, water and yeast before distilling it, the cheapest way to make quick alcohol. Everything was homemade, the sour cream we spooned into the soup, her potatoes, her sauerkraut, her meat. All her work was here in the home, the pigs, the cows, the vegetable growing. Her son worked in forestry, she said with a trace of pride. I asked about her husband and Luda told me he worked abroad in Russia, coming home for a few weeks every six months. We made a face at each other: this was sad but so normal that it was barely worth acknowledging. The tragedy of people leaving their families to work abroad was the lesser of two evils when starvation was the other option.

We drank three shots of vodka together. People quite often gave me alcohol in threes. I think there's one shot for welcome, two for being together and the third for being friends. I joked that I needed to walk in a straight line, not a wiggly one, using my hands to emphasise. It was 7.30am.

Finally I left, full of breakfast soup and warmed by booze, giving Luda a quick hug, my heart light and happy at my unexpected night indoors and the generosity of a stranger.

Only 10 miles more, along the valley bottom before I reached Rakhiv, where I was going to take a week's rest. All these weeks had led to pain – tight hips and glutes that couldn't swing freely, aching lower back and shoulders, solid calf muscles; the gradual creeping tension of muscles that never quite had time to relax before another day strapped to a rucksack. Climbing Hoverla and the 18-mile race to the bottom had added extra strain, pushing me into injury territory. Sharp pain shot into my feet, the final place for the stress to rest when my body couldn't disperse the tension upwards. I imagined my hostel there ahead of me, the food I would buy, the protein I would eat, the daily showers, the daily yoga. Just 10 miles more of long straight road, mostly one village bleeding into another, houses scattered high up on the hillsides. Logging lorries came and went, cars passed me, horses with rackety carts on fat tyres, people on single gear bicycles. I walked and smiled and said hello, '*Dobryi den. Dobryi den.*'

My head was swimming with all I'd experienced (and the trio of shots before 8am): the mountain, the bears, the frost, the views, Luda. It was time to pause and rest my body. It was time to stop.

Rackiv was almost at the border, just 12 miles north of Romania. I'd planned a longer break here; a time to let my body calm down and relax a bit more than it could in a single day off, plus the chance to receive a support package from home with replacement kit I needed for the change of seasons. This one would contain a thicker sleeping bag to cope with the Romanian winter ahead, as well as a fresh bundle of maps.

I went into a hostel and met other travellers for the first time since Kyiv two months previously. It was really fun to meet people my age who were out in the world, with the freedom to choose enjoyment over responsibility. Relaxing into their lightness felt immediately familiar. There was Gosha, the beautiful Polish girl who talked to all the babushkas selling their produce by the bridge and took us to meet her new friends; sarcastic Josh and lively Beth, the Canadian/Australian couple on a world tour, maintaining their fledgling YouTube channel and stressing over the statistics.

That first morning I walked out of the hostel and purchased a selection of offerings at the first food place I saw, which turned out to be a variety of three deep-fried dough parcels; one containing mashed potato, one mince and the trio rounded off with green cabbage, an oily carbohydrate cacophony that I struggled to finish, even after a week of mountain rations. It began a luxurious week of leisurely hostel time, playing cards with my fellow travellers, mending clothes, washing my tent to try and remove the must of damp earth and leaves. I went for small walks, stretched every day and found myself getting truly, groggily tired for the first time in almost three months.

I made a mistake the night before I left Ukraine. I'd walked on the road all the way down from Rakhiv and camped where it turned west and began to run alongside a river. I thought I'd found an ordinary secluded camping spot but a few hours later, once I was tucked up against the freezing dark, a strong light shone onto my tent and a dog started to bark ferociously. Peeping out of the bottom of the door, trying not to move the tent fabric, I saw the dark silhouettes of two men standing in the near distance, one holding the barking dog, the other training a torch on my flimsy shelter. My heart burst into a flurry of beats, a prickly adrenaline rush flooding me. *Something is happening. What to do? Cower inside the tent until they come to me?* A moment's consideration. *No.*

I gathered myself, grabbed my knife and stalked towards the silhouettes, demanding to know what he wanted. '*Sta hochesh?*'

They didn't answer.

One man stood apart, holding the dog lead just taut enough so it couldn't get at me. The steam of its hot barking plumed into the torchlight, which was angled low to highlight the edges of a masked face under a peaked cap and the black metal sheen of a rifle. I tucked my knife in against my leg, hoping they hadn't seen it.

'*Pasport.*'

The man explained calmly, with no noticeable change in tone, that he was a border guard. His authority showed in his lack of irritation; no need for alarm, especially not when faced with a plump, homely woman with furry pink bed socks bulging from her unlaced boots.

The bright lights across the river were the beginning of Romania, I realised, where the borderline falls down from the mountains to run along the river. I held the knife flat against my leg as I went back to rummage in the tent. I was a fool to bring it out with me. I'd learnt years ago while hitch-hiking that my greatest defence against danger was my brain, not any paltry weapons I might inadequately arm myself with.

They checked the passport and dismissed me; I was not a threat and that was the way I liked it. I wanted to be a nobody during this journey, both to authorities and to predatory men; non-sexual, non-threatening, not worth noticing.

The next day, after a sleepless night where patrols returned every two hours, shining torches over my tent in lazy animosity, it didn't take long before I was walking alongside razor wire strung in coils along the river edge. At first I thought the patrols were to stop people crossing, then I realised it was more likely to be against smuggling, tobacco in particular. Tobacco companies in Ukraine manufacture way more cigarettes than their country can consume, and figures I found online showed that in 2008 almost a quarter of the 130 billion cigarettes produced were illegally exported. Big business for smugglers.

'People are richer in Chernivtsi Oblast,' someone had said further north. 'The houses are like palaces because they are all smuggling.' It was true, the houses lining the road on my final day of walking were gigantic, multi-storey concrete mansions compared to the rest of the country.

This was where the system changed, I realised. I'd arrived at the European Union – just on the other side of that river was the great organisation that stretched more than 2,000 miles to the Atlantic Ocean. More than just a change of country, I was crossing a border into freedom of movement, freedom to work, access to funds, access to help, a collaborative system.

Here was this joining together of countries for a common good, to increase standards throughout their membership, to improve living conditions in poorer countries, to allow access to cross-border work and education. This club that Britain had voted to leave.

The Brexit decision had happened two summers previously, while I was serving pizza at Glastonbury Festival, commiserating with shocked festival goers as they woke up with more than a hangover to realise that the world outside the bouncy, colourful festival dream-world had changed unexpectedly. The illusion of a festival where you can forget about the outside world for a while and plunge headlong into a hedonistic fancy-dress wonderland had abruptly been shattered by the chill fact that people had only gone and voted leave.

The subsequent two years had seen much political bluster and no decisions, sleepwalking towards the deadline. Entering the EU, I would experience, with sadness, what Britain had voted to separate from.

Unpolished Ukraine had been full of tough people who spend much of their lives surviving, embodying the grit of a life with rough edges. I didn't think I'd see much like it again as I walked onwards.

ROMANIA

Passing the final few cigarette sellers squatting at the roadside, I crossed the wooden border bridge into Romania, alongside many other pedestrians. The glossy difference on entering Sighetu Marmației was an immediate shock; wide, paved street, cafés everywhere, shops of all different kinds: clothes, phones, household goods. I'd become used to the sparse nature of Ukrainian towns, small settlements with only a few tiny shops where there never seemed to be a defined commercial centre.

I walked into a café which offered green smoothies, paninis, and a variety of coffees. Calm piano music played through hidden speakers and there were framed quotations on the exposed brickwork: 'There's no place like home.' 'Laugh Every Day.' 'You are someone's reason to smile.' These tepid, trite decorations make me roll my eyes back in the UK and here they seemed especially pointless.

As I left Sighetu, I passed the drearily familiar layout of a large supermarket and chain stores lined around a central car park: a pet shop, DIY chain, sports shop, clothes, shoes, electronics stores. The EU meant commercialism, it meant a car-centred lifestyle, it meant polished professionalism and it meant homogeneity.

The sleazy way men on the street looked me over, eyeing my body up and down in lascivious assessment, was both new and drearily familiar too. Such distinct, brutal objectification had been completely absent in Ukraine, and I hadn't even noticed until it returned full force.

The roads were in much better condition: thick black tarmac smoothed all the way to the lane edge, white lines carefully painted. There were road signs with distances on them, something that had been completely missing from the small roads of Ukraine. The cars were newer too, the effect of thirteen years of EU scrappage schemes.

Out of Sighetu Marmației I headed towards the village of Breb, a day's walk south, to stop and wait for a supply package.

Planning this journey, I'd imagined regular deliveries from the UK, containing fresh maps, seasonal changes of clothing, replacements for things I couldn't source locally such as high-quality vitamin tablets or kinesiology tape. I had a helpful friend who was storing my kit in her spare room and picking out the things I needed to courier them to me. The package I tried to get sent to Rakhiv, Ukraine was the first test of the process, but instead of taking the quoted five days, it took a nail-biting wait of two and a half weeks.

The first problem was the lack of courier delivery to Rakhiv; DHL didn't cover that area. When I fretted over how to get my resupply, a stranger called Cheryl offered stays at her smallholding to an online women's group I was part of. Incredibly she was only about 50 miles away across the border in Romania and, reading my plea for help, she offered to receive the package and have me to stay while I waited for it.

My UK friends sent the box and I aimed to arrive in Breb at the same time as the parcel. Unfortunately, it didn't arrive as expected and disappeared from the tracking, so I found myself faced with an awkward wait in a stranger's house, sleeping on their kitchen floor and feeling in the way.

There was nothing to do but exist while I waited for my parcel to arrive, tracking its infinitesimal progress for four agonising days, stuck in a constant rollercoaster of being overcome by tension and trying to release control, allow time to pass without gnawing my fingers off.

Cheryl and Roland were very kind and patient with me but I was climbing the walls. I was supposed to be walking, that was all I existed to do. Having to wait for this parcel showed me how much of my life during this journey was focused on constant movement, my only sense of progress towards the far-distant finish line. Winter was coming; I was running out of time.

I'm fine when I can solve my problems myself but, after a childhood of suffering constant parental unreliability, awful at relying on other people, and in this delay an anxious, restless rage set in.

The calm, slow lives of the Magyars orbited around the basic self-sufficiency tasks of feeding the fire for heating and cooking, collecting and chopping their wood, drawing water from the spout outside, washing food, crockery and bodies in a sequence of metal bowls. They lived in a traditional rural Romanian wooden house with a huge weathered front door leading into two rooms, one for living, one for sleeping, carved decorations adorned the length of the large verandah outside.

As the days passed, I began to realise the breadth of their knowledge, in herbalism, animal keeping, clay and cob building, spinning, weaving, sewing, shoe making. Every other evening, Roland would take the small milk churn and a couple of lei over to the neighbour and return with fresh milk, still warm, to be kept on the windowsill of the unheated bedroom. 'We wash our hair in walnut leaf infusion,' said Cheryl. 'It's an astringent.' She made me an anti-inflammatory willow bark tea when I had hip pain after the first night on the kitchen floor, my legs stiffening up after four days of repetitive road walking.

I felt calmer for my stay with the Magyars. Theirs is a life that seeks self-reliance, acknowledging the impossibility of true self-sufficiency. It's a lifestyle I recognise from Wales – there are plenty of alternative spirits there. I have friends who live off grid, friends who pay attention to moon cycles, friends who practise herbalism, friends who hug trees, who harvest seeds, who walk barefoot, work with natural materials, who think responsibly about community and ecology and our effect on the planet. But somehow, the life I was lucky enough to be invited into in northern Romania felt more authentic than many back home. Their lack of car, fridge, washing machine or shower; the moving of the bed to sleep in the kitchen during the coldest months. In my experience of modern Britain, compromise creeps in. Even if every easy online purchase comes in a recyclable bag, it's not good enough. Even if we take our own reusable cup for our takeaway coffee, it's not good enough. Living a life more in tune with the planet means giving things up, means not having it all, and just because I choose not to fly across land doesn't mean I'm not part of this global hedonism. Most modern lifestyles are breaking the planet apart and we still can't stop sucking the marrow from its bones because we are utterly unable to give up a single comfort.

Roland and Cheryl were unusual in this village, just as similar hippies are back home. Roland regularly went into the stream at the end of their land and cleared out the plastic that other people had thrown in upstream. I noted the rubbish littering the field edges and the stinky ditches full of rotten fermented plums, run-off from the neighbour's large home distillery operation.

On leaving Breb, I was heading south-west towards the Apuseni Mountains, not sure how much of the heights I'd be able to tackle once the full depth of winter snow fell, but it felt like a more interesting challenge than a route on the lower land running south-east between the two mountain ranges of the Southern Carpathians and the Apuseni.

My worst-case scenario had come true: the courier delays had kept me still during the final period of clear weather and now the blast of a Siberian cold snap was on the way, no snow but freezing dry cold air, with night-time temperatures dropping to minus 15c a few days ahead. The weather forecast was minus 5c for the night I gave the Magyars grateful hugs on the wooden verandah and walked away to cross their local mountain, a volcano crater named the Rooster's Crest, Creasta Cocoșului, which twinkled white and icy in the blue sky.

When walking and camping in temperatures like this, life becomes reduced to the battle for body heat. The wind had teeth, scraping my cheeks raw. Frostbite is a cold gnawing at your skin, squeezing you, shrinking life. All the actions of the day required thought – *Am I warm enough to sit still for a while? How are my fingers? Have I eaten enough? Am I hydrated?* There was a constant addition and removal of layers – gloves, headband, neck scarf, fleece, down jacket, waterproof jacket – making sure I stayed warm but not dangerously sweaty.

Walking in cold weather, as I lost water, in my sweat, my urine and my breath, I didn't notice the lack. I had to force myself to eat and drink, consider it a mechanical necessity rather than a desire. It was too cold to sit and eat. I couldn't keep my hands out of the sleeping bag for long enough at night. My water bottle was freezing solid at night, too leaky to keep inside my sleeping bag (something that would be resolved at Christmas).

All I wanted to do at night was put the tent up and get inside my layers of sleeping bag as quickly as possible. If I'd cooled down too much while putting the tent up, then I made sure I jumped around, jogged away from the tent and back again to get hot blood all the way to my fingers and toes.

My body ached from the walking, my hips were tight, it hurt to lie still in the restrictive sleeping bag cocoon. With no room to stretch properly, all I could do was curl my feet up and down, stretch my calves, and rub my lower back and bum, trying to release the big thick gluteus muscle. I changed position a lot, my body unable to slip into deep sleep while it was still so tense. Every time I moved I had to rearrange all the layers of bedding so I didn't smother myself or lose heat.

Every point took focus. The tent was covered in ice in the mornings, frost on the outside and my frozen breath on the inside. I had to take it down without getting my woollen gloves wet, but my thicker ski gloves made my fingers clumsy. I wanted to pack away the tent without scattering too much frost into the inside, keep moisture away from my down sleeping bags. Even if I was still tired, I couldn't stay in bed too long, there weren't enough daylight hours to waste. Once I'd made the decision to unzip the sleeping bag then I was pouring my conserved heat into the icy air and had to act quickly. I had to eat something, usually a banana, unpleasantly semi-frozen, before stopping for proper breakfast later, once I had thoroughly warmed up. I needed to drink but the water was full of ice crystals and hurt my throat.

As I walked south-west on flat land towards the next mountains, my initial impression of Romania was hostile; there was very little conversation, I was more likely to receive sideways glances from uninterested faces. The houses felt shuttered and inward facing, with blank white plaster and small windows on the street, high gates enclosing unseen yards where the real life of the home was.

The village dogs were awful to deal with, much more aggressive than in Ukraine; frothing in a white fanged frenzy at the limit of their leashes, or making rushes at the back of my heels, scattering at the swish of my stick before nipping in again as my head turned away. They snarled more and followed me for longer, their owners making irregular, ineffectual attempts to call them back.

Occasionally, which was deeply unpleasant, people watched in passive hostility as their dogs harried me along the street.

'Beware of the feral forest dogs,' people warned me. But when I saw dogs in the wild, well away from villages, they completely ignored me – plenty of territory for everyone and no need to fight.

Shepherd dogs would come bounding at this new threat, spying me, the unusual movement, from far away and cantering to be the first to explore the alien up close, sheep flowing in the background, shepherd invisible. They would be huge dogs, paws like thick workman hands, as if they could reach out and cuff me, spiked collars with dangling stubs of wood or metal spikes, designed to protect the throat from wolf attack.

I learned to shout. They ignored insipid, soft voices, and trying to beat them away with my walking poles only confirmed I was a danger, but if I bellowed until my voice cracked, sometimes they listened and backed off. For a human, a raised voice is a sign of anger, of weakness, but for dogs it's a show of strength.

Slowly, as the days passed, I started to experience human connections.

A man beckoned me from his yard and invited me in for coffee. I said yes on impulse and found myself in a warm room crowded with furniture, fabric covering the walls, floors and just about every surface. Nelu and his mother, Margarita, didn't ask me anything about myself, just offered me food; a meatball broth, chunks of bread, then mashed potato and fried sausage, a mug of coffee, glass of fizzy drink. Nelu poured me glasses of his homemade wine. He tried to give me vegetables to take away but my pack was too heavy, so we settled on a single apple.

There was Ioana, the girl in the empty café who started telling me how she wished she could do something like me but was too scared; how she was stuck in a job she didn't like, trying to encourage her small children to be braver than her, telling herself every day that this was the day she was going to do something for herself. We compared nail varnish, mine chipped and shabby, hers shiny and perfect, and she gave me a hug before I left, asking if there was anything I needed.

What I needed was for winter to be over, although it was only just beginning.

A priest found me on the steps of his church where I'd stopped for a quiet place to eat lunch. He asked if I was OK and offered some food, then brought his wife around the corner to invite me for tea. We had a short conversation where I told them what I was doing and they told me I was courageous, before it was time to go.

I walked another hour and found somewhere to camp. It had been an extremely cold few days, below minus 10c at night, difficult camping conditions. I woke up to a pale pink dawn, peeking out of the tent to see a line of deer crossing the frozen field. All was crisp and crystalline as they picked their way over ploughed clods and corn stubble. I was slow to pack away, having to stop to stamp my numb feet and rub my burning fingers. Pulling up my neck scarf to cover my cheeks, I stopped at the first café for an omelette breakfast and to thaw my solid water bottle on the top of their wood-stove.

At midday, a car stopped ahead of me and a woman got out. It was the third time in two days that she'd passed me on the road, did I want some tea? Her name was Bianca; we chatted a while and she offered to find me somewhere to stay the night. I agreed – my tent was covered in frost from the night before and another night in extreme cold would be difficult. We arranged that she would pick me up in a few hours, once it got dark. She did, the temperature already reading minus 8 at 5pm and, as we drove towards my hosts, she said she'd phoned her brother and told him about the woman she'd met. He'd met me too, the day before, 15 miles away; he was the priest.

Bianca called some friends and took me to the house of Nelu and Maria, a retired couple. I could stay a couple of nights, keep walking during the day and hitch-hike back to theirs to sleep. They invited me to stay for an extra day off too. 'They're killing the Christmas pig, a great treat,' said Maria.

In my culture we are distanced from our meat eating, encouraged to let the dismemberment be done in secret, left only to pick out our end product, plastic packaged, sterile and safe, the details of death kept separate from the eating, behind closed doors. This distance from the origins of our food allows unnatural processing and ingredients and unnatural living conditions, all in the name of profit for the food processors. Maria's brother owned the farm and he delivered the body on the back of his tractor. They'd have killed it themselves but the EU says you can only kill animals at the abattoir these days. The huge body lay on a pallet in the centre of the concrete yard, a plump, pink lump of dead pig.

It was a family celebration day; the two sons helped Nelu gut and dismember the carcass, feeding in the meat leg by leg, chunk by chunk to the women in the woodshed, who were chopping and mincing. I helped a little but mostly watched in fascination. Nelu poured us all regular shots of *țuică*, home-distilled plum brandy, and showed me the box where he salted down slabs of fat, for them to come out months later as *slanina*. Called *salo* in Ukraine, it's a favourite Slavic delicacy across Eastern and Central Europe, eaten in thin, almost translucent slices with raw garlic and bread in Ukraine, or used as a cooking fat.

This break for the day of butchery saw me through the last of the extreme cold. The Siberian blast passed over and the weather turned to a manageable grey drizzle. Romania felt like very slow progress. As November flipped to December, I seemed to be crawling across the land, way behind where I expected to be. I was crossing dull, brown, faded agricultural landscapes, often under a heavy grey sky. Many tracks were churned by tractor or the passage of sheep to a sticky mud that weighted every step.

Yet I was often thrilled to be there, excited by this feeling of survival. It's invigorating to be cosy in my sleeping bag, feeling the warmth build inside my nest when the chill in the air outside would numb my skin within seconds. To exit the tent and see the pale lilac of a cold dawn, the rose pink of first light tinting faraway mountain tops, to know that I had survived another night sleeping outside in the cold. How could I possibly feel let down by what I was managing when just staying alive was hard enough?

I regularly heard a roaring blowtorch as I walked through villages and knew that somewhere behind a wall there would be a couple of men in dirty jeans standing around a pig carcass, probably with cigarettes firmly in their mouths, as they burned off the bristles with jets of flame.

One day the air was full of stars; thousands of perfect star-shaped snowflakes falling from the sky to sit, brilliant and distinct, on the frozen mud. It was almost Christmas.

I went to Bucharest for the celebration, to meet my brother who had flown out for a week. The city was bustling and expensive, with fairy lights decorating trees, ethereal blue lights twinkling in the snow and bare branches. We met a couple of his uni friends, now app designers and financial analysts, and went to their home for a family meal of pork and polenta, with Christmas *cozonac*, a yeasted cake with cocoa, jelly and raisins twisted into the dough.

Last time I stepped out of the central train station in Bucharest, in 2011, I had faced a pack of stray dogs and a bunch of teenagers huffing glue fumes from plastic bags crunched in their fists. Now it was a glossier city, cleaned up, homogenised. We went to a pub with imported ales, one from a Cardiff brewery. Then a Christmas market with a specially constructed skating rink, just like hundreds of others across Europe, where we drank overpriced mulled wine from cardboard cups and browsed expensive traditional artisan crafts displayed in open-sided wooden sheds to the ugly noise of a sound system blaring distorted singing.

There was very little unusual or interesting graffiti around, just a scrawl of names on every available surface. Some of the grit of Romanian city life may have been washed away by a wave of EU development money but what remained felt like all consumption, lacking soul.

Wealth disparity between a capital city and its rural far reaches is normal for any country, but Romanian capitalism felt soulless; furniture was often cheap and badly made, shops full of plastic goods that would fall apart within a few months. I struggled with the differences I saw. It was lacking zest – Romania had no zing. I missed Ukraine in comparison, the simplicity, the honesty and the rawness. I'm romanticising poverty and survival, true, but in a hyper-capitalistic, over-processed world, where the focus is on a clean, recognisable, same-in-all-the-franchises product, then the spirit of life is the first thing to die and the last thing to be missed.

New Year came and I spent a final few days alone in Bucharest, feeling worn down by the stress of winter. I knew I was returning to snowy mountain conditions and had no idea how to approach the next part of the route. Anyone I shared my fears with would strongly urge caution and it was undermining my self-belief.

I was making route decisions on the hoof; I'd been too busy working to earn the funds for the trip to do the gargantuan amount of research necessary for exact route planning. Before setting off, I'd drawn a line across the continent connecting the countries I wanted to visit. These eastern countries had very few marked footpaths, let alone long-distance walking paths, so I was free to follow my nose, head for areas that looked intriguing, and work out exact paths week by week, sometimes day by day. I preferred to plunge into the unknown anyway. There was a sense of fuzzy logic about my journey style; I wasn't certain of what would happen to me, who I would encounter or what conditions were coming, but I equipped myself with the high quality kit I expected would be enough to survive, based on previous experiences, and then went for it, trusting that I had the skills to successfully respond to whatever situation I found myself in.

It meant freedom to choose whatever route felt interesting or fitted my energy levels. I always wanted to achieve the most, imagined myself climbing the highest peaks or pushing through the snow, but without the experience to know when enough was too much, I was always pushing and retreating, pushing and retreating. Choosing a route based on how brave I felt, meant it was easy for me to get put off by anxious advice online, which inevitably urged caution over wild abandon.

On the first night back in Bihor County, I had permission to camp in the garden of an empty house. After three weeks off in Bucharest, I trundled up the hill from Bratca, my apprehension growing. At the edge of town I stopped and drew a line in the snow. 'No more tiredness and stress,' I said to myself, geeing myself on, 'from this point on, I will step forward into positivity.' I walked upwards into thicker and thicker snow, none on the road but all around me on the hills; there was a bite in the air that had been missing from the lowland city warmth of Bucharest and all felt very silent and still. Finally at the house, a traditional wooden building with a red tiled roof, I wiggled the frozen gate latch open. As the garden was knee deep in fine white powder, putting up a tent was unappetising and I decided to sleep on the large verandah. Windblown flakes drifted thick across the planks but I was good and cosy, despite a moment of strong sensory dissonance when I opened my eyes in the morning to see snow around my bed.

It had fallen thickly overnight and for weeks there was snowfall every day, sometimes just for an hour and sometimes all day and night. Icy pinpoints rustling against my jacket like sand. Sometimes it came in hard, thin dots that were barely seen until they blew against my face like fine needles. Sometimes it was fat, feather flakes, floating down soft and slow like a demure lowering of eyelashes.

The sudden increase in effort was shocking after my Xmas lethargy, leaving my body stiff and complaining. I was often the only person outside on head-down trudges through closed-up villages, gardens quietly blanketed and smoke from chimneys the only sign of life. The fields were covered, every tree branch carrying a thin layer, the concrete lumps of bridges, posts and telegraph poles all softened by their rounded snow hats.

Shân, who had been so helpful when I was walking the Conwy Valley, had given me her useful Romanian contact, a city dweller who had previously worked in rural tourism development; we had met for a coffee in Bucharest. He couldn't really understand why I was doing this and strongly urged me not to go up into the Apuseni national park area, a mountain wilderness where there were definitely wolves, but did offer his contacts to help me get accommodation, usually people he'd helped to get grants. It was a great idea in theory but rarely worked smoothly, mostly making me divert from my route to reach the accommodation, meaning wasted hours hitch-hiking. The local host was several degrees removed from knowing anything about me, usually forcing a disinterested welcome, and I felt like a package that had been passed into someone's care for a while – a completely unrelaxing experience.

But the alternative was snow camping and I felt completely unrelaxed about that too. There's a particular intimidation to walking through a snowy landscape without knowing where you're going to sleep. Mountain struggles or busy road dangers, unsuitable hosts or snow camping; all my options were difficult in some way.

I chose a wriggling route through the Apuseni, trying to keep up in the mountains and away from the main roads. The back roads were a network of veins, and plenty of valleys had a single road leading off the main road up into the mountain and back again, but access to the next valley was restricted to thin tracks that were covered in a metre or more of snow.

Walking along main roads was an awful endless trudge on painful tarmac; vehicles spraying me with dirty slush as they rushed past; having to break my stride and step into the verge to avoid a lorry passing so close I could touch it; cars overtaking from the opposite side suddenly appearing at my shoulder in a shocking boom of sound and air. But the other option was snowy mountain walking. Even wearing snowshoes, I'd still be floundering around for hours, committing myself to slow progress in remote areas with minimal food, water and shelter. I was repeatedly told not to walk up in the mountains and, fear-weakened, I listened to them. Maybe I could have done it, but I didn't have the experience to be certain, and at least on the roads I was making faster progress.

Climbing mountains felt like success and road walking felt like failure, but this was an illusion I had to get over; it was my walk, my creation, and I was in charge, both of my route and my attitude. The only rule of this whole journey was that I walk across Europe – no further conditions or additions – yet somehow my ideas about what that entailed were pretty hard to change. Berating myself for not choosing the hardest option – what was this self-flagellation? I was pushing myself to my limits and then only focusing on the tiny step back I took at the last minute.

So, I walked on roads and took detours up side valleys in order to get to places to sleep, which is where I got the real taster of Romanian village winter life.

One afternoon as I hitch-hiked away from the main road up a dead-end valley, the road covered in a few centimetres of packed snow, an Orthodox priest stopped for me, driving a 4x4. We passed through a couple of villages, roofs layered in a foot of snow, pathways shovelled from doorway to road, and eventually he dropped me at a bridge in the final village before a semicircle of high white hills, right next to the village bar. I decided on a hot chocolate and cognac before battling what I'd been told would be very deep snow up the track to my Couchsurfing hosts.

Some village stores and bars were modern, the bars in particular – leather seating, TV blaring dance music, generic cityscape or flower pictures on the walls. Others, like this one, were simply a room for men to come and sit and drink and chat, as they have done for years, without minding the dirty walls and tattered furnishings. There was a TV in the corner showing folk music, the fast violin tunes that I heard from many houses, videos featuring plump contented women in traditional white blouses embroidered with colourful blooms, standing and singing in sunny flower meadows or snowy churchyards.

I was shocked by the emptiness of some of these stores, used to shops and bars that are designed to soothe or sell. In supermarkets or corner shops in the UK, no space is unused: there's advertising, bright lighting, crowding cardboard displays. This assault to the senses has become so normalised that a large room with minimal strip lighting and products piled haphazardly on handmade wooden shelves, prices scrawled on them in marker pen, seemed dingy in comparison.

The majority of the food I found in small village shops was low quality junk, over-processed empty calories. Crisps, tinned pork pâté, biscuits, instant coffee, chocolate, preserved meat, processed cheese in plastic tubes. Very minimal fruit and vegetable selections. I was too tired and it was too cold to put thought and time into preparing meals – during the daytime it was too cold to stay still for long and in the evening I just needed to shovel food into my body and sleep. Cold beans straight from the can were a saviour during this Romanian winter. Every shop seemed to stock decent beans in tomato sauce with passable quality meat floating around in there. It wasn't about haute cuisine, nice china, or the intangible pleasures of eating, just calories spooned in to fill my stomach as quickly and efficiently as possible.

This village bar was particularly dingy, with battered wooden tables, worn metal chairs and the most ramshackle pool table I have ever seen in my life: baize rubbed smooth to a dirty grey green, a scattering of duct tape covering the many holes. The blank gaze of four men greeted me; I'd chatted a little to one of them outside and understood enough Romanian to know that he was explaining to them where I'd come from and where I was staying in the village, but not enough to follow the remainder of the conversation. I stayed quiet, dipping my stale, packaged croissant into my black coffee, pouring in the cheap cognac and ignoring the complete lack of eye contact or acknowledgement from anyone else in the room, as they discussed me.

It had quite often been like that since Christmas; most people weren't explicitly unfriendly, just seemed uninterested. Broadly speaking, back in Ukraine I was used to being pleasantly welcomed as an intriguing novelty by people fascinated by who I was and what I was doing there. In Romania, if I said hello, people would say hello back but that tended to be it. I could go a day or two with no conversation beyond '*Bună ziua*'. Maybe it was down to winter conditions, everyone a little shut off, focused on what they needed to do with no time to stand around and chat in the cold. But there was a closed feeling to most villages; I think a lot of Romanian life takes place in private.

That night was wonderful, though. I'd been accepted by Couchsurfing hosts in a tiny cottage high above the valley; to climb to it, I had to cross a stream and follow a track thickly covered in snow. Eventually, after an hour of wallowing in drifts, I found the house, a peaceful and welcoming place. With the tracks inaccessible by vehicle, a visitor was a rare occurrence and Flaviu and Lydia stayed here all winter, dug in until the thaw of spring, calling it a deep meditation.

Even better, thick snow fell overnight and I had the wonderful experience of walking two hours down to the road in thigh-deep snow, following a path to the south, as a quicker way to leave the valley. The dogs of the house bounded and barked around me as I opened the door into this white wonderland, the small black one following me for quite a distance. We walked high above the valley bottom along a long curve of the hillside, a thin line of depressed snow my only indication that a path existed. The air was full of thick flakes whirling around me as I carefully stepped on, using my walking poles to balance while the small dog followed along in my wake, the snow too deep for her to break her own path.

As the path led into the forest, I heard the other dog barking in the distance. The black dog stopped and looked behind her, then turned and began plodding through the snow towards home as I walked on into the forest. After a few minutes, a huge animal pushed past me. It was the other dog, much bigger and shaggier, bounding in and out of the trees, branches shaking down shivers of snowfall to mark his hidden path. He accompanied me all the way to the road as I plunged down the steep hill in hip-deep drifts. Young trees arched over the path, bowed under snow weight, and he would wait as I knocked hanging branches, clearing them to spring upwards in rustle and mist. As I checked my map, he stood calm with me in the black-and-white silence of the sleeping trees. It was as if the dogs had decided I shouldn't be without a companion that day and made sure I came safely down the hill.

Thanks to Gabriel's web of contacts, I climbed a solid 19 miles of road to sleep in a mountain rescue base up at the ski resort of Vårtop. That was the most spectacular day, starting on the flatlands and wriggling up into the mountains, back and forth on the curves of the ascent, snow getting thicker, dribbling from the trees, fine flakes collecting on my hat and coat, walking all day, timing my breaks, not allowing myself to stop for too long, until finally I saw the twinkling lights of the ski resort, glowing high in the darkness of the mountain.

The snow was thickly piled around the buildings; bright windows in steep triangular roofed lodges made tiny openings that shone golden steam from hot showers inside. Incredibly, there were even stray dogs up here; two shaggy snow-coated heaps, matted and dirty like old mops, curled sleeping on the snow under the tangy orange glow of a streetlamp.

I arrived at the base too tired to speak, going straight to bed and lying there, body too painful to sleep. In the morning, up in the spartan dormitory, before I went downstairs to face the conversations of the busy team, mainly catering to ski slope injuries, I watched the snow out of the window. The air was white with a mist of tiny flakes. Pine trees surrounded the back of the building;

tall, thin black columns shrouded white, swaying slightly in the wind, branches drooping. In between the trees came a scrappy black squirrel, thin, sparse tail, pattering and leaping, bouncing easily on the frozen surface that drifted up almost to my first-floor window. The pine trees felt cloaked and smothered, held in the stillness of the deep winter sleep that is a near death and I stared in amazement from my artificial bubble of hot air, admiring how easily the ragged squirrel moved here in this inhospitable, white wasteland.

As I descended from the mountain I joined the main road between Brad and Deva, a busy transcontinental route, totally cleared of snow and ice, with heavy traffic running fast. With no hard shoulder, each lorry slammed past me in a racketing mass of metal, close enough to touch. It was deeply unpleasant walking, even for a couple of miles, and I was very glad to escape onto a parallel side road. Immediately I was walking more slowly on packed ice and taking a longer route as the road wriggled and rose into low hills, but I didn't care. The relief of not being oppressed by dangerous heavy traffic felt more important.

There was very little colour in this muted landscape; the bright whiteness turned all the browns and greys to black. As the valley twisted, I could see the scattered villages ahead, each one with its high, pointed church spires. For my bed, an ideal barn presented itself, fenced and snow-covered. I checked the ground for prints, not wanting to be surprised by a shepherd returning to fill this place with fifty sheep, but the snow was pristine and I snuck in at the back, finding a perfect, fenced-off corner full of haybales and loose straw. After I stacked bales against the draughty open slats of the wall, it wasn't long before the straw began to give me back my body-warmth and I slept a cosy night, woken only by rustling mice and wind buffeting the roof. By morning yet more overnight snow had spread into the centre of the barn floor. I left a small pile of broken biscuits for the mice, and walked a final 14 miles on packed snow to achieve my Deva day off. The red tail lights of occasional passing cars were vivid points of colour in an intense black-and-white landscape of snow and rocky gorge, until I came off the winding back road and entered the city.

Looking south from Deva, I had to decide how to cross the Carpathians for the second time. When I entered Romania, they'd curved around to the east as I'd come west to walk south through the Apuseni Mountains. I could have walked south-west to cross the Danube into Serbia, but I wanted to loop to the east and include Bulgaria in my route. I'd cross the border at Ruse and give myself a few hundred miles of Bulgaria before reaching the Balkans.

The simplest way to cross the imposing barrier of the Carpathian Mountains was to continue directly south on the E79, a main transport link full of lorries, but I was loathe to walk a full 90 miles along a very busy road with no hard shoulder; even an hour of lorries thundering past within arm's reach was too intimidating; a whole week would be torture. Many of the north/south smaller mountain roads further east were closed due to heavy snowfall and avalanche, but I fixed on one possibility.

It was a toss-up between what was navigable and what was bearable.

I was walking across Europe: that was the only constant I needed to stick to. Road walking, sleeping in hotels, or mountain climbing and wild camping. As long as I walked every step, everything else I did to stay alive and keep on walking was good enough.

A few days of simple walking through the flatlands of the Mureș river valley, which separated the Apuseni and main Carpathian ranges, brought a distraction of dog drama. A mile outside a village, on a back road, I met a yellow dog barking at two patchy brown puppies that seemed to have crawled out from a box in the hedgerow. They were too cute to pass by without a fuss and I soon found myself feeding them my entire stick of salami. Yellow Dog circled nervously, snatching pieces from my outstretched hand, while the pups crawled all over me. Feeding them made it hard to walk away – the tiny puppies were obviously abandoned, only four or five weeks old, one barely had its eyes open. I decided to take them to the next village, maybe find a vet. They toddled after me, mewling, short bandy legs bowing around big bellies, until I scooped them up, tucking their soft sausage bodies into the front of my down jacket, where they snuggled down to sleep.

I let out a wail on Facebook, feeling so sad about these animals callously left to survive in a frozen field, and some dog-loving friends kicked into action, contacting their Romanian animal charity links. My phone kept buzzing with notifications: someone could come and pick the puppies up the following night, I just had to walk 12 miles to meet them in the next town. It was a strange thing, this passionate reaction to two abandoned puppies, the swooping in to save them when there's so much wrong in the world, both back then in 2019 and now. Trump was in power in the USA, racism and xenophobia continued to blight society, Brexit limped ahead, Ukraine was at war, we continued to approach climate catastrophe, Romanian politicians were openly corrupt, and here we were fussing over dogs that sleep outside. I suppose, in the face of such awful global events, achievable small positives involving innocent animals are easier to focus on than such human-made catastrophes.

Walking with the pups tucked inside my jacket was difficult; the weight of them bent me forward, awkwardly hurting my back, but I loved to feel them wriggling against my stomach, sleeping happy and insulated. The other dog followed along but pretended he wasn't, looking away whenever he saw me watching. He seemed uncertain, wouldn't interact with me and growled and snapped at the pups when they went towards him for a sniff.

I called them all Eric, for my friend's dying father, sending her cute pictures as she sat at his bedside back in Wales.

The puppies naturally followed me into the tent that night, and then my sleeping bag. They'd wriggle out for regular explorations and come back to gnaw my nose and tuck under my chin, my bag filled with grit and the hot peppery smell of their skin. It snowed overnight and I found Blond Eric curled under a tree near the tent, a melted circle around him marking the circumference of his body heat.

I had no food left to share with them but dry bread. Blond Eric hunted around for extra scraps. *I shouldn't be feeding him.* A little warning sounded, as I packed away my frosty tent. *He's not part of the puppy rescue and I can't get near him, let alone hand him over to someone else. Do I want a dog? I don't want a dog. They're extra responsibility and mean I can't stay in hotels so easily.* January was not a time to have a dog limiting your hotel access.

The miles were long that day as I trudged along a straight, flat road, a thin layer of snow slippery underfoot, ploughed fields stretching either side, the snow there melting into stripes. Far away across the ribbons of river and main road, there loomed the broad wall of the Carpathian Mountains. I would walk east until I reached the road I had judged would be clear enough to climb over to the south.

The puppy pickup was accidentally arranged for a very posh hotel, an imitation chateau with a long driveway and tailored gardens. Fortunately the receptionist was enchanted by the bundle of puppies I was badly concealing in my jacket and we found a sheltered shed for me to wait for the charity workers. When she brought out a mug of fruit tea, Blond Eric wouldn't let her near the shed at first, barking and growling. I wasn't sure what to do. How could I start controlling him if I wasn't going to make him mine? But after she left, he came near me for the first time, sat down at my outstretched feet and faced away from me, licking the accumulated snow water from his fur. It felt settled.

Puppy rescue arrived and they didn't really know what to do about Blond Eric either. Romania is overwhelmed by stray dogs, a few of them flitted around the edges of the car park as we spoke. The charity was struggling, not for money but for homes; too many dogs and not enough takers. The public dog shelters had high kill rates, and the animals were crammed together, left to attack each other, they told me. Blond Eric came close enough to sniff one outstretched hand but otherwise avoided us.

Maybe I'll keep him, I thought, then anxiety started whirring; the border crossings, the vets visits for vaccinations and a dog passport, the cost of it, the weight of the food I'd have to carry, how to prevent him from barking at people, the lack of access to hotels. My mind whizzed further ahead to the UK: where would I live with him, what would he do while I was at work, how could I get him on a lead and train him away from the feral impulsiveness of life as a Romanian street dog?

I thought about telling him to go away, hissing and shouting until he felt unwelcome, and it melted me into tears. I started to realise that immediately thinking of all the things that could possibly go wrong just because I was letting a dog follow me for a while was not a calm, reasoned response. Neither was feeling distraught about upsetting him.

It was obviously bringing up all kind of fears in me that were nothing to do with a stray dog. This was about trusting myself to be responsible for another living being. I grew up in a very negative house, everything wrong and broken, never receiving praise, never being good enough. Gut fear shrieked that I'd get angry and abusive like my parents, that I couldn't care for Eric properly. '*You're a bad person, unworthy. You're not capable of this,*' whispered the childhood conditioning that permeated my inner psyche like a malignant mycelium.

Having grown up full of fear about my flaws, a key part of trying to become a functional adult has been about accepting failure and imperfection. I was so scared of revealing my imagined profound and unacceptable failings that I wasn't trying at all. The immediacy of the walking and adventuring that I began in my late twenties, was essential – to go out into the world and let things happen without trying to control them in advance; to get them wrong, to allow myself to fail, to realise that the world wouldn't collapse when I did, and instead to learn how to do better. This was a clear next step in my healing, to accept the possibility of failing in the care of another living thing, committing to a lifetime of dog, something I couldn't run away from. If something was upsetting me this much, then maybe I should go with it.

Once I'd packed up the chaos of the hotel room, pulling the clothing and sleeping bag and tent from the various chairs and lampshades where they'd hung to dry overnight, I went outside to find Eric was hanging around at the door. I sat down and let him smell me a bit. He still wouldn't let me touch him, but when I walked away he followed and after a while I said something and he did a few little skipping jump steps so I knew he was happy to be setting off again, just like me.

We walked five hours together, all the way to Sebeș. He tinkled along on his little corgi legs, nosing around in the verges when I decided to have a wee or a sit down. I talked to him a little but he didn't respond, just trotted along nearby, pretending he wasn't with me. There was an awkward incident at the supermarket where I assumed he'd wait outside but he followed me in and then froze when the security guard started shouting, looking sheepish while I ineffectually tried to usher him out. *This isn't how to have a dog*, I thought. *Everything has to change; I'll have to have him on a lead, I suppose, I'll have to tie him up outside.*

I shopped for four days' worth of minimal mountain rations – bananas, cheese, potato, peanuts, salami, oats, chocolate. Then I added the smallest bag of dog food there was, 1.5 kilos. I was really pushing the limits of what I could carry now; with full winter kit my rucksack was heavy and bursting. But there it was, the dog responsibility started here.

We sat for a while in the sunshine. I ate my lunch and emptied a tin of dogfood onto the concrete for him. He ate, sniffed at me and then went to lie under the nearest tree. *I look like a proper tramp now*, I thought, as I sat on the kerb eating yoghurt and preserved strawberries from the jar given to me in a village two days earlier. My legs were spread wide to dry my muddy trousers and I noticed the sideways looks from the better dressed customers, without particularly caring. As I heaved on my rucksack, Eric was ready, springing up to follow me to the city centre.

Suddenly he wasn't there. I looked down behind me and there was no flash of yellow. I turned, thinking he was on my other side, but for the first time in two days there was no dog. I was about 100m from the street corner and stood for a long while, thinking that I wouldn't walk back and check for him, but then I did. I waited at the corner for another long while but he didn't appear.

It was a loss – a huge sadness weighted my chest. But I knew immediately that I wouldn't search for him. If a dog was going to randomly appear in my life then I had to allow it to randomly disappear. What would I say if I went to find him? 'Come on, keep following me and pretending I don't exist whenever we make eye contact.' It was a relief, a coward's way out, but he was only a good idea if I just saw what happened. I might have let him follow along with me for a bit and found that our lives grew into each other. But they didn't; he turned a different corner.

The next morning, after a final B&B on the edge of town where I had a big cry and left the dog food in the room, I headed out on the small road, going up to cross the Carpathians. The road might be closed ahead but it would take me a few days to find out.

I had the sensation of small puppy noses pushing against my chest, warm bodies wriggling inside my jacket. I felt Eric's absence, a small trotting thing missing from the edge of my eyeline.

I was glad they weren't there. I didn't want pets, it changed things, made more work for me at a time when I was already stretching myself to my limit. But it showed me a lot, the Eric incident: how much I'd like companionship, while also pushing it away. This journey was really testing me, who I was, what I was lacking, why did I choose to be alone, how did I really feel about those choices? I saw how my life had been created by my own trauma-driven decisions just as much as by what had happened to traumatise me.

White mountains ahead, billowing lines in the sky, above the hills, like clouds until you realised they stretched the width of the horizon. I faced four days of following a road up and up, as the hills rose higher either side of the valley, until the road became a thin strip blasted from rock, a steep fall to a river on one side and overhanging pine trees on the other, snowballs and leaves dribbled down to the roadside hinting at mini avalanches above.

My mood lightened now I was actually there, tackling the mountains which had loomed ahead for so long. It was much warmer than two weeks ago, I could walk along without gloves, hat or scarf, once I'd heated up. The trees were black and the villages had a stark and grubby look against the bright white ground. There was hardly any snowfall, just a few tiny flakes for a short time every day.

As I walked the winding road, a car pulled up alongside me. It often happened, especially in these remote areas, and I had to stop and explain that I wanted to walk but thank you for the offer. This car was full of happy smiling faces; they told me they were going to stay in a monastery.

'I'm walking over the mountain,' I said. 'Can I stay there too?'

'Yes, yes of course.' A woman bundled out of the back seat to hug me in her excitement. Andrea wanted me to go with them that minute but I said I'd see them there in a couple of days. We talked about directions, they looked at my map and showed me a barrage up ahead. 'Turn right here and it's another 7km,' they told me before driving off, waving and grinning.

I walked through the town of Şugag as the sun set in the grey sky and light started to fade. There were very steep hills behind the houses and I wondered how easy it would be to find somewhere flat to put up a tent. Wonder of wonders, a car stopped for me and there was a jolly old man inside, talking lots and quick to laugh.

He understood when I told him I was searching for camping but not 'camping official' and offered me his land, 8km ahead. 'I'm so sorry,' I told him, 'my feet are too tired to walk that far and I need to stop here, within a kilometre.'

For anyone impressed at my fluency, the actual stuttering Romanian I used was:

'Feet tired. Finish here.'

'No problem, come with me!'

We drove back through the village in the darkness and up a steep driveway to a wooden cabin in a garden full of beehives. Inside there was a bed, a wood-stove and a table full of honeycomb frames. Ştefan pulled out a bottle of *ţuică*, showed me how to turn the electricity off, where to hide the key in the morning and, after a couple of chuckles about the many family photographs hanging on the walls, showing him in varying stages of baldness, he left me to a magic night in a warm cabin, with honeycomb to finish my dinner, brushing away my thanks.

The next day was more of the same, more winding tarmac, snow piled on either side, steep hills above me, the colour of the trees changing in infinitesimal graduations of ombre, from bare branch black up to ethereal frosty white. There were no large villages anymore. I'd climbed into tougher territory and only passed an occasional snow-coated cabin, plumes of smoke, and paths broken through snowdrifts telling me whether they were inhabited. Forestry lorries were the main traffic, roaring past me with their loads of snow-smeared logs, obviously dug out of deep drifts. I realised that it was the same lorries coming up and down over the days it had taken me to walk this far and I could see the drivers noticing me; there I was again, the weird little human snail trailing her incremental progress over the mountains, for reasons unknown.

That night brought me the perfect sleeping opportunity. About 200m away from a farmhouse was a small wooden barn, roadside, with a ladder leading to an open hayloft, a black square hole I could climb into and burrow into the hay for warmth. I couldn't resist.

I waited a while, listening to the animals moving in the barn below me and eventually a woman came plodding along the road. She was short and stumpy, wrapped against the cold in a black headscarf and thick cotton coat. I held my breath as she uncovered a pile of hay at the foot of the ladder and took it inside to give to the animals. Then the ladder started shaking as she climbed. I was about to be discovered!

I winced out a '*Salut*' in greeting. She paused, said something about getting hay for the animals, forked down a pile in silence, climbed down the ladder and went to walk away. I honestly cannot imagine a more laconic response from a farmer on discovering a human hiding in her hay. I called to her departing back, 'Is it OK?'

'Yeah.' She carried on walking.

'Thank you very much!'

'Don't make a fire,' were her final words.

The husband and wife returned later, as I was sitting eating bread and cheese in the twilight, husband with a big belly, leaning on a stick. He brought the animals out of the barn, three cows, two heavily pregnant, and took them for a short walk up and down the road. While the cows walked, the wife scraped muck out of the barn below and when they returned the man climbed the ladder. 'Are you OK?' he said. 'Do you have food?'

'I have everything I need.'

'You will be cold tonight!'

'*Nu! Bun equipament!*' I said, and gestured to the hay. 'Super!'

This made him chuckle. 'Oh yeah,' he said. '*Paradis.*'

I did have a wonderful night, snug and smug in the hay, thinking of centuries of travellers doing the same. I hoped for a monastery at the end of the following day but just had to get through more remote road walking, more winding upwards, more snowy pine trees.

A man stopped for me on the road, said he was going walking up in the hills and did I want a lift to Oașa? Dacian was his name and we had a long conversation about the area. He was obviously an experienced outdoors man, opening his boot to show me trekking poles, climbing rope, first aid kit. I grilled him about the conditions ahead and he gave me all the answers I wanted to hear. Yes, the road was closed to vehicles between Oașa and Obărșia Lotrului, but I should still be able to walk it without snowshoes. He got out a map and told me about the most beautiful and wildest mountains of Romania. He was an accountant, escaping to his beloved mountains at the weekends. There was a sadness about him – he scuffed at the road as we talked, looked away a lot. When he warned me about the lack of roadside barriers further up, between the tarmac and the drop to river gorge, he went silent for a minute and then talked about how communism was still affecting the country, how the people in charge were uneducated and careless, that only the younger generation are changing, getting better but too slowly. He was obviously a person who felt the problems of his country very deeply and was passionately upset about its failings, where other Romanians seemed to shrug helplessly as if to say, 'What can you do?'

I had stayed earlier at a Couchsurfing place in Cluj-Napoca and met a woman freshly returned to the country after twelve years abroad, who spoke about the brain drain – the mass exodus of Romanians to live and work elsewhere meant decades of the best and brightest energy of the country leaving, the people with the impulse for change, the creators. Between 2007 and 2015 the only country with a higher percentage rise in the number of people emigrating was Syria.

Romanian salaries were less than half the EU average, but food prices were not correspondingly low. People here were running to stay still. No wonder they were leaving to work elsewhere, even when they didn't want to. Two men told me, on consecutive days, they'd worked abroad to raise cash, but eventually returned home because they couldn't spend their lives in a country that wasn't their own.

All my ways of seeing this country were through EU eyes, about Romania gaining membership and subsequent migration numbers, focused on the influx of incomers rather than the conditions they were escaping from. I'm distracted by Brexit, my country voting to refuse economic migration, to refuse to fund improvement projects in other countries, to refuse to join in. I see Romania through a lens of shame. Whenever I asked Romanian people how their country had changed, they didn't mention the abstract question of the benefit of the EU's existence; they talked about their corrupt government, the limitations their leaders had placed on the opportunities available to their country, the way that money had to pass through many greedy hands before it could make the difference it was assigned for.

Finally I reached the barrage and across the icy lake I spotted a white dome in the dark forest: here at last was the monastery. The road twisted, tracing the jagged outline of the water edge, until the final corner brought me to this huge building. It was a big complex, a couple of domed buildings, plus the spiked peak of an older church, then long concrete dormitories.

There were surprising numbers of ordinary people wandering around, interspersed with thickly bearded monks in long black robes, but fortunately, during a confused conversation about who I was looking for and what I wanted, Andrea, the woman from the car, appeared and gave me a big hug.

She needed to check with Father Stefan that there was room for me to sleep in the women's dorm, so we hung around in front of the church. It was all a bit awkward now that I'd actually turned up; no one seemed sure what to do with me. One monk stopped to talk, with a surprising American accent, incredibly tall and thin, with large, round glasses taking up most of the face space between black head veil and long grey beard. He invited me into the service, and, as we walked together, started talking about James Herriot. Yes, the books about idyllic veterinary life in post WWII Yorkshire. My brain began to unravel, but fortunately he quickly positioned me at the rear of the church and told me to wait there until after the service, when I could receive a hot meal.

As I sat there, listening to the priests' monotone drone, the swinging incense censer was paraded the length of the aisle and people walked around, prostrating themselves in front of a picture of Mary and child, kissing the glass over their feet and hands. I surreptitiously stretched my feet and legs as much as I could manage without feeling disrespectful and after a while the Herriot fan, who'd been leading the choir, came back to take me to tea.

Andrea and Ana reappeared and the three of us crammed onto a bench that would comfortably seat two, with me in the middle. The room was crowded with rows of tables; the monks had their own section in the corner; someone stood at a lectern and read from the bible as we ate. Irrepressible Andrea kept whispering in my ear, asking me if I'd like soup or some water or if I had any brothers or sisters. She was also talking across me to Ana on my other side, passing cutlery between them. There was a bowl of small raw onions and cloves of garlic on the table and Ana picked out an onion for herself, saying it was a good antibiotic. Then she peeled and handed me a garlic clove. While I was staring at it, wondering if I was in the mood to chew down on raw garlic out of politeness, Andrea loudly whispered the word, 'GARLEEK,' very close to my ear and I absolutely lost the plot. Andrea laughed too, because she's the giggly type, but me most of all, face in hands, shoulders shaking.

After three days of difficult solo walking on packed snow, surrounded by pine forests, I'd burst into this busy mountain monastery where the surreal juxtaposition of James Herriot, Orthodox Christian rituals and eating in a warm steamy room, crammed shoulder and thigh between friendly strangers, had overwhelmed me into hysterical giggles.

It was a bit of an anticlimax to such a drawn-out journey. Andrea showed me to my single room and went to hers. The next morning, she came in at about 7.30am and we took a quick picture together before I left. There was another 25km to go over the closed pass, potentially breaking my way through thick snow and I wanted to cover as much of it before sunset as I could.

First I had to walk 7km back to the barrage, before continuing around the other side of the frozen lake, where the road ran towards Obârşia Lotrului. 'It's open,' people said. 'It's closed,' said others. Well, here, standing at the 'road ahead closed' sign, where all the tyre tracks turned left into the final wooden lodge, was the result of my decision, where all the reasons people had been telling me to avoid the snow might become terribly real.

At first, the road wasn't especially difficult to walk on, but as the hours passed, the snow became thicker and thicker, until it was mounded chest high on the verges. Fortunately there was a set of tracks I could follow, some thin flat strips; I wasn't sure what they were until a snowmobile came buzzing around the corner. With the road no longer accessible to wheeled vehicles, the snowmobiles had free rein and their swooping tracks up the sides of the snowbanks showed their dancing freedom.

Every corner brought new beauty on such a sunny day; glistening white snow dripping from trees in misty shivers, animal tracks curving across the frozen lake ice far below me. As I pushed on upwards, the steps became difficult as the snow banks deepened. It was silent now, had been for hours, echoes muffled by the trees, just an occasional bird call sounding. I continued to pace upwards, feet slipping, occasionally sinking deep into a patch of loose snow even in the compacted snowmobile tracks. Not long before sunset, I reached the high point of the pass, with a wonderful view of miles of silent pine forest and bare white mountain tops beyond. The snow glowed blue white in the fading light, and the cold air burnt in my lungs. Here was where I would sleep.

Fear came to the fore as the distraction of movement faded away and I began to put up the tent. I could die here if I made a mistake. I used one of the snowmobile tracks and set about treading the snow down further. It was a difficult job on loose powder, and I had an occasional unexpected plunge to knee depth that would then force me to tread down the rest to the same level. I talked myself through it, as I do when I'm under pressure. *First make your bed, then get the kit tidied into your tent, your feet are cold so you need to make sure they get warm first, then eat something to make sure you have enough energy.* All while standing at the side of the tent to blow up my mattress, and carefully parcelling my sleeping bags inside one by one, trying to keep snowflakes out of the tent. I couldn't stand far away from it without sinking down to thigh depth. I felt clumsy and slow as I spread out the sleeping layers on the uneven floor, made sure I had everything I needed, brushed the snow off the rucksack and levered it inside. Once I lay down in bed, I felt scared and unsteady. The sense of the earth a metre underneath my body, rather than directly supporting me, made me feel as if I was floating. These compressed flakes of cold water were no kind of a mattress.

I didn't really sleep that night, just laid and dozed, checking the time every few hours. It took a long time for the sleeping bags to get truly warm. I had to go for a final wee, which was an adventure in itself, and then a wind started which, every time it rustled the icy tent, sounded exactly as if some terrible beast was padding around outside.

But I woke to see the sunrise, that's the main thing. I had camped in deep snow and come away in good enough shape to keep going, that was all that mattered. The morning began in a glorious flash of pink-and-yellow light before subsiding to ordinary grey and I plodded down the mountain to the road and the anticipated comfort of a hotel. It was a long slog; I hadn't eaten enough and was out of energy. When I finally reached a clear, ploughed road, down in the valley bottom, after five hours of descent, I felt as if I was bouncing on the tarmac, my feet so used to the sinking, slipping give of the snow. The hotel owners refused to believe I'd walked over the mountain until I showed them photos.

After a rest day, I walked on road all the way down off the mountain, painful but I'd soon be on easier ground. The roadside snow dwindled from chest to calf depth and the trees turned back from white to green. Branches littered the ground, snapped under snow pressure. Water ran across the road in the thawing sunshine. A thin blue sky permeated the morning mist as it slowly cleared for me to see the hills surrounding the town ahead. The snow was patchier here, about ankle deep. Turkeys gobbled to each other and a calf paced its cleared patch across a garden. Thin plumes of smoke rose from chimneys and humans appeared, getting into cars or pushing wheelbarrows full of snow across the road to tumble away into the stream. All was quiet and peaceful. A distant cockerel crowed. It was the 1st of February, another month or so until spring.

Descending from the Carpathians I came to an altogether different land, a wide flat flood plain that stretched a few hundred miles down to the mighty Danube River. As the mountains shrank away, the sky bloomed in their place and the horizon became a faraway flat line again. Long marches of electricity pylons strung away in belays. I was thrilled to get out of the heavy snow, with the freedom to go off road again. Tarmac was so boring, and painful on my body. Leaving the extreme cold meant the cracked and crusted skin around my nose and lips could finally begin to heal. I walked through ploughed fields churned to mud, awaiting their summer crops, wet earth clung to my boots and weighed me down, meaning painful stretched ligaments. This was oil and agriculture territory; I saw rusting hammer head pumps, dipping and rising, spaced regularly on the horizon. It was poorer here: plenty of horses and carts, the back roads packed earth again, the houses older, their lath and beam bones appearing behind crumbling plaster and long-faded bright paint, some obviously abandoned with vine growth over windows and holes in roofs, others with well-walked paths to the door.

'*Abandonat, abandonat,*' said Alina, pointing at the houses facing her shop window. I'd come in for a drink and been invited to sit for a while. She fed me chicken wings and *coliva*, a boiled wheat cake served at funerals and memorial services, which continue regularly for a decade after the bereavement. This one was for her mother-in-law, three years dead. She bemoaned the cost of the food and all the other customs, such as the clothes that must be bought for the people who wash the body, annoyed that she couldn't skimp the ritual lest she be talked badly about.

'When I die, give my good organs to others and just put me in the fire,' she joked.

Maria, leaning behind the till, said that Alina made a really good *coliva*, putting in the extra bits like coconut and sultanas; she hoped that Alina would make her a good one when she died from these chest pains she was having. Alina scolded her, told her to go to the doctor. We sat at the counter, chatting in a mixture of Romanian, Spanish and Italian. Maria and I ate, and Alina smoked, breaking off to serve the occasional drunk from the shambled male gathering outside the shop. They'd come in to buy single cans of beer and individual cigarettes, probably so nobody could cadge off them. Most village shops had a cabin or porch attached where men could sit, drink and wile away the day. Alina moaned about Romanian men and their working habits, doing less and less, leaving women to take up the slack; modern feminism may mean that women can work outside the home, but in her opinion it just gives them more to do.

Somewhere in this flood plain, I passed the thousand-mile mark, for the second time in my life. During the Welsh walk this was a major milestone, but it felt very normal this time around. I'd just taken steps until I got here, not so monumental.

I was amazed at how well my body was coping this time. Of course I was tired and in pain, that's the nature of a physical challenge like this. But I wasn't exhausted, I wasn't injured, and I felt pretty pleased about my physical resilience. My biggest issue was back pain. I really felt the effect of being so solidly strapped into a rucksack, meaning my hips and spine couldn't flex as they should. It made my whole body stiff, with shooting pain down into my legs making it hard to sleep. I was carrying my heaviest kit, thicker sleeping mat and extra sleeping bag, ice spikes, extra clothes, insulated trousers. Soon, as spring came and the temperature rose, I'd be able to send winter things home and drop a couple of kilos.

There was enough daylight to take a relaxed lunch break now, sitting in the fields under the huge empty sky on a thin track between ploughed mud, weeds rustling around me. The days felt warm but there was ice in all the pools, still minus 3 or 4c at night, but after the minus 10c nights of December, camping didn't take a lot of effort.

At night I'd hear the calls of migrating birds, long skeins of geese flying over the plains, and feel the stirring energy of their adventure to new lands, the call of spring, of heat rising, the pull to move. They honk and herald change. Calling to each other, as nomads, to stay together, to move as one. 'Exodus! We go! This way! Don't get lost!' And I lay there, deep in the thrall of my own solo migration urges, feeling the blast of their exultation whoosh over me before the night silence returned.

As I came over a rise, I saw the great River Danube far in the distance, a mile wide. For a faint flash, I felt I could smell the water; a deep, green, living smell.

For the first time on this journey I had trouble with the police. Crossing open fields one afternoon to camp by the side of a long straight track, there was absolutely nowhere to hide the tent in this wide flat landscape and I shrank behind a sparse roadside hawthorn. The moon rose large and yellow that night and I was disturbed by a single vehicle which rushed past me twice at great speed. The following morning I was hailed by a police officer as I reached the small town centre, who asked to see my documents. She was very mild and gentle about it, I didn't mind at all. When another police car stopped me a few miles down the road, I told him I'd already been checked and he called the first officer to confirm. He was polite, but stopped another two or three times to talk to me, polite conversation but it set me on edge. I was stuck on one road, very visible, walking a long straight line towards the big town and the border crossing point.

The final encounter was much ruder and I got angry in return. Stopping to buy jam at a roadside stall, as I walked away, an unmarked car screeched to a halt beside me. '*Paşaport*,' demanded the plainclothes man inside, with a surly belligerence. Something about his attitude made me say no. The third interaction with authority that day and I refused to be treated this way. I asked to see his ID, and he opened his wallet to show me, with all the slow, deliberate movements of a man controlling his anger. Obviously not someone used to being defied, which only made me all the more certain that I wouldn't show him my passport.

I argued back, telling him that I'd shown it already and he should call the station to confirm. We had a back and forth where I repeated myself several times. 'This is the third time I've been stopped this morning. If you call the female officer in Putineiu, they will confirm I am not a problem.' He asked if I even had a passport and I tapped the top of my rucksack to say, 'Yes, it's in here but I showed it to an officer this morning and you need to call the station to confirm that.' Eventually, through gritted teeth, he did exactly that, and let me walk away.

We were close to the border here; migrant paranoia was already making itself felt in the Balkans. I'd refused to comply with a police officer because I didn't like his attitude, which felt like a victory against an abuse of power, but one that contained all my white privilege and the self-importance of the country on my passport. 'How dare you challenge my right to go wherever I want?' Classic coloniser. I passed through the town (avoiding the police station) and stayed at the hotel closest to the bridge that crossed the Danube. Lorries rumbled past my window all night as I slept fitfully. I'd walked eight days to get there, covering 125 miles, and my body was too tense to let me sleep, in need of a day off to relax my muscles.

This was a major transit route for lorries from Turkey, they turn north through Bulgaria and then west once they've crossed into Romania, to avoid the paperwork of non-EU Balkans as they take their consignments to the richer north-west Europe.

Paying for my final breakfast in Romania, I tried to give the waiter some of the coins and small notes in my purse, in order to receive a large note as change. He refused the coins, saying he had no use for them, and pulled the 50 lei note from my hand, saying he'd only accept that; then, worse, gave me a handful of 5s and 1s as change.

Irritatingly this meant he'd left me with a bundle of unchangeable currency; the money exchange booths wouldn't accept coins or even a Romanian note smaller than a 10 and now I had about 35 leu in 5s and 1s, worth almost seven quid. I could buy a few days' food with that money, but only if I diverted a mile back towards the town centre, and I needed to look for maps in the Bulgarian city across the river, rather than scratch about spending a few quid on unwanted food weight.

As I made my way towards the border bridge, across a crumbling concrete wasteland, feral dogs made flurries of barking at me and I shouted back, obviously still angry about the rude waiter.

It was a long way to the border point and I tried to think about why I was annoyed, besides his rudeness, and the unfair refusal to accept coins of his own currency. I grew up in scarcity and have never earned enough to be profligate. I was mostly living on savings but money was constantly coming into my life through Patreon subscriptions, and gifts from strangers were plentiful. I should be more relaxed about the loss of £7; I could have paid that much extra for my hotel room with little more than a sigh.

As I paced the long straight road towards the bridge, frontier police regularly checking my passport, smiling, wishing me '*drum bun*' – 'go well', I saw three Roma women in high-vis jackets sweeping the side of the road. They called out to me, smiling widely, wanting to know what I was doing. We had a short conversation about the usual subjects; where I'd slept and whether I was scared to travel alone, before I pulled my purse out and offered them the money the waiter wouldn't take. I have no idea how much it meant to them, a day's wages or pocket change. Some information I've found said that the Romanian minimum wage is £450 a month, someone else told me it was £250. These women may not have been working officially, with contracts. One thing is certain, what constitutes poverty in Romania is far below what we call poor in the UK.

My side of the road towards Bulgaria was clear, but a long line of lorries queued to get into Romania. The drivers stood in groups on the central divider, chatting and either staring lasciviously or completely ignoring me. Further on, one called out. 'Hey, do you want some food?' As I turned towards the voice, he was already climbing down from the cab waving a tin at me, cold from his on-board fridge. I accepted it. 'My final present from Romania,' I told him, and packed it into my rucksack, nestling it down alongside the jar of homemade cherry jam that I'd bought at a roadside stall the previous day, the thick fingers of the seller reminding me of gardening friends back home.

I didn't want a tin of cheap pork pâté, but here it was, this unexpected cadeau and I accepted its obvious symbolism, opening myself to trust the flow of gifts in and gifts out rather than huddling, miserly, over my dwindling hoard.

The line of lorries started to rumble and the man jogged back to climb into his cab, shouting goodbye. I turned towards the pillars that marked the beginning of the bridge with rising excitement. Goodbye Romania, here was the Danube, my beloved river; here was the beginning of Bulgaria.

BULGARIA

Facing the Giurgiu-Ruse bridge was an emotional moment. I'd taken trains across this 2km bridge, hitch-hiked over it several times in various cars and lorries. I'd kayaked underneath it seven years previously, age 31 and in full health, with no idea of the cancer tornado that was about to crash through my life. Now here I was, back again, standing over the rippling grey-blue water that was the keeper of so many of my memories.

I thought this Europe walk was simply a continuation of plans interrupted by illness, but as I stood at the centre of the bridge, wind whipping at my hair, I realised it was impossible to return to my pre-cancer life. I had changed irrevocably, through cancer and walking around Wales and heartbreak. I'd experienced intense vulnerability and weakness, therapy and learning. I was stronger now, crossing the bridge at 38, and I was more jaded. I could no longer identify with the joy, hope and innocence of being 31 and setting out into Eastern Europe to find adventure, free from the presence of the possibility of death. That naïve state of mind was as impossible to return to as it was to reach down and touch the water far below.

This journey wasn't what I thought it might be. I'd expected a tough, exciting adventure of walking and wild camping, but this was harder, lonelier, and now I was here in sight of the Danube, the reason to continue with my pre-cancer plans had melted away, dissolved into the mighty river current.

I had wondered if I'd be able to walk without such a strong mission as the Welsh challenge's charity fundraising driving me forward. Yet somehow the impulse to walk was automatic; my journey had its own presence now – like the river, there was no denying its solidity.

I didn't know exactly why I was doing this and yet here I was, continuing on, walking until I was sweaty and sleepy, then waking up with a grin to say good morning to the dawn, thank you to the place that held me as I slept, and setting out to do it again. Perhaps I was just doing it – perhaps it didn't matter why.

It was almost my birthday and I had received enough money to treat myself to two luxurious massages in the underground spa of a posh hotel in Ruse, a big city on the banks of the Danube. The treatments were enough to relax my body but not heal it, so that once I put exactly the same weight on my shoulders and resumed exactly the same walking motion, my muscles screamed as they struggled to resume the stress position they'd only just been coaxed out of. The following week was a struggle with sharper pain than usual, as I made my way towards Veliko Tarnovo.

I walked south through the Rusenski Lom national park, alongside the wriggling River Lom. It has high gorge sides, big buttresses of rock standing large, with wetlands at the bottom and gentle ripples of ploughed land up high either side. Herons flew from their sentinel posts at riverside and there were hare prints in the snow, but I saw almost no other people as I followed a track along the curves of the river. Fish swam in hollowed stone pools, glowing in green-brown water light. At the end of the day I made camp in a barcode stand of white birch, amongst bare lines of black and white, where I was warm and happy in the patchy snow, even when I woke up with a stiff, sore body.

I heard dogs howling every night, on my way through gentle hills that were growing higher as I headed towards the Stara Planina, the central range of mountains that run east/west across Bulgaria. It was an unusual, rippled howling, almost trilling. *Strange that the dogs would howl in every village here,* I thought to myself. My next host told me of the Balkan jackal, prevalent throughout Bulgaria. They'd pose no danger to me, no more than the wolves.

I pushed myself hard, walking to the deadline of my planned break. Twilight was getting later and later every day, and I could feel summertime twinkling in the far distance, calling to me with heat and long daylight hours – how much easier everything would be there.

Friends Joel and Beth from the Rakhiv hostel had a long housesit in a hill village near Gabrovo before they were heading to Greece to volunteer at a migrant camp, helping at an activity centre near the notoriously overcrowded Moria camp, the first landing place for refugees crossing by boat from Turkey.

We celebrated my 39th birthday with cake and wine, then I had a week to enjoy their company, dog walks, market visits and lots of lounging. I'd been feeling a few injury pains towards the end of Romania, sharp stabs in my feet and knees, and this was a good time to release the stress and struggle of winter walking.

Nedellin, the local taxi driver who spoke good English, agreed to give me conversational Bulgarian lessons and we spent a few afternoons together talking about his country. From here to Slovenia I'd be walking though the same language base and wanted to improve on the Serbian swear words I'd learnt on my way down the Danube.

He arrived one day with a handful of red-and-white striped bracelets, and solemnly tied one onto each of our wrists. They were to welcome spring, he said, 1st of March is Baba Marta Day. '*Chestita Baba Marta,*' (Happy Grandmother March). The bracelets could only be given as gifts and had to be worn until we saw a stork. Next market day I saw red and white everywhere, large tassels on cars and bracelets in thick profusion on teenage arms.

When I started walking again, I was exhausted, realising that, in all the goodbyes, I'd been tipsy three nights out of the previous five. No good, if I wanted to push my body to athletic feats. (This is an aspect of my story that strongly diverges from the style of esteemed travel writer Dervla Murphy.) I slept long and deep that night on the edge of a freshly seeded field, the grass growing thickly enough that my tent wasn't covered in earth as I packed away. These fields had developed in recent weeks from bare earth to a mist of fuzzy green, coming tentatively, like breath fogging a mirror.

After the south-easterly route meandered through Romanian snowy mountains, turning west into oncoming spring brought a lift of energy – time to make progress. I returned to my normal routine: heading out between small villages, avoiding the bigger roads, trying to walk more than 15 miles a day but settling for anything above 12, finding good food to eat and searching for small conversations.

The problem here was that there was barely anyone to talk to.

Bulgaria felt more isolated than Romania, the villages emptier, shuttered and quiet.

There were more tumbledown houses here; broken windows showing dusty fallen plasterwork, sometimes rubbish and clothing lying tangled in creeping vines, the ground outside covered in walnuts that nobody had picked. The old houses were a solid yellow stone, built in square blocks to head-height and then finished with lath and packed earth, or earth bricks. Where roof rafters had tumbled inside the house, earthen walls were exposed to soften in the rain.

I passed empty stone troughs, where water used to trickle down through a series of levels, providing access for animals and for washing clothes. The stone backs of the springs proclaimed their dates, 1975, 1962, as the grass choked them and the cement crumbled.

However empty the streets were, I would usually find a crowd of men in the bar. It was always faintly intimidating at first, to be stared at both blatantly and subtly. Clothing was usually black, stubble abounded. Bulgarian men tended towards the round and hairy, thick swollen hands, big balloon bellies, a profusion of moles. These were bars where the pensioners spend half a day playing backgammon, gossiping and teasing the friends they've spent their entire lives around; where the younger unemployed guys hang out, pretending they have something to do; where the men home from work abroad come and catch up. People came and went, groups hunched together at small tables, cigarette smoke filled the air, a television singing folk songs or droning the rolling news cycle. I would sit in the corner with mini feasts for brunch: coffee and *ayran* to drink, a banana and *banitsa* (a delicious Bulgarian snack food of folded puff pastry and *sirene*, the salty white crumbly cheese).

It was like a switch had been flicked as I crossed from Romania and the dogs were much less aggressive, a wonderful relief. Outside a supermarket one day, a couple of street dogs milling around, few passers-by, someone driving a gaggle of goats down the street, I was on the stone wall munching my snacks. One dog barked at the other and there was an instant noise from all the nearby humans. They hissed, they tutted, and they shut that dog down, a significant difference to behaviour across the river border.

There was no hostility, as I had sometimes felt in Romania; instead of narrow sideways glances or cold deliberate silences, people felt curiously disinterested in me here.

A woman passed me by one morning as I ate porridge on a bench, rapacious cats prowling for leftovers. She spoke to me a little but when I struggled to understand, she just sighed and walked away. In Ukraine people would rabbit away, regardless of my lack of comprehension. Perhaps Bulgarians were tired. Tired of people leaving, of buildings crumbling around them, of the genuine lament that things weren't like they used to be. I saw mainly pensioners in the villages, pottering in their gardens. Funeral and anniversary remembrance notices papered each village centre, covering entire walls, insulating the bus shelters; pictures of the deceased staring out from the past, in impersonal portrait posings. There seemed to be a quiet resignation about Bulgaria. Organised crime had a stronghold in government and corruption was rife. The minimum wage and pension rates were the lowest in Europe (€250 and €190 a month, respectively); food prices were not proportionately low. Nedellin, the friendly man who gave me Bulgarian lessons during my rest week, said simply, 'Bulgaria is crime. Everyone is struggling here.'

The Bulgarian population was shrinking: in 2005 it was down by more than a million from its communist peak, and it had shrunk further since. Just under 7 million people lived in the whole country, a sixth of them in and around the capital city, Sofia. In terms of population density, Bulgaria is 118th in the world.

I thought of desperate people going abroad to work when they'd rather be in their own culture, rather be raising children in the country their hearts belong to.

'Everyone has a relative abroad,' said Nedellin. 'The country would fall into chaos within one month if they stopped sending money home. We run on tick. All those small shops, they have a book where people say they'll pay in two weeks. I have a book in my taxi. People must get places but they can't afford to pay. My book is full.'

He had worked in the UK in the past but came home because he wanted to raise his children here. He wanted to go back. 'In the UK I didn't have to worry about money. I had a good job as a lorry driver and didn't have to look at food prices. Here I am always worried about whether we have enough, every month.' He showed me his letter containing a National Insurance number. 'Is this enough? Can I go back and work?' I had to tell him that I had no idea. Britain's future relationship with this Bulgarian man, post-Brexit, was a complete unknown to me.

I felt sad and ashamed.

So many versions of statistics exist, so many distortions of truth, that it felt impossible to know what the real situation was. Even if Britain was a net contributor to the EU, even if I only focused on what the EU cost my country and not what we got in return, we had voted to stop giving. An ungenerous act. Tricked into thinking we did not have enough, when our living standards were amongst the highest in the world. Austerity was a manufactured concept that brought us to resent what others seek, to guard our pile fiercely, the rats squabbling in the garbage heaps at the foot of the castle walls. Capitalism tells us that what we have isn't enough, that there is always a higher standard to aspire to, so we're deluded into bemoaning our comfortable, warm, well-kept houses that don't have a pool or a wine cellar or a third toilet.

It was a strange feeling, to be walking through the EU, heading towards a country that had chosen to give this up. Bring back visas, customs taxes, keep people out. I'd rather choose a world that heads towards integration, not separation. But separation is what keeps rich people rich, isn't it? We plundered the world in the time of empire and now we can't allow those subjects equality because they'll claim a share of what we have gathered. We want to reach out from our island and stir our finger in world politics, sell arms, drop bombs, create tax havens, but then shut the gates, turn away from the consequences of those dirty decisions, the desperate humans turning up on our actual island.

British politics was mired in toxic treacle; from here the administrative struggles of Teresa May looked like nobody was going to end up on the winning side. What could I do? Nothing. Pretend it's not happening.

I continued walking; just as many dissociated using social media or by avoiding the constant gloomy world news, this was my own way of sticking my head in the sand and avoiding the unpleasant future.

Bulgaria was beautiful, even in its crumbling, unattended glory. Every night the jackals howled with the onset of darkness. They were the happiest things about Bulgaria to me. I imagined the camaraderie of waking up and calling out to the sky, listening for where your cousin-neighbour has got to. I would hear the closest of the pack clearly, reaching their noses up to yodel out with all their strength, then others echoing across the valleys.

One night the spring seemed to coalesce and I felt part of my surroundings, more at peace with the journey than I had done for quite some time. The woods next to the road were flat and clear, there was something inviting about their openness, no scratching branches or poking undergrowth to struggle through. I turned in, checking the fallen leaves for signs of wild boar; any of their rooting and snuffling would turn the leaves aside in piles, but they lay in an unbroken carpet of orange oak. There was a fallen tree a distance from the road, caught between two stumps, creating a triangle of trunk, with drooping branches trailing to the ground; once I saw the way the branches framed a bare spot, big enough for a body to lie, I knew I'd sleep there. It gave the illusion of shelter, a curtain that passing jackals would have to brush aside in order to reach me; with my rucksack at my head, I felt safe.

The weather had become warm enough to bivvy out now. I could lie on the ground in comfort, without needing to keep my hands covered. I put out my tent liner, my sleeping pad, ranged my belongings close to me in the leaves, ate a tin of beans and meat, and laid back, satisfied.

I lay there for a long time as the night fell, listening to the jackals' yips and howls that rose from the hills around me, different groups communicating, and wondered what a jackal would do if it found me here on the ground. Sniff and run away, probably.

The night was quiet, apart from the occasional howling, and eventually I realised just how utterly still the silence was. I heard the gentle rattling of dead leaves hanging on the branches near my head as they shook in the breeze which blew with no more force than a wide-mouthed breath. I heard a mouse rustling out from a hole close behind my head, then the scritch-scratch of nibbling as it gnawed on foraged kernels. I heard moth wings fold in a burr of vibration as the creature settled in the twigs immediately above me and I heard the whistle-whish of feathers as an unseen night bird flew over my bed.

Above us all the moon shone bright enough to see by, riding the night, and I bathed in its calmness.

There were no jackal visitors that night, no rustler more threatening than morning birds and I woke happy in my forest bed, thankful for another night at peace.

Rain came the next day; I smelt it first, then followed the wind and looked west for the clouds. Instinctual, without even realising it, I was changing, animal instincts coming to the fore.

I would often see deer now, sometimes early in the mornings or late afternoon in remote fields. I liked it when birds fluttered away from the track, meaning nothing human had passed there for a while. I saw hares, bursting from undergrowth and bounding away from me.

I passed through clouds of scent, hawthorn was the first bloom of the year, thousands of tiny white flowers foaming up like suds in a washing bowl. Every tree sounded a low hum of attending insects. The sky was clear blue with squiffs of cloud in marker pen scribbles.

The geology across the north of the country formed gorges and I was surrounded by high hill ridges at times, rubbles of rock and exposed cliffs running above me. Stone burst from the hillside, blooms of rock where I was used to trees and scrubland. The colours were yellow, with the grey of winter grass and the occasional shocking green of manmade ploughed and seeded fields. Soon it would all change, leaves were budding in a faint fuzz of green, like the stubble on an unshaven face, and I had already seen bright blotches of violet flowers nestled in shady patches.

Forty miles south of me there was the great wall of the Stara Planina, ghostly pale mountains in snow-covered whiteness, wreathed in mists and barely seen. My route headed parallel to them for two weeks, in bright sunshine, and then turned to pass over the snowy peaks, aiming for a border crossing point into Serbia. With better quality food and longer daylight hours I was getting more power in my body and could keep a good pain-free pace for a couple of hours at a time.

At the end of March 2019 I shed my Martinitsas, the red-and-white bands that I had been so excited to tie onto my wrist on the 1st of the month. I must have been keeping my head down, focused on my feet, because I didn't see any storks for weeks after I heard they'd arrived.

But that morning I walked into a shop and the owner gestured at my wrists, flapped her arms to signify the bird and took me outside to point across the small town square where people gathered in groups, children running and swerving between them. Over the small river, on top of the tall chimney of an empty, crumbling factory, sat a fuzz of spiky sticks and a bulbous bird, standing still, long beak hanging down onto its breast. Here was the stork, returned from its African winter to herald the Bulgarian spring. Now I'd seen it, I must take off the bracelets and tie them to a fruit tree – that's what the shop lady was showing me.

The north of Bulgaria had felt like a limbo where I remained parallel to the mountains, never reaching the point where I would cross them. There had been conversations with goat herders, small sips of *rakia*, swerved propositions. Looking up at the cliff sides, I'd watched swifts swooping from crevices, bees tending honeycomb bulging in long crystalline structures, safe from theft, and marvelled at fully grown trees blossoming vertically from tightly clinging roots. I had found ticks crawling on me, swallowed flies, watched pheasants fighting and heard the eternal jackal whoops and hollerings.

I walked and the Brexit mess churned. A last-minute petition, garnering millions of signatures to try and reverse the decision to leave, had no effect. Everybody seemed dissatisfied. We were all in limbo. I was walking to a destination that never seemed any closer, on an earth that was turning underneath me so I never made progress. I could have been in a magic lantern, the scenery rotating behind me, while for all my efforts, I stayed in the same place. Bulgarian pensioners went to the same shop, talked to the same people, dug their gardens, tired of a government that never gives.

We are living in the age of the eternal crisis, climate, political, economic, and everybody feels distressed.

Only the stork had changed places, flying up from the south with the rising of heat and light to herald the new season.

On the way out of the village I stopped at the fence of an empty house, with newspapered windows and the garden choked in long grasses. I tied my Martinitsas to the branches of an apple tree, pink blossoms flowering bright for nobody. I tied them to join in, to belong to Bulgaria, to be more than transitory and to honour tradition. I tied them to connect to those who went before me.

A week later the magic lantern juddered to a halt and it was time to leave limbo and cross the mountains, to climb up from sunny scrubland where the sunshine was beginning to brown my arms, back into patchy snow. There were horses in the forested foothills, watching me climb towards them, swishing their tails. I looked again and they were gone. Only the sound of hooves clattered further into the trees, like heavy rain.

Through the grey-green grass of last year, flattened by winter snow, poked delicate purple crocus. I flew up on the mountain tops for a wild forty-eight hours in the wind, crunching through frozen snowfields, and came down to a subtle seasonal shift. On the warmer southern side of the mountains, hawthorn petals billowed like confetti with every breath of wind, a frill of fallen petals rippling from the force of each footstep.

***

As I shared my walk online I'd connected with other people making their own journeys across Europe on foot, all coming towards me from west to east. I had found three different points where I could leave my own route to visit theirs without too much detour and delay, and I felt compelled to go and meet these other walkers, seeking kinship and perhaps a different perspective on my own journey.

Dragoman was a good moment for me to travel south to intercept my first adventuring kinsman. It would have taken me a fortnight to walk there, while he walked further east towards Turkey, so I used public transport and didn't count it as part of my own walking route. Instead of continuing west into Serbia, I wandered up to the bus station early in the morning, bought myself a *banitsa* and a bottle of water and got on a bus to Sofia. Then south from Sofia to Thessaloniki, the high, snowy mountains accompanying me all the way to the border with Greece. The climate was different once I came through the mountains, I saw leaves on the vines, a green fuzz on the trees, where I'd left bare branches behind in Dragoman.

I took more buses to the north-west of Greece, then finally started hitch-hiking, knowing my target's route but unsure of exactly where he was. Eventually I saw a dark figure by the side of the road, pushing a laden trolley very slowly up the steep hill. 'Here! Here!' I called, and the driver pulled over for me to tumble out of the car and embrace Jan.

Here in Greece, I was in the area of one of the main human migration routes, from Turkey towards the EU. Bulgaria pursues an aggressive policy of migrant detention. A strong right wing contingent forms part of their governing coalition so people desperate enough to seek illegal entry into Europe would flow through Greece and up north through the Balkans towards the coveted Schengen Zone. I had friends in Greece who were volunteering in refugee camps, providing community centre facilities to the asylum seekers doomed to months of camp dwelling, waiting for their applications to be processed. They'd been to see the life jacket graveyards, huge piles of thousands of buoyancy aids discarded once the desperate reach the European side of the water.

Jan is Spanish, with thick black hair, dark eyes and a deep reddish-brown tan from constant sun and wind exposure, the weather mottling his cheeks and roughening his skin. Back in Croatia, he'd had a pistol fired in the air by a vigilante anti-migrant gang, determined to halt him and check his passport. He'd seen groups of tired and shabby men walking with small rucksacks detained by police and ushered into vans. He'd been constantly stopped by police himself, on the border roads from Albania into Greece, where there are many paths through the mountains, away from frontier checks. He had people ask him if he's Arab. I had people ask me if I'm German. I'm goofy. I'm very white. I'm safe from racist xenophobia.

Jan was documenting his walk from Barcelona to Australia with enthusiastic videos and plenty of pictures of birds. My immediate impression of him was weathered skin and an angular, bony body that jutted through his layers of jacket and jumper. He was a bubbling burst of gabbling conversation, jumping straight into all the reasons why he was pissed off that day, showing me different pieces of kit that were broken or not working properly.

I had asked to come and join him for a few days, which meant I was the acolyte, essentially, and for that reason I didn't mind that he talked so much, spending two days telling me about his love life and interrupting me shortly after I began any story of my own.

I wanted to know why he was doing this, why had he chosen to leave his life in Spain and walk thousands of miles on such a difficult quest. He responded with tales of a dozen girlfriends from a sequence of overlapping relationships, irritatingly blasé about his infidelity.

He only mentioned low paid jobs; call centre work, sales, food delivery. Eventually I saw the thread of what he was saying; he'd always followed the women in his life, said yes to their lead and gone with their ideas over his own. 'This is the first thing I've ever done that is my idea, and I almost gave it up when my ex-girlfriend came back to me, wanted me to move to Portugal and get a job to be with her. I said yes until I found out she was still with someone else.'

He may have been seeking character development during this adventure but he seemed blind to the way that his relationship to women was so distorted. Maybe this man only saw himself reflected in the desire of others, as I have too.

My sexual attitude was the opposite to his and felt prudish in comparison. The rare times I'd been propositioned on this walk, it had been easy to say no. With only a short time to make connections, if you agree to stay longer for a twinkly-eyed man after such a minimal introductory period, you can be damn sure he thinks it's a done deal and won't put any effort into the bedding of you beyond ensuring his own satisfaction. I wasn't interested in a quick bunk-up, I wanted to be in a relationship, and for many years had been choosing ways of living that made that impossible. Realising that my loneliness was the result of my own choices, rather than an intrinsic unloveableness, was part of the awareness my own journey was bringing me.

Jan worried about money. He had worked day and night to save for this journey, whizzing a pushbike to deliver takeaway meals around Barcelona. He had €6,000 left in his bank account, had spent a mere €4,000 during his first year of walking, but his kit was fraying and in need of replacement. He estimated it would take at least another two years to reach Australia and was trying to live on €10 a day but still his savings were slipping through his fingers.

I remember this inescapable stress from my Welsh walk, my gnawing worry over diminishing funds, always feeling guilty whenever I splurged, usually on food. I'd saved more thoroughly this time, living in a van while I worked as hard as I could, and had an ongoing income thanks to Patreon subscribers.

He told me he went without food for long periods, through missing shops in villages and then being forced to walk miles on an empty stomach. But on the second morning he showed me a forgotten packet of oats in one of his panniers.

Stories like this made him seem erratic and incompetent, but he couldn't be. This man had laser eye surgery in preparation for this trip. He'd walked thousands of miles already, and was winding his way towards Australia between beautiful places he'd researched online, having a wonderful time.

It was nice not to have to justify myself with him. There was no questioning of whether the hardships balanced the rewards, we both understood the call, and shared the unspoken knowledge that this was a totally worthwhile, wonderful experience. The irritating incomprehension on strangers' faces ('But why?') was totally absent.

There was a lot that we had in common; a mutual understanding of how to cope in the journey, the importance of flat, hidden sleeping spots, of regular café time to sit and rest.

We poked each other's rock-hard calves. I showed him my sleeping mat, he showed me his GPS. The major difference between our kit was his monowalker – a single wheeled trolley modified by him to take three wheels, that he pushed along in front of him with relatively low effort required to transport almost 50 kilos of luggage. I was impressed with it but also saw how limiting it was – restricting the walker to roads and simple tracks, missing out on tiny paths or climbing mountains. Jan loved the cumbersome beast, and although I felt the weight of my rucksack after I swapped to push the monowalker for half a mile, I still didn't want to saddle myself with one.

'What is failure to you?' I asked Jan.

'If I don't reach Indonesia,' he said at first, but then talked about home. 'Failure would be to return home with the same ways of thinking and to return to the same behaviours. To return to a job as a waiter and still not be able to hold down a long relationship and still have the same insecurities would be no progress. I'd like to find out what I'm made of, what is my purpose in this world.'

I glimpsed hints of his sad history behind the deluge of sexual content. He described painful childhood circumstances, parents who were absent or mentally unwell. It seemed that like me, inadequately loved and nurtured, he had always been building an adult life on broken childhood foundations. For him this journey was a way to raze to the ground and begin again, just as healing from cancer had been for me.

Walking for thousands of miles reduces you to the bare bones of self, and brings forth the inner parts you are shying from. It's all there if you can bear to face it, both the festering hurt and the time to process it.

We hugged goodbye and turned our backs to one another, him to keep walking towards a national park and me to the next village, where I was hoping for a bus to begin the two-day journey back to Dragoman. I wasn't too sad to say goodbye; he'd been singing a very crude sexual song over and over that morning, and his lack of awareness about how I might feel about it had grated on me. Overwhelmed by an onslaught of information, I had wished he would stop talking and give me a little peace. After so much time alone, I was unused to such intense interaction. But I was pleased I'd met him, seen the stubbornness and strength of this man on his mission to walk across half the world, experienced him, in all his rambling, joyful, charged intensity.

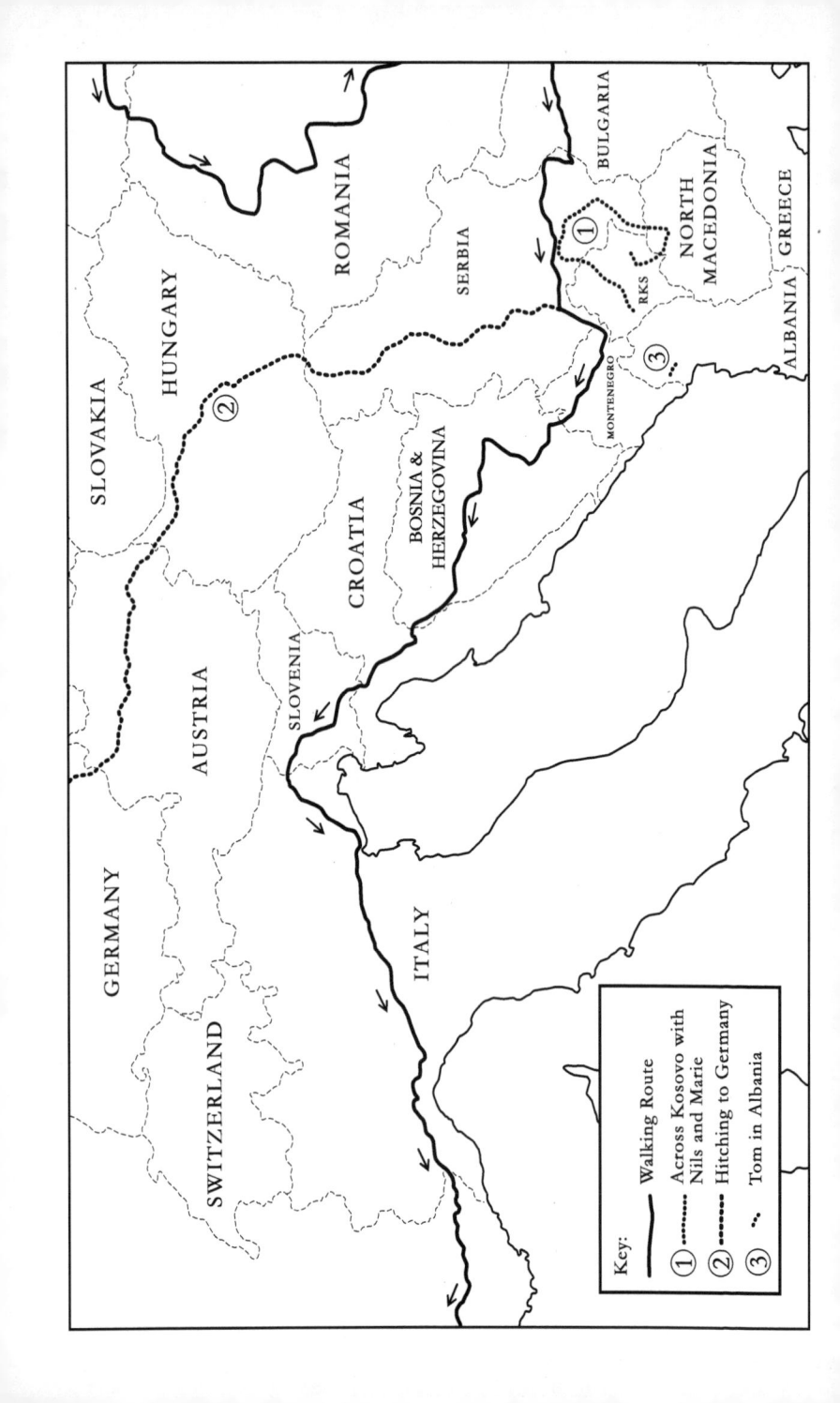

Key:	
——	Walking Route
①······	Across Kosovo with Nils and Marie
②▬▬▬	Hitching to Germany
③- - -	Tom in Albania

SERBIA

Back on my own route and heading into Serbia, I spent some time at the service station on the Bulgarian side of the border, calculating prices of peanuts vs almonds, trying to spend my Bulgarian lev down to the last stotinka. I had to walk nervously alongside the wide motorway that led from the border point before cutting away into Dimitrovgrad, my first Serbian town. I waited half an hour in the bank queue, reading my book, raising eyebrows with my neighbours, and listening for the heavy double thump of stamps on paper that meant we could all shuffle forward. £200 brought me 26,000 Serbian dinar, a thick wedge of notes that I hurriedly packed away into my rucksack, embarrassed at my apparent show of riches.

I had my first detailed topographic map in a while – they'd been hard to come by in Bulgaria – and decided to make the most of it and go north, for a meander into the Stara Planina, the Balkan Mountains, before turning west across Serbia.

I had what felt like plenty of food; some instant mash, oats, a tin of tuna, a tin of rissoles and beans, two bananas, one apple, a jar of Bulgarian *lutenitsa* (delicious roasted red pepper and tomato paste) and a small salami. I could see plenty of villages dotted across the area and would soon come to a shop, so I thought.

I climbed a hill straight out of town, cutting under the concrete cathedral arches of the motorway, following a path through well-spaced young oak trees on a thick carpet of orange leaves, that would lead me over to my first village, Petrlaš. Peeking through occasional breaks in the forest, I saw the town far below, the Bulgarian side of the valley gradually disappearing behind a dark blue haze of rain. Eventually the shower reached me, fat, soaking droplets, and I covered up, pushing on until the ground flattened out. The village seemed occupied; the surrounding fields were freshly seeded and there were groves of fruit trees, trunks limed and gleaming freshly white. But closer still, the red tiled houses showed extreme disrepair, windows papered over with yellow newspaper and torn curtains hanging ragged in empty frames. Some were falling down, showing the skeletons of their wooden frames, thin cut woven lath, with earth and straw packed in to flesh out the walls, wildly undulating roof tiles signifying collapsed rafters beneath. Others were entirely gone in a tumble of beams, their stone walls only built knee high.

I walked up into the centre of the village, uncertain of what I'd find there, hoping for a small bar or shop. But there were only more dishevelled houses and a long official building with smashed windows, a rusty padlock on a mighty hasp. I sat on the verandah for a while, put out my tent to dry off and checked my maps. A couple of people appeared with buckets and I called to one of them, asked about a shop.

'No shop, only ten people live here.'

'In the whole place? But there are more than sixty houses.'

'Almost one hundred houses, but empty. Empty.'

She pantomimed resignation and walked away, gumboots flapping.

The village was silent, only the gurgle of water toppling endlessly from the spring.

The soft sudden rain came again, falling gently on the ground, and I waited it out, refilling my water bottles and peering through the windows to absorb the dusty quietness of plaster crumbling from the walls in tiny trickles, the abandoned single chair askew in an otherwise empty room. It was close to 6pm when I left the village and I camped in a nearby field, streetlights visible in the distance, lighting the way for nobody.

The next morning I walked through forest for a while before

realising that the trees looked bushy and squat, a dozen sprouting shoots bursting from every single root, like fountains. This was coppice wood, trees such as hazel or chestnut, cut regularly, encouraging multiple branches to sprout straight upwards so they can be regularly harvested. These trees had provided the empty village with their fences, house walls, tool handles, walking sticks. I sent photos to a friend to be sure. 'Yes,' he said, 'it's grown-out coppice, last harvested about twenty years ago.'

What was happening in Serbia twenty years ago? NATO bombs and international sanctions. I wondered how it had affected this rural village; the natural migration of young people with no taste for peasantry hastened by conflict? Just the old people left behind, too aged to do anything but live it out at home. There came a cuckoo call echoing through the forest; wildflowers were growing in the forgotten coppices, spaces where humans no longer came.

Searching for a shop, I drew another blank in Odorovçi, the next village north, across a wide flat plain, with an ancient road running straight across the centre. 'Military road,' it said on the map. 'A Roman road to Constantinople.'

All was quiet again, and I climbed the hill, listening for the sound of voices. Eventually I found someone to ask, 'Where is the shop?'

'It's up the road but it closed an hour ago, won't open until Monday.' It was midday on Saturday.

It was another day's walk up and over a mountain to the next village of Rsovçi, and I'd have minimal supplies remaining by the time I reached it. If I couldn't get food there, I could walk on and hope for a shop soon or detour 10 miles down the mountain pass to the big town of Pirot to resupply and return, wasting time.

No sense worrying about it, I had enough food now and all I

needed to focus on was the mountain ahead. I spent the entire afternoon and early evening climbing slowly upwards, following a clear track. The village disappeared beneath the dome of the hill, leaving a view of a wide, flat plain that led back to Bulgaria, and eventually I curved around into a flat open space held in the mountainside, with nothing but forest and grass in view. The clouds had lifted from thick grey to billowing white, and I walked in sunshine, with a chill wind blowing. I was thrilled to be there in such remoteness, picking my way through long grass folded over by a season of snow and then, higher up, over rocks and thorns. I crushed the leaves of sparse, wiry plants that crawled around the rocks. I passed the shepherds' summer huts and the track dwindled until finally I pitched my tent in a hollow at the dip between two peaks. I heard no jackal calls up there, only the deep burr of fluttering wings as birds chose their final perches in the fading of the light.

In the morning my hollow was white with cloud, bright droplets furring every grass tip.

Checking carefully between compass, map and GPS, I descended on forest paths marked with the snuffling of boar, grooves in the leaf carpet showing their search for tasty morsels.

The open meadows and shepherds' huts marked the beginning of human territory again and I stopped to peek in through the windows, marvelling at the simplicity within – a stove, a bed, bare walls and coats hanging on the door.

Finally, down in the centre of Rsovçi, with plenty of people around, I asked and yes, there was a shop. Saved! A kind woman unlocked the door to a small room and stood waiting as I assessed the contents of the shelves. Only bread for carbohydrate, sadly, but there was cheese, salami, tuna and pâté to go on it. No bananas but

I bought a few apples. I asked for a coffee to drink outside and bought a packet of biscuits to eat with it. A couple of other people turned up and we all sat down together. The woman, Mirjana, spoke good English and we chatted about what I was doing. I told them my troubles finding places to eat. 'Ah yes, Petrlaš,' she said, 'nobody there anymore.'

'What happened?'

'They left,' she said, 'like everywhere. Half the village lives in Pirot now, they come back here at weekends.' She told me that they have a house in this village and some land nearby where they used to harvest firewood, but they don't go there anymore. She got bitten by horrible bugs the last time, and mimed for me the sizes of the lumps on her arm, getting an injection in her bum from the doctors. The bugs only showed up here after the NATO bombings. 'We call them "*Clintonche*".' Little Clintons, after the president who ordered the attacks. I ask if they were bombed here. 'Not here but Pirot. We were safe in the village that night, but we could hear the explosions echoing up the valley.'

I realised as I walked across Serbia that it was the twentieth anniversary of the bombing of this country. The seventy-eight-day Nato bombing campaign ended on 9th of June 1999. I didn't pursue it, not wanting to bring the Balkan Wars into my first proper conversation with Serbian people and the conversation moved on, without rancour, to bears and wolves. There were wolves here, apparently, but no bears. I thought of the empty uplands I'd seen in the last twenty-four hours where the lack of humans meant plenty of space for wild beasts to roam.

We drank our coffee and Mirjana bought me and her husband Vule (short for Vukašin, meaning 'son of wolf', a popular Serbian name) a beer. He was a thin man who spoke no English, with big eyes and a funny, naughty look on his face. We got out my map and pointed out the different villages. 'No shop in Gostuša,' he told me. Rooting in her bag for a pencil, Mirjana brought out an apple and handed it to me, bringing strong memories of all the apple gifts of Ukraine. We ate from a communal plate of bread and homemade cheese. The shop owner asked what the food was like in Bulgaria, how it compared. I had to tell her that I hadn't really been invited into houses in Bulgarian villages, that people would say hello on the street but not really take it any further. She mimed for me that Serbian people had big hearts, took a small piece of cheese from the plate and demonstrated that if it was all she had she would give me half. I understood; Bulgaria felt weary, ground down by systemic neglect. Serbia was different, it had more of a sense of cohesion, felt less broken.

They showed me the old border between Serbia and Bulgaria; this area had been part of Bulgaria, but the border moved after WWI where the Serbs took territory from the Bulgarians and villages changed passports but not languages.

We all got ready to leave; it was 1pm and I was heading for the gorge path towards the next valley. 'I feel like I know you well in a short time,' said Mirjana as we walked away together, before offering me their village house for the night. I started to say no, mid-afternoon was too early to stop walking, but took a breath and accepted.

Saying no was more than refusing an opportunity, it was refusing connection. I was meandering through these mountains, not racing, and sometimes offers should be taken, even if they felt like a delay.

The wooden house was basic; a kitchen/living room and two bedrooms off a long balcony with barns underneath. When I pointed to the large bread oven across the yard, Mirjana told me the story of her husband's grandparents; everything they grew they ate, their only money came from hiring out the bull. His parents had the same life too, then finally in the Socialist Yugoslavia of the 60's, Vule and his brother were able to stay in school to become an architect and an engineer. They had renovated the house very slowly on their weekend visits. Next project was to get an inside bathroom. We hugged and kissed and they left for their main home in Pirot. I was to give the key in at the shop the next morning.

I made a fire and rejoiced in the warm, comfortable space. The next morning, I sat on the verandah at a simple plank bench and table, painted green, leaning back against a coarse lime-washed wall, with a view of sunshine on the house opposite and the steep hill covered with bare brown forest. I sipped coffee from a small, perfect espresso cup, painted dark blue with ornate golden edging, topping it up from the *cezve* – a Turkish coffee-making vessel used throughout the Balkans – enjoying the undulating softness of the crisscross lines of red-tiled roofs, aged and weathered. Birds sang nearby and one brave bullfinch even came to assess me, sitting for a few confident seconds on the balcony rail. It was a rare moment of perfect fulfilment, and I sat in happiness, letting the weight of that realisation sink down into me. It had been a while since I wasn't rushing to be somewhere else.

The route that day took me north out of Rsovçi and along a path above a steep gorge that twisted back and forth in horseshoe loops towards a huge lake, 3 miles long. First, as I left the village, close by the river, I passed stone streets and grassed yards, ancient cars kept undercover. Sheep rustled and bleated inside the barns; only one more month until they would be shepherded up to their high summer grazing grounds. This was a living village, thanks to the main road towards Pirot, with full-time inhabitants and many others who came from the city to visit their inherited homes on the weekends. It was a day for planting potatoes; the shopkeeper had a tractor outside the door when I went to drop the key in, loading sacks of seed potatoes onto a trailer. As I left the village, there were two older couples planting together, the men working with hoes to pull ploughed soil into furrows and the women bent at the waist, picking potatoes from boxes. Another woman chatted from the field edge, leaning on her stick and laughing. She was in her late 50s, black headscarf, bobbled, saggy cardigan, wrinkled layers of socks and tights above rubber work shoes, her seven sheep nibbling nearby.

I thought of all the ways I could feel pity for these people, forced to work so hard to survive, describe their poverty, their struggle. We can frame this life as simple, as old-fashioned or backwards. But isn't that to bolster our own choices? If I only see their world through the lens of capitalist labour then it's worse than mine, but if I see it through the lens of community then maybe it's better. Perhaps it's their life that's normal, and ours that has lost its way, peering down from castle walls through crystalline phone screens, wondering why everyone isn't eating cake.

It was a beautiful sunny April day, clouds passing over to give occasional shade and keeping the heat from becoming overwhelming. There was a marked trail here which would lead me all the way through the gorge – all I had to do was follow red and white flashes painted onto protruding rocks, climbing away from the river through young oak forest. I caught flashes of movement as deer sprang away from my noisy footsteps, barking a loud cough of defiance once safely hidden from view.

Halfway along, as I followed the road's contour curves, I stopped, struck by an interesting sign. '*Vrtibog Plateau,*' it said, with a symbol of a walker. As I checked the map I saw that this was the beginning of an incredible route that rose from 800m to a plateau, showing circular contour loops of billowing terrain, before climbing sharply and curving in a 20-mile semicircle around the mountains that formed the border between Bulgaria and Serbia, culminating in Midžor at 2,167m. I was stunned and wished I had enough food to go straight up there but it didn't feel like a good idea when the only carbohydrate in my pack was a loaf of bread that I was rationing by the slice. *I'll go back there one day*, I thought, *once I finish this walk, I'll plan another*.

I added it to the mental list of future journeys, imagined myself coming back in ten years to walk it, maybe taking a break from writing a book to take a walking holiday, perhaps even in my 60s, weaker, wrinkled, but still heaving a rucksack on and walking slowly.

Past the lake and miles up into a dead-end valley, I came to the last village of the day before I'd climb my final foothills and then down to Ćuštica, out of the mountains.

I made the mistake of walking into the village too close to sunset, and as a couple of men walked alongside me, one cadging a cigarette from the other, I got paranoid that they'd know I was due to camp somewhere. Cigarette cadger, a big, gruff, pot-bellied man, was talking a lot at the other one, a smaller, older fellow with kind eyes, something about a lot of euros in the bank, and I fancied that it was about me, with my brightly coloured, expensive clothing, newer than anything either of them were wearing.

I said goodbye to them at a junction and walked ahead, worried. With only a short time until sunset and a single track ahead, it was obvious where I was going. It's a shame that I had to push on quickly because it was a beautiful village, well populated and nicely lived in, wooden beam and plaster houses either side of a shallow stream, with goat and ewe prints pattering the ground, ducks babbling in the water. A couple of women, chatting over an open fire, stopped and stared as I walked past, and said hello as I hailed them.

It would have been a friendly place to catch a coffee and a chat but I wanted to get as far as I could before darkness fell, just in case hoarse, pot-bellied man had a couple more shots of *rakia* and got an idea in his head. It's something I avoided as much as possible, walking through a village close to sunset, advertising the idea that I am a woman alone who is clearly going to camp somewhere nearby. *I should have stopped before the village and appreciated it properly the next morning,* I berated myself.

The track wound onwards through a deep valley, with plenty of nice, flat spots by the stream but nothing suitably hidden. Eventually a side valley opened up and I went up a short way before doubling back on myself into a cleared field above the track. It wasn't perfect, but perhaps slightly unexpected if someone was looking for me. My paranoia didn't last long; as I listened to the owls hooting for each other in the dark, dropping down into tired unconsciousness, I felt safe.

In the morning, I shook the glittering flakes of frost off the tent, jumped around to warm up, and set about climbing upwards, seeking a sunny spot for breakfast. I wound back and forth over the stream in dim icy air as the sun inched slowly down the gorge side, but eventually the track climbed away from the water, up into the sunshine and I breakfasted in the ruins of a shepherd's hut, with a view of a dozen forested hills and just one small building in sight. A cuckoo call echoed nearby, getting gradually closer until it sounded from the apple tree whose branches gently rustled against the top of the stone remains. I gloried in my surroundings, red rock and dry grass, so happy to be here, wandering free in these mountains.

My walk from Dimitrovgrad to Ćuštica completed, I took a day of rest in Kalna. While I lay in my bed staring at the ceiling, I thought about the mountains. Was I done with the Stara Planina? That unwalked route of the Vrtibog Plateau was niggling at me, a glorious piece of mountain beauty missed out on.

Why would I leave it for another time? I was 10 miles away from a beautiful mountain walk and telling myself I'd come back in the next decade. Come on now. Surely other things would take over once I got back to Wales; unexpected events that would change the course of my life. Maybe there would be a child? Maybe there would be a walk around the world, even another cancer? Why add this mountain walk into such a pool of uncertainty and expect to pick it out later? I was here. I should do it now.

Why such stubbornness about not leaving my planned route?

I knew, in a way. The fact that I walk in one direction and complete the original challenge I set myself had to become the entire and only idea; if I deviated from the plan, I made it possible to abandon the whole thing. It was only my stubbornness that made me devote myself so utterly to an unusual goal and push onwards to completion.

But here I was 10 miles away from a mountain with a strong feeling that I should climb it.

It was an intimidating prospect, no matter how inviting. There was snow up there and, once I'd descended from the mountains of Romania, I'd posted my ice spikes back to the UK to remove 500g from the weight on my shoulders. There were also wolves. As I'd walked into a small village one day, I'd been accosted by a shepherd, walking his small personal flock of twelve around the outskirts of the village. He thought I'd come down from the mountains and I didn't have the language to tell him it had only been the lake. 'Oooooh, *ley ley ley ley*,' he clucked, in the noise they use to show surprise here and he mimed the bite and snap of a hungry jawed pounce. '*Vukovi, vukovi.*' Wolves, the shepherd's nemesis.

I shook my stick to show how I would fight them off, 'Nema problem,' said I in performative bravado, and we laughed at the foolishness.

I took a risk for my withdrawn British nature, and contacted

Mirjana and Vule, the friendly couple from Rsovçi to ask if I could stay with them in Pirot and leave non-essential kit there while I walked the mountain loop. They said of course! So there it was, a plan being set in motion; I just had to follow along to make it happen, doing all the things I knew how to do.

I walked along the river to Niš through delicious smells of meat on a grill, passing families who'd come to the river for a Sunday of drinking and relaxing, then took a slow train back to Pirot, chugging along and stopping every ten minutes at small, crumbling stations, people descending directly onto the gravel trackside. I was welcomed into the hugs of Mirjana and Vule, up in their 8th floor apartment in the centre of the town, looking down across the sprawl of high-rises and hotels, mixed with the familiar red-tiled roofs of single storey older houses, shrouded in trees. They made me feel instantly at home, pulling out the bed in the study room.

They fed me well, laid on ornate breakfasts of cured meats and cornbread, yoghurt to drink and cream cheese to spread. Coffee and hot milk, honey and rosemary tea.

I gorged on the delicious spread and then went shopping for a correspondingly sparse set of rucksack provisions, four days of food that looked like a very small bundle on the conveyor belt.

I emptied out my rucksack, putting aside the non-essential items (keyboard, books, spare pants, swimming costume, extra pens, boot grease). The extra food and water I was carrying made the weight back up to the usual amount, around 13kg.

'Will there be wolves up there?' I'd asked Vule the night before I left the city, through the phone translator.

'Yes, where there are sheep there are wolves.'

'But will they attack me?'

'No. Man is the worst animal.'

I had at least a day of climbing ahead, to get me up to the plateau at 1,500m and then a steep ascent to 1,900m, before another 20 miles of walking, around the arc and up to the final peak of Midžor.

I'd brought myself here, so nothing to do but get on with it, and I heaved my bag onto my shoulders and set out to walk.

The lake grew smaller below me and I eventually came up onto the plateau, covered in grass and scrubby trees. At the noise of bells, I looked up to see young cows, silhouettes moving across the skyline. Once I climbed further I saw the man with them; clothes stained with layers of filth to a shiny black and carrying a bag over his shoulder, hooking a great thumb into the handle loop to hold it, his fingers and nails engrained with grime. He was a younger man than the usual pensionable shepherds, with a woollen hat pulled low down over a gnomish face that bore scabs and signs of sun damage; talkative, although when I asked him where his dogs were, I understood little of the reply. I told him I was going to Midžor and, as a warning, he pointed to the huge rump of land to the north-west to show me the dusting of snow on top of it, speckled with thicker white patches like the broad back of a Friesian cow.

This man and his twenty cows climbed up into the mountain clouds every day from the village of Gostuša, far below to the west of us. He had three dogs but they stayed down in the village. I asked about wolves, no, he wasn't bothered about wolves. Perhaps I was overestimating the danger, listening to warnings from people too nervous to actually come up here.

He wanted to talk more but I left him there and moved away to a valley head where I found a small spring; a pipe jammed into the mountainside, trickling water onto the ground in a sea of cow-trodden mud. I drank to fill my stomach, not knowing when the next opportunity would be. Climbing further up, small steps in long wiry grass, I came to the ruin of a building. The walls were about a metre high, showing two rooms; one for cows, and in the other a huge stone sat in one corner, pieces of wood and stone laid above it to make a corner roof, just large enough for one person to shelter. The shepherd. I sat there for a while, on his seat, and imagined the silence of entire days spent with the cows and the mountain and your own thoughts. Did he have a book in that bag? Did he have a knife, to work at wood? Did he spend the entire day in a beatific state of zen nothingness? Being a person who requires regular distraction from her negative thought spirals and is also addicted to her smartphone, I could not imagine the ability to spend such time without stimulation.

I wedged a portion of halva into the stone wall, plastic blue wrapping clearly visible, hoping he'd see it and eat it, a small sweet thing melting in his body heat, a softness for him up there where the wind blew hard.

The next day, oats and halva and banana for breakfast, no wind and the beginnings of a blue sky. Perfect.

Snow patches became more frequent and I started to see animal tracks, a preserved record of recent days. The first track I saw was badger, strong claw marks in an even line. There were hares, showing as an unusual triangle of holes with a single trailing imprint. There were plenty of deer.

I was waiting for the cat prints that might be lynx, for the dog prints that would be wolf. Eventually, higher up, I saw both. Single lines of solitary animals, loping their way across the land, hunting. Up to 1,900m where there was a small picnic shelter, a summer Serbian tourist destination, and down again, slipping up to knee deep in thick snow drifts on the north facing land, as the track wound downhill towards pine forest and a pass between peaks. The snow here was speckled with pine needles, sometimes frozen so hard

I could step onto it and sometimes unexpectedly soft so I'd sink down and have to catch myself with walking poles. Crocus began at the pass, where a small pond caught the snowmelt that was trickling from every slope.

As I climbed again, here now was my first sight of Midžor, seemingly far away but still looming large, a gauze of snow on the entire peak. It was high enough to freeze the overnight rain that had smacked against my tent at 5am.

I thought I could get over there that day but should have expected the slowness of walking at such height; the panting steps of climbing hillsides, feet stumbling on lumps of grass or tentatively finding stone footholds; the illusion in the clear air that the mountains are at a touchable distance that is really many miles away.

Another obstacle presented itself once I'd climbed to the beginning of the huge arc of high peaks. They formed the border between Bulgaria and Serbia and paths on the Serbian side encouraged walkers to stay at a line 20m below the heights, winding in and out on the ripples of grassy slope. I clambered through the low-lying bushes to find the path, having moved off it to admire the view, and gasped when I saw where I had to go next. The route dropped steeply down onto a north facing stretch and there was a huge swathe of snow, stretching hundreds of metres up and down the steep mountainside. It was only 30m across but the slab was smooth and incredibly steep, cliffs up to the right of me and a drop of a couple of hundred metres to my left, nothing to break my fall until tiny pine trees deep in the valley. I'd been walking for twenty-four hours to reach this point – I couldn't go back and find another way. I could climb the cliffs to my right but there would be snow on every north slope I needed to cover.

I took a deep breath and stepped onto the snow, stopping after a couple of steps to breathe through a sudden rise of choking fear. The crust of the snow was frozen with a softer layer underneath and I had to concentrate on every step, drive my walking poles down, kick a foothold, place my foot solidly, make sure I was balanced on three points before moving the fourth. Clumps of snow rolled away each time, skittering to crystals on the steep frozen slope. I focused on the snow at my feet, not allowing myself to look around and lose balance, not allowing myself to stare for too long at the drop. Safely done, I stepped onto the grass, the snow still on the slope above me but with a nice line at the edge of the flat path that I could walk along. I turned to look at the line of footsteps marking my descent from the rocks above, clumsy potholes compared with the agile deer prints that barely dented the surface.

I walked miles that afternoon and every time I turned a ripple of the slope there was a snow field covering the path in an unbroken diagonal. My thighs trembled as I held the weight of each kick, the snow absorbing much more muscle force than solid ground. Each time I told myself to remain steady. I couldn't start doing this on autopilot, but had to stay present, laser my focus on every step.

The crocuses grew thickly here, covering the path that was gouged out of the rockside, a purple haze of colour stretching away and marking the route ahead.

It was clear that I wouldn't make the final summit that day and I set my mind to push on until the last twenty minutes before sunset at 7.30pm, stopping at a ruined building at a flat point that jutted out from the slope. Once I put the tent up I collapsed with a headache; I should have brought my sunglasses to protect against snow glare but had taken them out of my pack down in Pirot. I peed, checked hydration, ate a little, took painkillers, and slept for eleven hours, fortunately waking up the next morning feeling fine.

There was a momentary flickering of fear as I stepped onto the first snow patch of the following day but I urged myself back to calm focus. The hill was a little less steep here; yesterday had been the worst section.

The crocuses grew thicker, the slopes ahead tinged faintly purple. I stalked bumblebees for a while, as they hummed happily in the crocus flowers, diving to the bottom of each bloom, just their back legs and bum visible, coming up from their sweet supping and, pollen covered, perching on petal edge to clean themselves in an all-over body shimmer before taking a long hop to the next flower. Larks sang in the air above me, startled up from the ground to sound an alarm. It was a silent mountain, on the whole; I felt no singing from the ground, no sense of the presence of the land.

Hearing bells, I looked down to see the small dots of horses grazing on the slopes leading up the peak, far below me. I was close now, just a final 150m to climb. Small steps, stopping often, looking back along the entire semicircle of mountains, my first peak glowing snow white, far away in a hazy distance now. Eventually I made it, passing hoof prints in the final snow patches as I hauled myself to the top, a thick blanket of snow falling away on the steep northern side.

I may have been the first human of the year to walk this path to Midžor but the horses and the hares had been there before me.

The other side of the mountain had easy access to the peak, it was only 5 gentle miles to the nearest car park, at a ski slope, and the peak was covered in human footprints. There was a hotel there; maybe I could get a coffee, even use an inside toilet.

I passed a family on my way down, kitted out in tracksuits and trainers and smiled to myself, thinking I was so wild and remote.

Eventually at the hotel, I went inside to claim my coffee, but the waiter tried to usher me outside onto the terrace and when I went to the toilet I understood why – I sported greasy, windblown hair sticking straight up in the air and ghostly smeared remnants of suncream on my cheeks. I tidied myself up as best I could, but still apologised for the many crumbs of earth I left scattered on the floor.

To the woods then, for a night of camping with the loud crashes and barks of deer nearby, before waking up on day four to walk a final 10 miles to the road. Storms had held off but were still threatening.

I followed a thin 4x4 track that traced a ridgeline path, rippling downwards over many hills. It was marked on the map as 'under construction', but was years away from anything more than tentative jeep passage. Eventually I found myself pushing aside branches and descending the hillside at random, holding onto a tree trunk to lower myself the final 2 metres onto another red earthen road, hazy and humid in the sunshine. The leaves around me were the bright lime green of fresh growth and butterflies flickered nearby.

I saw my first boar of the journey; the dark, squat animal on the track ahead looked like a bear at first, attuned as I was to the fears of the wild mountains, but as the creature snorted in alarm it morphed into the barrel roundness of boar with a sagacious, hairy snout. I realised there was a group of them as they squeaked and crashed down the hillside away from me, a few waiting, poised, for me to appear again, to confirm that yes, this terrible creature was coming their way and they should definitely run, snorting. *So that's how I shall know you*, I thought, realising that a cloudy puddle in deep forest was no longer a sign of recent vehicles passing, but the rooting of pigs. Reading the forest, in all the ways it was communicating, would help me learn what I was living amongst.

Almost as soon as I came to the tarmac and crashed my rucksack to the ground, panting and sweaty, a car stopped for my raised thumb. A happy family, man and woman in the front and older grandmother in the back, headscarfed and smiling, squeezing my arm, pretending to have heart palpitations when I said I'd come down from the mountain, telling me I should get a good Serbian man who worked hard. They passed me a bottle of water and I gulped greedily, my own stash reduced to the final centimetre. At the first shop they stopped to buy everyone in the car a beer. Folk music played, an echoing melodramatic tremble of male voice, with trilling trumpet and hyperactive violin and the grandmother raised her arm in the air as she sang along. I looked out of the window, sipping the cold beer and smiled, happy.

Back in Pirot I returned to Mirjana and Vule, the couple who had opened their home to me in a way I was coming to recognise as typical Balkan hospitality. People talked to me more often than they had in Bulgaria or Romania, expressed more interest in what I was doing and more freely offered me food and drink.

The night I returned I fell asleep early, sitting quietly on the sofa, rubbing my feet and drinking beer. Mirjana made ceremonial meals for the Orthodox Easter weekend, fried fish and potato salad, dyed eggs for an Easter breakfast, a huge chunk of slow-roasted lamb, brown and greasy, with roasted potatoes. They'd procured a bottle of *rakia;* Vule normally stayed away from it after years of drinking heavily but we toasted each other, and kept pouring small shots. Mirjana told the comedy tales of his drinking years, saying that most men turn bad when they drink but Vule turned better.

Mirjana spoke basic English, remembered from school fifty years ago, sometimes losing herself in a sentence but mostly getting her point across. Vule spoke none, and his patient eyes waited as we talked, watching the TV and smoking in silence.

I felt nervous around him, wondered if he was tolerating me for the sake of Mirjana's obvious soft spot, but the day before I was due to leave, he spoke and Mirjana translated: 'It feels like you are our third child.'

I looked strangely at him for a brief moment, trying to imagine him as a father to me, and realising I didn't know how to have a father I wasn't scared of. Mine was either absent or angry, violent sometimes and callous at others. I was four when I first witnessed his domestic violence. His outbursts made me frozen around him and I never got a sense of who he was as a person; he remained a monster, who I stopped visiting at age fifteen after cringing through a few years of awkward custody visits. A great deal of my childhood is remembered as a miasma of fear, awkwardness, uncertainty, paranoia and sadness. I always felt lost and out of place.

Eight years later he was diagnosed with terminal cancer. The remaining two years contained a few frigid interactions where I challenged him on my memories of childhood violence, only to receive stilted, insufficient answers about working too hard or not having his needs met. Otherwise, he remained emotionally constipated; there was no apology, no real connection and once he died the relationship froze in time, unable to evolve further.

As a child, my home was never a place where I felt loved or accepted by either parent and, when I realised that this was what Mirjana and Vule were offering me, I decided to try going with it, trusting that they were happy for me to be there, just for a couple of days.

Both in their sixties, Mirjana and Vule had seen years of a successful Yugoslavia under Tito, lived as adults through its collapse, the subsequent war, then the bombings and sanctions that punished Serbia for its brutality. Mirjana told me about her family: born to a Croatian mother and a Serbian father, she married in Croatia and then lived in Montenegro, settling in Pirot, Serbia. She made sure to emphasise the mixture of countries and nationalities that have so often been used to draw lines and make divisions. 'My mother was not Ustasha,' she said, 'my father was not Chetnik' – the vicious Serbian and Croatian militia groups of the many historic Balkan conflicts of the 19th and 20th century.

When we hear about a country, we hear a simplified version of the majority opinion. There are dissenters in Britain but we have a Conservative government, the country voted for Brexit, Farage gets his regular airtime and Tommy Robinson is the talk of the internet.

'When Milosevic first came to power, we were big supporters,' said Mirjana. 'We had all his speeches on tape and we would listen and ahh...' She mimed listening rapturously, clapping in awe. 'But in the early 90s we went to stay with my mother in Croatia and a family friend said to us that Milosevic was like Hitler. We were so shocked; why would she say this?' They had a serious conversation when they got home and began to question: if it makes sense for the Serbs in Croatia to have autonomy and schools in their own language, then why not the same for the Albanians in Kosovo?

'We started to listen to the independent radio stations, avoiding the government-controlled propaganda on all the main news channels. Every day I would rush home to the radio at a certain time for the real news of what was happening, and slowly our opinion of Milosevic turned.' She mimed a slow half circle in the air.

Vule pointed to the TV, a quartered screen showing commenters from Zagreb, Sarajevo and Belgrade waiting to say their piece to the presenter, telling me that it was better now, it used to be a single point of view where now they had multiple. I thought about the modern problem of distinguishing an unbiased opinion amongst so many competing, easily manipulated sources of news.

I thought about asking Mirjana what they did to oppose the war but it seemed an uncomfortable question when they had probably done nothing but stay at home and be scared. The experience of disagreeing with your government does not equal standing up against it. There are many people in Britain who stick their heads in the sand, ignore the worry of climate change, our country's profits from global inequality and suffering, to concentrate on their own lives, their own small gains and losses. It's easier that way, let's face it.

They had both been engineers, in their working lives. Vule had a car parts shop that he was desperate to sell but nobody would buy it. Their youngest son, Alexander, still lived with them, an unemployed 27-year-old who stayed in his room for most of the day. I got the sense of a disaffected man; he talked of spending a few years as a waiter in Malta and then, once home, the only job he could get paid a quarter of the money he'd earned abroad, so he'd quit. He'd tried working for his father but had given that up too, didn't want to inherit the old-fashioned shop, where metal parts sat on shelves in dusty boxes, prices scrawled on slowly desiccating paper labels.

He described work as futile – why bother when he received so little in return? His next subject shocked me. When I said I was a writer, he said he didn't know any Serbian writers and talked about the poor quality of the Serbian language. 'English is better, it's more advanced. Serbian language is plainer, more basic.'

I wondered how it feels to be born into a conflict that is blamed on your nationality; international tribunals set up to prosecute atrocities committed in the name of the country that all your propaganda is telling you to support. Alexander was born in 1992, as conflict flamed and communities collapsed. He was seven years old as Nato bombed his town and the family fled to shelter in his ancestral village home; grew up in a Serbia that suffered years of sanctions and international condemnation. How does that feel, to be the child of a government explicitly labelled as villainous by world leaders who 'control the narrative'? Some Serbs ran away to new lives abroad. Others stayed and stewed in bitterness, chewing the flavourless nationalist gristle of always being hard done by.

Spending more time with Mirjana and Vule was tempting. They had a programme for me, a stay planned out for three further days, the restaurants they'd take me to, walks along the river, but I couldn't stay, I had to keep moving on.

I cried as we stood together on the train platform for my return to Niš. I didn't expect it, I say goodbye to people all the time, but they were dear to me.

Walking out of the city centre took 5 miles before I saw my first tractor. Five miles of walking on pavements, then roadsides, then dirt tracks alongside the river; 5 miles from glamorous cafés with Wi-Fi, a range of coffee options on a bilingual menu, beautiful waitresses swishing their slick ponytails as they marched outside to serve people on cushioned seats under patio umbrellas, to a set of planks balanced on empty crates outside the only shop in the village, forming a low table sticky with spilt beer and a fine dust of cigarette ash, where a group of men with work-thickened fingers and tatty clothing drank and joked around. One elderly gent came shuffling in on crutches, holding out a 100 dinar note to the shop owner for his beer, but they were busy with a potato delivery.

There was an intriguing lump of land north-west of Niš, the mountain of Jastrebac, a strong patch of green on a white map, with roads that seemed to creep up the sides but never connect to each other – there was no way to cross from east to west. I decided to go onto the green lump anyway, before taking a second break from my own route to go to Kosovo and meet more walkers.

Eventually I came to the final village on a string of small roads across the base of the mountain, where forest rose up from the wide plain, and was able to walk away from the houses and into the trees. It had rained all night and into the morning, and the wet earth meant that the forest was humid. Sweat dripped from me in the effort of climbing a steep and winding earthen track, the thickness of lush forest around me, mosses and leaf mulch. I was startled to see salamanders at my feet, the brightness of their yellow blotches shouting poison! They would ponderously slide away from me with a complete lack of urgency, their pudgy feet scraping at the earth to move a few feet to safety. A hunting dog whiffled at me from behind, then ran past in a light, flickering motion. It was in its element, the liquid sway of an animal in full immersion, its perception of its surroundings coming through nose not eyes. I heard voices far below me and hastened as much as I could, not really wanting to meet anyone here. It worked, or they took another path, one of many tyre-marked tracks through these hills, diverging for hunting and harvesting.

Boar prints were higgledy, large and small. I hoped the occasional canine print were dog and not wolf. They'd warned me of wolves in the village below, as they always do. The spectre of the wild haunts every rural imagination which lives at the boundary of conquered land.

Two days later, after a night sleeping in an open-sided cabin as snow fell and winds blew grit and ice all over me, I came off the mountain a little cold and shaken, back down to the gentle cherry orchards, where I could look for the first village and the beginning of an asphalt road to town.

KOSOVO

It was time to take another detour from my journey, this time to meet Nils and Marie in Kosovo.

I stuck my thumb out in the rain on the edge of Prokuplje, an ordinary town in the south of Serbia, pacing up and down, treading footprints into the wet gravel at the side of the road. Two lifts brought me to within 20km of the border with Kosovo. I'd left Prokuplje late and it was 5pm, maybe too late to get another lift. I didn't know how heavily controlled the Serbia-Kosovan border was, how passively hostile; maybe nobody would take a hitch-hiker into disputed territory. I was just passing the minutes until it got dark enough to go and camp, but unexpectedly a van with a German number plate stopped for me. The man spoke in a mixture of German and English as we shoved my rucksack in through the back door, balancing it on piles of boxes and a deconstructed bicycle, continuing to talk as he cleared his clutter – bottles of water, cigarette packets – from the front seat, until I could get in, my feet balanced on sacks of compost. He was Ramon, a Kosovo Albanian, heading from his German home for a three-week holiday, and his town was 6 miles away from my destination, all the way over on the other side of Kosovo, almost at the border with Albania. I couldn't believe my luck, I'd thought it would be a two-day journey to get there.

Ramon laughed at my knitting; I'd packed a ball of wool and small circular needles, and knitted blanket squares as I went, posting them home with completed diaries and other unwanted kit. He took a picture to show his sister and offered me water and cigarettes. He was a solidly friendly person that I felt instantly comfortable with and we chatted in a mixture of Serbian and English. He was 50, with grey hair in a curly ponytail, and had lived in Germany for thirty years, sending money home to his parents, keeping them going. His father had been a farmer with three hundred sheep and he'd been sent out with them as a child, spending days alone in the fields. Now the sheep were gone and his father survived on a pension and smallholding; neither were adequate without extra money from economic migration.

The first thing I noticed about Kosovo was the buildings. They were all new. We'd drive past small villages on the fast highway, I couldn't see a single crumbling, decayed house. 'Bombed,' said Ramon. 'Both Nato and Serbia bombed here, many houses destroyed. My house too,' he said, and showed me pictures on his phone.

'Did the government give you money to rebuild?'

'No, we fund ourselves – people go west to work, France, Germany, Italy.' The usual economic exodus I've heard of elsewhere, but this time more urgent.

Ramon advised me against hitching in Kosovo, said it was dangerous here, that people were crazy; he made a twisting gesture against his forehead. The Serbian men who'd picked me up had also told me not to hitch in Kosovo, that the men there would be sexual, that it was dangerous. I was not about to pay attention to the Serbian opinion on a territory full of people they'd oppressed for decades, but a Kosovan view was worth listening to.

Fortunately I wasn't going to hitch again, not until I wanted to leave in a few days. Ramon said he'd take me directly to Gjakova and find a hotel for me. It was late at night and he twisted in pain against the prolonged driving position, having been on the road for fourteen hours. He swore against the road conditions, the everlasting roadworks, external rebuilding money that has poured into Kosovo but had to pass through many layers of grasping hands before the remnants went towards the public good.

After three hours of driving, when we reached the hotel, he went in to check they had rooms and came out to tell me he'd paid. There wasn't much I could do to argue, just hug and kiss him with the familiarity that comes of a shared journey in the dark, of shared spirit. A good man, he'd described himself as; just a divorced man who does nothing but work, but a good one. He was – I felt it in him.

Now here I was alone in a huge double bed with red leather chairs complementing the huge smoky mirror that covered one wall. I messaged my reasons for making this diversion – Nils and Marie. *Deux Pas Vers L'Autre* was their Insta handle, 'Two go towards others' their awkward translation. They were a French couple who were walking from Portugal to Turkey, seemingly over every single mountain en route. We'd been messaging encouragement for a while but as our routes crossed like swooping bird flights from opposite directions, here was the chance to meet in person and I'd taken it, seeking to learn from comparison. I was intimidated by their ability: they'd been posting nonstop snowy mountain pictures since September. Snowy mountains were my barriers to walking, where it was their destination.

It's a strange thing, to connect journeys where both sets of protagonists are hailed as heroes. Ego plays a huge part in the documenting of an adventure journey, or does it...? Maybe it's just my own low self-esteem that manifests as being hugely competitive, a part of myself that I don't like. Being the eldest of four siblings, and clever at school, winning was easy when I was little. As I've got older, competitiveness becomes pressure on myself, a focus on my own speed, my own ability.

Now I was meeting people who were much better than me, much faster, more capable, better photographers, more successful social media documenters, more glamorous. I shrank in the face of their heroics.

I felt myself wanting to match them, but at the same time with the knowledge that I was utterly outclassed, which expressed itself in imagining unpleasant behaviour. I anticipated that they'd be rude, curt, superior and prideful. Of course they were none of these things and my insecure brain was the problem once again.

I had come to follow them for two days, absolving myself of any route-finding decisions. It was a hugely different experience to mine in many ways, and also completely the same. We wound our way south-east across the flat plain towards the mountains that separated Kosovo from Macedonia. People called out to us constantly, beeping their horns, waving, beckoning us into awnings of cafés and shops.

This was an extension of their reception in Albania, they told me, where they'd had to refuse offers of food and hospitality multiple times a day. I wondered what their experiences would be in Romania, where I'd experienced so much silence and sideways glances.

Maybe it was different to walk as part of a group, not as a solo oddball, laden with unknown motives. In a group, each presence legitimises the others.

Nils would dive in, hand outstretched to introduce himself and I realised how he created interaction, actively inviting it, compared to my more reticent, neutral smiles. Many differences exist between the journey of a solo woman and the male of a couple; people would often talk to the boys – Nils' brother was also visiting – and include Marie and I as an afterthought, but I also realised that I could do more to instigate interaction in my own journey, that I'd been happy to let experiences flow past me rather than actively create them.

The sky was a clear blue and the sun shone hot onto packed yellow earth tracks and verdant green fields. As we tracked across a huge plain towards the mountains, I smiled with recognition at their route finding: the eternal oscillation between trying to stay away from busy roads or ending up on tiny tracks alongside fields which could disappear or turn to mud at any moment. There was plenty of pausing to stare at phones, of confusion and turning back the other way, of missing turns. I felt pleased, in a small way, to see these imperfections, that made their journey so like mine.

Every so often there came a ripple in the surface of our idyllic tourist experience. As we walked up a steep hill into a mountain village, there were bullet holes in the first house facing the road. I imagined troops coming to kill and destroy the village, the first defences at the entrance, shots fired. There was a man in the centre who spoke English and he gave us directions to the old road along the hillside. He told us that it was the day after Nato began bombing in Kosovo that the Serbs came down from the mountain to set fire to the village, killing three people that day. I saw names on the monument in the centre, faces of four men and one woman laser-etched into the marble; the two older men were 87 and 88 years old.

We camped on a piece of riverside ground just outside a small town. It was a fun night, *rakia* and a few beers, birthday cake for Marie, presented to her in an elaborate surprise created by Nils, his love very evident. I enjoyed the fire and the public camping without fear of being seen, both things I can't do alone. The next morning though, as I looked around the unnatural dips and curves of the ground, I was chilled to realise the entire area was grassed-over rubble, where destroyed houses had been dumped as war detritus, to be reclaimed by nature.

The trauma of this country wasn't far from the surface.

Place names were on bilingual signs, but in many instances the Serbian names were obscured with black paint. I only spoke Serbian as a last resort, when everyone's English, Albanian and French had failed.

'Deep Kosovo' we called it, joking about the time Nils asked where he could buy a Taser for self-protection and was taken by a hotel owner to an arms seller, returning with tales of a bunker two storeys underground, full of guns and piles of money.

But when the ripples had stilled and the smooth surface reflected only cafés and cheery hellos, Kosovo was completely unchallenging. The sun shone, we walked and chatted, there were regular bakeries where we could buy *burek*, oily layers of pastry folded together with cheese or meat and baked until crispy. We'd treat ourselves in the afternoons, finding a shaded place to rest and gorge.

Two days felt like too short a time to spend with these people. I was only just getting to know sharp Nils, with his impulsive outbursts, and softer Marie, with her smiles and silence, but I felt torn about staying longer. These weren't my steps and it felt like wasted energy while my own walking target hung paused and waiting. Their route climbed from Prizren at 400m up to a 2,100m gap between snowy peaks. The snow had been gleaming far away as we sweated in the sunshine and I both wanted to follow them and was unsure if I could. They were the mountain experts and I was a comparative novice. But it didn't feel right to duck out. I needed to join them in the mountains, to get the true Nils and Marie experience. We slapped hands in high fives: I'd cross with them to Macedonia.

In the end, it didn't turn out as hoped. We climbed up out of Prizren and camped above the original city fort, the web of city lights stretching out like a blanket over the plain. At the moment of sunset, loud fireworks boomed and hazy cheers floated up from the city. It was Ramadan and sunset meant time to eat together in communal celebration. The next day though, heavy rain came and we struggled. It was a hard route ahead and all we could do was cover up and press onwards. I knew I'd be the slowest; they had the slender, muscular bodies you'd expect of long distance walkers, rather than my short and chunky barrel shape, but it was still embarrassing to struggle at the back. They were getting cold waiting for me every five minutes and we transferred some of the weight of my kit onto their shoulders. I burnt with shame but couldn't go any faster – my mountain pace is a slow trudge and there was no changing it.

After a damp night in a barn, rats nibbling at our kit, we carried on in the forest. The path was steep and simple, winding between old trees, but when we reached the tree line, it immediately became much harder; the wind was wild, battering rain against us. We were still 300m below the pass, with an unknown amount of snow and wind still to come, when Marie lost the feeling in her fingers, a familiar condition for her, with pain that made it impossible for her to grip her walking poles. We hunched together for a quick consultation and decided to turn back, all soaked to the skin.

This was a relief too, to see them making sensible group decisions, rather than pressing on dangerously in the name of heroism. We tracked our way down the mountain in a new direction, stopping for coffee at a hunting resort, before arriving in a wet village where we could wait for a bus back towards Prizren. There would be no trying again; brother Noé had a flight back to Paris from the other side of the mountains, so we found a hostel and looked up bus times to skip around to Skopje.

As we talked about their project, I realised the strong philosophies lay behind it; that Nils and Marie were deliberately opening themselves to Europe, inviting as much interaction as possible, both with guest walkers and local people, in order to communicate to their audience the beauty of immediate neighbours, to see beyond Thai beaches or colourful Mexican glamour, and value traditional European cultures, especially in rural agriculture. The perfection of their social media display made more sense now, when related to Nils' photographic career in the Paris fashion industry. I saw that their documentation was an artistic creation, rather than the real life 'warts and all' I was focused on, and that underneath the glamorous achievement lay truly generous, open hearts.

Safely down off the mountain and back in Prizren, I wanted to hitch-hike back to Serbia, but our hostel owner advised against it. A Kosovo stamp in the passport meant trouble at the disputed border, still freshly and unjustly imposed in Serbia's eyes, and he had tales of tourists being turned back, seemingly at the whim of disgruntled border guards.

We said goodbye at the bus station with promises to meet again when I walked through France, unaware of the drastic journey changes that would come for all of us.

Nils and Marie would head south to Greece then a detour up into Romania and Bulgaria, a route planned to take in every European country on the 52nd line of latitude, before heading to Istanbul, aiming to finish their challenge before 2020.

I had no idea when I would finish mine; this journey felt impossible to pin down. In January 2019, I had told myself another year but here I was in May and felt I could still take another year about it. I was more at peace now, not feeling too much pressure to make progress or force myself to walk at any particular speed. I had expected to be further along my route, but I wasn't and that was fine. I felt the full freedom of this adventure; to sleep where I liked, in field edge and farm bed; to pause in cafés or to maintain a pace all the way to the top of a hill without stopping. I was free to break and go to Kosovo to meet other walkers. There was no deadline to return home. This was more than a charity endurance challenge this time. It was just a journey made by walking and I was free to give it whatever form I wanted.

SERBIA

I took buses back into Serbia and hitched to the small village I'd left a week earlier, continuing my walk from exactly the place I'd left it, without missing a single kilometre.

As I got out of the car outside the village shop, I was hailed by a group of farm workers sitting at the dusty, worn table under the awning. Fresh from my week with gregarious Nils and Marie, with their open attitude and desire to connect with others, I paused and said yes to a beer, where on other days I might have slid away with a polite refusal, to slink into the cherry orchards and find a hidden sleeping spot.

One beer became two and I listened to this group of friends discuss the planting of corn and the rain forecast. Nenad was the force of the group, a colossal, good-humoured man who shoved the plate of pickled peppers my way and made sure I had another beer before mine was empty. After what seemed to be an intense conversation about the weather, there was a general decampment to Nenad's porch with a couple of crates of beer for a party which led to a drunken drive to town to eat grilled meat, an ill-advised 3am bottle of wine followed by a snog, and the next morning we find me blearily cooking eggs on the wood-stove in Nenad's house, blindingly hungover. He refused all food and just drank Fanta, smoking incessantly, while a man came over for a serious conversation. Turns out they were all supposed to go and plant his corn the day before, and Nenad had thrown it over to get drunk with a girl.

I had the kind of hangover where you need to slump back to sleep for several hours, but there was walking to do and I'd had enough time off recently so I swallowed painkillers and got a lift back to the village on Nenad's ancient tractor, sitting at his side on the wheel cover like a proper farmwife. It was Serbian hospitality at its finest – spontaneous, generous and involving plenty of alcohol. There is a wildness to Serbia that I connect with, a fiery spirit and blunt attitude that's easy to read. Make a Serb laugh and you're in the gang. I vowed there would be no more spontaneous acceptance of beers with groups of men, though. I had to find a different way to be gregarious.

Walking west from Blace was slow; the maps showed the roads ending in forest a few miles ahead, but I had a new trick up my sleeve – Nils had showed me how to use photographic satellite mapping to source information that was missing from incomplete GPS maps on areas of land that aren't mapped for tourism or off-road travel. Satellite view showed me a lot more beyond the end of the tarmac and I saw that I could follow wriggling earthen tracks across the hills, to tiny settlements basking in the sunshine on long, high ridges.

I took a moment of appreciation for nettle-choked paths, for overhanging branches dripping cool wet blotches on my hot bare skin. For leaf mould, for fungi, for silent trees, mottled bark and birdsong. Thickly clustered undergrowth and faint wing flutters. The faraway sound of rushing water. Crackles of twigs as unseen lizards and snakes scuttle and slide from me.

The farms were high here, with raspberry crops making use of the later seasons. Cherry on the plains, raspberry in the mountains. Shortly after I left the road, I found a place to stay. A man bent over his potato plants, scattering white grains by the handful, looked up and almost immediately invited me for coffee. 'Sure, why not?' I thought; maybe this was a better thing to say yes to than a group of burly day-drinkers. I realised once I entered the house that I was a guest for his housebound wife, breathless with heart problems and unable to walk very far. They were happy to see me, welcoming my sweaty self with hugs and kisses, offering me the traditional Serbian welcome of *slatko* (fruit in syrup) and water. I was supposed to take a few spoonfuls of the sweet thing and when I was done, drink the water to signify satiation. I was invited to shower and stay the night and didn't think too long before saying yes; I was learning on this journey to be less apologetic about my presence, to accept that I am accepted. 'This place is your home, be comfortable,' said Miroslav, a square-faced man with a mustachioed smile, before disappearing back to his potatoes. Milijana took regular phone calls on the land line, their only communication outside the valley; announcing to each one that she had a guest. She asked my age and told me that she had a son the same age, would I like to be her daughter-in-law? I feel uncomfortable with such direct jokes so that time I demurred by asking to see a photograph before making any commitments and this was the right answer, resulting in peals of laughter. I was utterly shattered, hangover still very present, and asked to go to bed at 7pm. Miroslav showed me the way to the attic beds as Milijana couldn't make the stairs.

I came downstairs to a waiting tray of *slatko* and water again, before a breakfast of eggs, cheese, bread and salami and I left refreshed, restored by this simple hospitality and at peace with my ability to walk and accept what comes, whether it's a drunken night with farmers or a gentle bed with pensioners.

It was raining for much of the week, light summer rain that came with thunderstorms and black clouds hanging heavy over the deep clefts that form southern Serbia. I sweated in the humid valleys, grateful for breaths of slight wind as I climbed to hilltops of 1,000m, where the roads were pressed earth and my map told me there was only forest. Mostly I would only receive whiffs of rain, speckles from the edge of rain clouds that salted the earth elsewhere. But one day it really came, torrential, thunder crackling overhead. There was no shelter, only high valley sides and a snaking, riverside road. I stood under a tree for a while, still in my T-shirt, spitting out the tang of salt and suncream from the water running into my mouth.

The rain came relentlessly, the kind of summer downpour that you could shower under, but eventually it lessened and I changed my saturated vest top and walked on, a steep climb, stepping over rivulets of brown water running in the road creases. My hips hurt with every step and I leaned hard on my walking poles, trying to solidify my stomach muscles to hold my body upright. I realised I hadn't eaten for hours and felt a heaviness in my body; I'd run out of energy. *Walk through the slump until you start using your fat reserves*, I told myself. I didn't want to eat anything now, it was too close to camping time and the evening meal. It worked – after another ten minutes the effort became easier again.

The rain poured again, on a looping road winding up a steep, forested slope with no flat places to sleep. Just down off a horseshoe curve I saw a man struggling with a pipe and I stopped to watch as he connected an extension to a pouring spout, thoroughly splashing himself in the process. He called out once he saw me, tramping up between the cleared logs with long strides to swing his hand into mine with the clean, strong clasp of a country man, wet hands flattened large like mole paws, warm brown eyes under a faded baseball cap. '*Sestra moya!*' (My sister!), he called me and immediately invited me to stay at his house.

His name was Lyudi and words poured from him like water from the pipe, how wet I was, how I must sleep at his house, just him and his wife there. We walked together back down the hill as he talked and talked. I liked this, to be carried home on a flow of words. His wife was more silent, bigger bodied where he was slight, and she greeted me in the dark kitchen with three cheek kisses and a tray of sugar lumps and water. They talked and laughed and moved in silence like trees that have grown around each other, the deep intimacy of knowing each other's shapes, each other's patterns.

The electricity kept turning on and off, prompting a string of curses from Lyudi every time. We lit candles and made space for my things, hanging wet clothes above the wood-stove and laying damp notebooks at the edge of the oven. The rucksack went next door into a large, light, unheated room with two long tables, pictures of saints, heaps of clothes and trays of eggs. This was where they put the cheese to thicken, once they'd heated the pan of milk on the stove overnight.

Maria knitted as we talked, using homespun wool from their own sheep and Lyudi went out to see to the tractor. I went to bed early again, once I'd dried out and we'd eaten together. Maria came into the room and slept with me, meaning I couldn't sleep as I listened to her breathing, unused to having another body so close to me.

I made 1,000m of altitude gain the following day, climbing all the way up to a ski resort at 1,800m, with small patches of snow nestling in the pine shade. A ski resort without snow is a strange cartoon. The buildings are impossibly large and luxurious, designed to be intricate imitations of log cabins or turreted mansions at monstrous sizes and the mountain-top development bubbles up in a horrible cluster like a capitalist fungal infection.

It was surprisingly busy with glossy rich people going for short walks, jeans tucked into shiny leather boots, velvet jackets. There were Porsche Cayennes, Range Rovers, smart women in puffa jackets with blade-straight hair who stared at me walking towards them, not speaking until I said hello. The hotels were expensive but

I was tired and needed internet for map access, so I settled on the cheapest place I could find. I had no sleep though as the bar across the road played music until 4am. The worst moment came when the owner told me that the place was busy because there was a pharmaceutical conference at the grandest hotel. I cried, thinking of Maria's welcome 9 miles down the mountain, with her bad heart, struggling to walk up the road to say goodbye, knitting her own socks because she couldn't afford to buy machine made. And here the rich people were, making their money from illness and disease, cold eyes staring at my muddy boots without so much of a hint of welcome, coming from the cities to celebrate together in a mountain top largesse, safely insulated from poverty and struggle.

It took a day and a half to come down from the unnatural mountain eyrie on a long day of winding road in hot sunshine. I spent the intervening night in a plum orchard, mating frogs croaking their horny chuckle-squelch at the river edge, and midnight-blue dragonflies zooming past the tent mesh.

I joined the main road at 4pm but with still another 7 miles to Novi Pazar I gave it up, stuck my thumb out and hitched. This was where I planned to stop walking and return to the UK for a short time; I had to go back for a hospital visit, one of my regular checks to see whether my cancer had returned.

A sunburnt man with piercing blue eyes, driving a ratty white van, stopped for me. 200 metres down the road was another woman hailing passing cars, but this time for sex work. The risk I ran when hitching was that often the only other women who stand by the side of the road in Eastern Europe are sex workers. I turned to the man and told him I wasn't a prostitute. He laughed and said he knew. Safir is how I remember his name, a beekeeper, with his protective hat placed on my lap and a piece of hoof fungus at my feet. Freshly cut from the tree, this silver-grey half-moon was to burn in his bee smoker, he told me, through many iterations of explanation. We liked each other and stopped for a coffee so we could talk about bees and his family, whether each of us wanted children. He wanted to carry my bag to the hotel with me, I think in a platonic way, but I said no thank you, still wary of the way we'd met and how my perceived freedom might be misinterpreted. I was dazed with tiredness and only capable of shower and sleep.

This journey was sometimes nothing more than a series of strange interludes that I flowed between, dipping into other people's worlds like a bird on the wing.

HITCH-HIKING BACK TO THE UK

The following day I walked to the edge of Novi Pazar and started hitch-hiking again. I'd decided to hitch to the UK from Serbia, a gargantuan journey when you're standing at the start of it, facing the uncertainty of a journey of several thousands of miles that depends entirely upon the kindness of strangers. Hitch-hiking is waiting. Hitch-hiking is resigning yourself. Hitch-hiking is trying not to panic that you will be stuck somewhere as darkness falls.

Hitch-hiking feels hopeless sometimes. There's a loneliness to standing there, holding out an arm to each car as it whooshes past, holding a smile on your face, waiting for someone to decide that they're feeling generous.

You are a beggar, a tramp, a scrounger, a body in an unexpected place, something for people to stare at in mistrust, in shock, in derision; you catch flashes of their faces through each car windscreen, sometimes open-mouthed in shock.

You are a lone pillar that stands in the flow of human motion and waits for an invitation to come along, and sometimes it feels as if you might wait forever.

I wondered if anyone would pick me up that Saturday afternoon, perhaps no good for anyone travelling long distance. I was on the main highway towards Belgrade but wanted to get off it before I came anywhere near the capital city, and travel cross country towards the highway that ran east/west across Serbia, part of the transport route for many lorries between Turkey and Western Europe.

It was all up in the air, as hitch-hiking so often is. There's very little I can control; just place myself in a good spot with space for cars to stop, then wait and hope for someone who is going my way and in the mood to accept a passenger. It's a complete uncertainty, scary if you give in to it, there is the chance that nobody will stop at all and your journey will become a complicated jumble of emergency transport options. But if you hold your nerve and wait, don't give in to the paranoia, then someone, eventually, will stop.

I watched the cars, keeping an eye on the cloudy sky, aware of the background men walking around the car sales place by the roundabout edge. A series of cars passed, driving wildly, with Serbian flags draped from windows, men half hanging out, waving beer bottles and shouting in a cacophony of horn hoots. An election, I thought for a while, but then realised they were wedding guests. There were scrolls on all the windshields, tied in red ribbon, secret directions to the after party perhaps.

It was close to 5pm and I was getting worried. My body felt ungrounded, swirling with adrenaline and, realising I'd not eaten for hours, I knelt down to pull off a chunk of bread, cutting a piece of sweaty cheese to squash into it. I looked at the roads, wondering whether I'd travel into the city centre to find an easy, safe hotel or did I have the courage to scratch together a camping spot on the edge of industrialia? I didn't realise a car had stopped until it was suddenly behind me on the verge. The driver who got out to put my bag into the boot was straight-backed and solid, grizzled and gnarled in an outdoors kind of way. The car had a German number plate.

'Where are you going?' I asked in Serbian.

'Deutschland,' he replied.

'Can I come?' We stared at each other for a second while we both absorbed the idea that I was getting into his car for a twenty-hour journey.

I sat in the back, a small boy in the front seat, and smiled to myself, unable to believe my luck in getting a thousand-mile lift.

From hopelessness to complete success, all in the raising of a thumb, and my hardest task had been to hold my nerve.

We talked little at first, both aware of many hours ahead, the man's son taking most of his attention. Eventually the boy fell asleep and we swapped places. I knitted and we talked in short bursts between long periods of silence, as the car left the mountainous south to cross the open Danube plain of northern Serbia and Hungary. He was going to drive all night, he said, to Köln, where he'd been working for the last twenty-four years.

As I always do when someone tells me about leaving the Balkans, I calculated backwards to see at what stage of the war this Montenegrin man would have left. So many people escaped the conflicts to seek refuge elsewhere. Canada gave many visas. There were those who dissented to acts of violence in their name, those in fear, those who were driven from their homes. I thought about the silence migration leaves behind. All the people talking about leaving the UK once Brexit had taken place were absenting themselves from any future decision-making in a country they saw as having taken a wrong turn, leaving the ship to be steered by the victors.

'Serbia. Liars.' He repeated it several times. 'Everything they say is lies.' I lacked the language to ask why, my phone wouldn't be able to translate any deeper meanings for us until we entered the EU and I had free data again (data access that would be lost once Brexit was enforced).

The man gave his son regular food and drink, but without taking any himself and it wasn't until I learnt their names that I realised they were Muslim and observing Ramadan. I heard the stickiness of his dry mouth speaking, watched him pinch his eyelids as the sun grew closer to setting. Eventually he asked me to pass him a bottle of juice from behind the driver's seat and I fumbled for it in front of his son's sleeping body, then held the juice as he prayed while driving, turning his head in small movements, gesturing and mumbling. Eventually he drank in long, thankful gulps and I imagined the intensity of fasting; small moments of suffering every day, constant reminders of your faith bringing you closer to your God.

A strip of land called the Sandžak was the reason that I'd been meeting Muslims in southern Serbia. The Sandžak was kept by the Ottoman Empire for long after Serbia and Montenegro became countries in their own right, finally being divided between the two in 1912, almost one hundred years after the Principality of Serbia was established.

The man told me about his home up in the mountains on the border with Serbia, where he'd been buying pieces of land for years and years; his village consisted of two houses and he owned them both. 'You can walk for 5 miles on my land,' he boasted, and I looked up the word for king to tease him with. There was a relaxed feeling between us, he was easy to be silent with. At first he said that he'd drive all night but eventually, at about 1am, he pulled into a rest area, one of many that appear regularly on the sides of European motorways, and we all wound the seats back to curl up and sleep as best we could for a couple of hours.

He said he'd take me as far as I wanted towards his house, gave me his address, which turned out to be in Düsseldorf, part of the terrible conglomeration of cities in the west of Germany. For the hitch-hiker, it's a hideous snarl of seven cities and numerous towns that have melted together in a confusion of motorways that are impossible to hitch around. In desperation I searched for buses and found that I could travel from Köln Airport to central London for €25. A bargain too good to miss, it just meant that I'd have to spend the night somewhere, waiting for the 10am bus the following morning. 'Of course you can stay,' said the man, who'd already invited me home anyway.

After twenty hours in the car together, we pulled up, slightly dazed, at his apartment in a small block in a bland suburb of a German town where every street looks the same. There was a strange emptiness to his place, the plain walls of a bachelor pad, where normally he lived alone, his wife and son back in Montenegro, growing and living while they waited for his infrequent visits. It felt strange to be there; I felt dull and exhausted, so I went for a long walk into the town on an incredibly hot afternoon, where people strolled in shorts and dresses. I tried to compare the cleanliness and sterility of this German town to the worn jumble of houses in any Serbian suburb, but couldn't even remember where I'd come from. I thought I'd be shocked at the prices but it all seemed suddenly normal, to pay €15 for a small bag of fruit and vegetables at a market that was made for luxury eating; watermelons and aubergines on sale, no onions or potatoes.

I went back to the quiet flat, all the windows open, flies buzzing slowly in and out. The man told me he'd go out that evening, to the mosque for Iftar. We'd slept through sunrise that morning so he'd had no chance to eat or drink before daylight and now he sat next to me, no food or hydration in almost twenty-four hours, a tired and drained man. We turned our bodies towards each other in the easy comfort of attraction, the faint stirrings of breeze that signified the potential of a sexual storm. I wasn't going to do it, he had a wife, so I went for another kind of intimacy and asked him about his life.

'Why don't you retire? Don't you have enough land yet?'

His life in Germany felt so empty, all his cares and loves were back in Montenegro. 'It's not easy for me to go back. For almost fifteen years I have rarely been home.' He'd only gone to collect his son to renew his German passport, keeping the boy's options open for the future. He told me that he used to be a high-ranking police officer but couldn't support the Serbian regime of the late 90s, or his corrupt superiors. We talked through a translation app, typing in silence as his son played with a football and waited, bored, for us to be done, bouncing the ball through the dimly lit flat, blinds drawn against the sun. The translation apps give a scrambled version of any conversation.

'I had a political problem. I did not work for the regime but for the people. I am afraid of high police officer X, because of injustice he kept everything and I went to claim asylum in Germany. If they had been arrested for corruption, I would be dead by now, in retaliation.'

I looked sideways at this solid, silent man, working far away from home in exile from his culture, and thought about the peaceful kingdom he was building, up in the mountains where nobody could touch him. 'When will you have enough money?' I asked.

'I don't know. Last summer I went home and built a road on my property, 13km. I couldn't have done that with Montenegrin money.'

He told me that in Balkan tradition, it's customary for hosts to share a bed with guests for their first night's stay; I twinkled my denial at him, telling him it was a story. It didn't matter anyway – they went to the mosque to break the fast and I slept early, tired from thirty-six hours of travelling on very little sleep.

Once I have shared intimate parts of life with a stranger, slept in front of them, spent hours talking or in silence, shared food together, I am a little bit in love, we are linked.

The next morning we hugged at the train station as thunder rumbled overhead and the heat flattened down under torrential rain.

Hitch-hiking goes deep and it ends neatly. Exchanging a flash of eye contact that was as brief and intense as our time together, we turned and walked away from each other.

After ten hours on a crowded overheated bus, broken fans blowing warm air onto cramped, moist bodies, watching Agatha Christie over my seatmate's shoulder as I knitted and waited for the time to be over, I disembarked in London. Not the way I wanted to enter the country at all; I'd imagined heading straight from Serbia to Bardsey Island at the tip of the Llyn Peninsula, giving myself a decompression chamber to weather the change from Serbian rural simplicity to UK luxury. But somehow it wasn't too shocking to find myself looking at rows of chic, overpriced snacks in a Sainsbury's Express at Victoria Station: disposable plastic pots of edamame beans and celery sticks; readymade mashed potato and soup, sitting sterile for busy people to heat and eat. The frightening thing was how normal it felt.

I hitched over to Aberystwyth then took a train, a taxi and a boat in order to join my friend at her warden post on Bardsey Island. Three and a half days to travel from Serbia to Wales, total cost €25.

I hitch because it's cheap, I hitch because it's a method of travelling that has many ethical benefits (both ecological and community). I hitch because it's exciting, because it brings me into contact with people that I would never otherwise meet. I hitch because it's an adventure.

Despite the intimidation of standing at a road edge while cars reject you over and over again, the worry of feeling stranded, the difficulty of relying on a belief that you will receive help, I continue to hitch-hike because I believe in it. I believe in lift sharing. I believe in community. I believe in trust between strangers.

The world feels very tired and scared at the moment. The immensity of climate change and the complexity of what to do about it. Politics is intractable, peaceable solutions very far away. Proven liars can continue on in public office. The way that every proclamation, every public decision, every piece of statistical information is subject to distortion and denial, until we have lost our faith in the traditional tellers, we have lost our ability to perceive truth. Smartphones have sucked us in, searching for satisfaction that is always another click away.

I feel like people want to avoid the discomfort, numb themselves, sink away from all the awfulness. But ignoring something you dislike doesn't always make it go away and leaving a void where your voice of opposition could be only allows those in control to maintain power for longer.

In a world that seems to be crumbling and full of hatred, reaching out against hopelessness is all we can continue to do.

VISITING TOM IN ALBANIA

I had left Serbia at the start of June, when the cherries were just ripening on the trees and I could walk on shaded forest trails. It was summer 2019 and I felt no sense of urgency to get back to the walk – I had all the time in the world. After my successful hospital appointment (no cancer), and other boring life admin like opening post and paying my taxes, I went for an exciting week of working at Glastonbury Festival, and a few visits to friends. Six weeks later I left the UK again, hoping that the next time I'd return there wouldn't be until the very end of this walk. I hitch-hiked back from Wales to the Balkans and took a sequence of buses down through Croatia to Albania. It was late July and we thrummed past bare, dry, rocky hillsides, wiry bushes and the unceasing rattle of cicadas.

This wasn't where I wanted to be; I wanted to be in the green, wet mountains, where there weren't any restaurants and the people were welcoming, where the deer barked at night and the tortoises crackled sticks in the undergrowth. I wanted to be away from salty wind and hot tarmac, in the place where deep dew fell and the streams ran clear, where tractors rumbled and women waved from their perch side-saddle beside the drivers.

Instead of returning to my own route, I was taking buses to Albania, the city of Shkodër, to find the man I'd been chasing down the Croatian coast.

His name was Tom, he was 30 years old, and he was walking around the world.

He and his dog Savannah had been walking together for almost four years, covering 16,000 miles to date. They were heading east from Europe all the way to Mongolia, and then skipping down to cross Australia, possibly New Zealand and Japan, then finally the width of the USA, back to where Tom started in New Jersey in 2015, having covered an expected 25,000 miles.

This was my third and final detour to meet other people on their journeys; it had felt as if Jan was a look to my past, to see how I used to be, how far I'd come. Nils and Marie had shown me how to operate better in the present, how to use more efficient mapping and say yes to more interaction.

Tom was a target moving away from me at 24 miles a day. I thought I could catch him in Croatia, then it had seemed he'd made it to Montenegro, then, as my hitching times grew longer and I gave up in favour of buses, we agreed to meet in Shkodër, Albania.

The final bus was a minibus, not so crowded. I was the only passenger waiting to get on at 6.45am. As we crossed the border into Albania, I saw my first herd of sheep scurrying to flatten their shape against a wooden fence as the bus passed, a small boy with stick in hand chivvying them onwards. The bus flowed out into the opposite lane to pass three cows pacing slowly behind a horse and cart. *Phew*, I thought, *I'm back to the places where my coffees will be priced in pence not pounds.* The smell of lavender wafted through the open windows and we passed a lorry in a crushed stone car park, a man squatting at the front of it, cooking on a gas stove with a stained piece of cardboard to protect the flame against the wind. It was a relief to be back in places that have character, that are unhomogenised, unsanitised, worn and human and full of life.

Tom was sitting in the street outside the apartment I booked; a tall lean man, browned with the scruff of the road, pushing a wheeled cart and accompanied by a yellow dog, who ran past me to smell inside the yard. Savannah was adopted from a shelter in Texas to ward against night-time marauders, and she'd walked beside him ever since. Her paws were so strong, her nails so hardened, that she left pinprick bruises on my thighs every time she jumped up to sniff hello.

My first impression was of a calm, pacing man, slowly walking his walk and totally immersed in it. He felt a little separate from his surroundings, a little reclusive perhaps, certainly not leaping to shake hands and make conversation as Nils and Marie were.

I felt like I was meeting a star. This man was the medalled Olympian to my lower league semi-professional status. I was there to see how we were the same. I was there to see how we were different.

We walked together for half a day. I skipped ahead in the afternoon, not wanting to hold him back. Tom covered a minimum of 20 miles a day, more than I was comfortably capable of, especially when fresh from a month off and overloaded with a too heavy rucksack.

The heat was a shock, the sun beating down from an unforgiving blue sky as we walked out of Shkodër and along the road between the plain and mountain's edge; pacing and sweating on never-ending tarmac is my least favourite type of walking. Tom stuck to roads because of the cart, which turned out to be an extremely expensive baby buggy for 'Manhattan moms' to take jogging.

I told him about what I was doing – coming away from my own challenge to meet other walkers in the middle of theirs, trying to contrast our experiences to learn about my own, to see myself more clearly.

He asked what I was trying to do better and I admitted that I was always competing, even with myself, and that I rarely felt good enough. I knew that I was making life difficult for myself, but couldn't see how to be different. Tom started talking; he's a philosophy and psychology graduate and it showed in his calm wisdom. He spoke about 'being there', as in finishing a journey, and never being there, and that the most important thing we could do was accept we were in a constant state of uncertainty, because if we didn't then it was possible for nothing to ever be enough.

'The important thing is not to try and control the outcome, only your stages of preparation, that's where you should be satisfied that you have done your best. I don't worry about anything anymore. I worked out all my personal problems. During the first year and a half of walking, I thought every thought I possibly could, I chewed over every memory, turned over every stone. By the time I reached Chile I was just walking through the desert with an empty mind.'

I was in awe of this; his lack of mental fretting was my holy grail. He'd gone through to the other side of his brain and it had taken a year and a half of walking, from Philadelphia down to the tip of his continent; longer than I'd ever managed without a break. This was what I wanted to achieve, to calm my chattering brain and stop thinking so much.

The scale of what this man was attempting was staggering. My entire challenge was something he was seeing as 'the easy bit'. The immersion of committing many years to one project amazed me, knowing that this is all you will do, month upon month, time stretching into the future filled with the same repetitive movements.

There was a zen-like calmness to him, a detachment from the small things. He was a cool, deep pool of water, undulating with his own ripples, undisturbed by the agitations of plans going awry, shaking off irritation as his dog Savannah shook away the dust of her resting place before readying herself to walk beside his cart yet again.

I only walked with him for one day, wary of slowing him down, of my blisters that had come with new shoes, not wanting to waste energy on hot painful tarmac that didn't contribute to my own mileage.

It meant that I only had a couple of hours of evening to ask him my questions, the ones I'd asked all the walkers, shaped by the problems I struggled with when trying to walk thousands of miles – loneliness, self-pressure, difficulty staying focused.

We were camped on a flat, cleared piece of land, blatantly visible to the few houses nearby, but Tom didn't mind. 'It's Europe, there'll be no problems.' I acquiesced, knowing I would never camp so openly by myself. We talked our way through sunset and into darkness, as the moon rose behind the mountains and dog barks echoed from their territory edges.

I asked him if he ever doubted his purpose, if his reasons why ever wavered. Never. This had been his dream since the age of 17, he'd only gone to university because his parents insisted. 'When we used to go on holiday in the car, I would look out of the window at the fields, imagine myself walking through them. Out there. I've always wanted to be "out there".'

The sense of human going towards wilderness, the urge to explore, to experience the unknown; for some, it's an impulse that bubbles from deep within. I know what it means, the sense of getting out there, when the 'there' is an indeterminate location, merely an intangible sense of 'other'.

We touched on the relationships we'd given up in order to pursue our challenges. We talked about how we both imagined the houses we'd have one day, shared fantasies of antique mirrors and homemade furniture, when the transience of travel was over, as it would come for both of us, either when there were no more fantastical targets to achieve, or our bodies would no longer let us try them. I said that, since I started walking in Ukraine, I didn't necessarily want to be travelling anymore. It had been harder to leave my Llanidloes home than ever before, and as much as I loved living wild, part of me was ready to stop challenging myself so masochistically. Savannah snuffed at me and I startled – I'd forgotten she was there.

I wanted to give him a huge squeeze of a hug goodbye next morning but he only committed with one arm, half his body turned away from me, staying detached, already moving on. Savannah walked once around me and then turned to follow him.

The only thing I felt was the sense of time stretching ahead. Before my June break, the knowledge that I'd have to leave the walk and return to the UK had been hanging over me. It was an imposed pause, the necessity to return to hospital and check my body contained no cancer. Now it was done with and I was ready to immerse myself in this journey. I had an entire year before I needed to return to hospital. An entire year where I would do nothing but walk. No more stop starts, complex transport or interesting diversions. Tom was the last journey maker whose route would come near mine.

I wanted to sink back into the rhythm of my own journey, to wake up every day and know that I would be walking. I wanted to live a solo purpose: to cross land.

SERBIA

I realised during my walk with Tom that I had a serious problem – the weight of my rucksack was insupportable. It was an embarrassment, struggling novice-like with an overweight pack in front of the great world walker. We took it in turns to lift it; 25 kilos he said, more like 22, I reckoned, months of lifting flour sacks back in Llanidloes giving me the sense of weight.

I had new walking sandals that had given me blisters. They'd arrived too close to my UK leaving date to test them out and I'd brought my trusty walking boots as backup, but quickly realised that 2kg of boot leather swinging from my pack was impossible to walk with.

After a sequence of buses back from Albania to Novi Pazar, I retired to a hotel room, surveyed the white puffy patches on the soles of my feet and considered my options. Dare I send the boots home? I wasn't sure if these sandals were a safe bet but struggling on under the unwieldy swinging weight of the spare boots was a terrible alternative. The sandals were comfortable, apart from the blisters, and I decided to take the risk.

I did a brutal cut down of my belongings and once I'd packed the boots, a few books and other small things like face cream and the emergency handwarmer, the package to send home weighed an embarrassing 4.5kg. With only 16kg on my shoulders it was incredible how light my pack felt. I realised I'd been slowly increasing my possessions, small thing by small thing, until I had hobbled myself, unnoticed.

But alas, my lightweight plans were brought sharply down to earth by a very unfriendly post office in Novi Pazar. They bluntly refused to take the package, at first saying it was impossible to send it to the

UK, then that it would have to go to Belgrade to be inspected and would be too expensive. My Serbian wasn't up to this conversation and I was receiving the information secondhand through a woman who simply shrugged when I asked why. A long queue of people watched with interest as five different staff members barked at me irritably and I withdrew, sweating and defeated.

Dispirited, I told my problem to Martina the hotel receptionist, who said I could send the package to Montenegro on the bus. It was an established system that I'd seen happening on other buses back from Albania to Serbia; pay the driver a small amount and he'd pass any item on to the recipient at a particular stop. I could walk lightweight on the scenic route over the mountains into Montenegro, text Martina when I got to town and she'd go to the bus station and send me the package. Given that new boots would be £180, the effort to send mine home from a different country's post office felt worthwhile.

It felt like a very tenuous arrangement but the best of a bad set of options, so I left the package with Martina in Novi Pasar and headed out to walk the final 70 miles of Serbia.

It was hot now, late July, and close to 35° in the sun. I had to be very mindful of my body; by 11am, after a couple of hours of solid sun, I was bothered, cells buzzing, feeling as if I was on the verge of heat exhaustion.

The paths were beautiful, small winding tracks through wildflower meadows. Serbia has the most incredible profusion of wildflowers that I've ever seen, probably as a result of continuing traditional shepherding practices, moving sheep daily and never fencing them in to overgraze fields. The plant biodiversity meant hundreds of butterflies too. There are over a hundred species of butterfly in the Serbian Stara Planina and every day I would see at least ten species in large numbers. Serbia is a richly fertile land.

My UK break meant I missed the cherry season, leaving just as the first precious harvest came into the market. I returned to shrivelled stalks on the final fruits, markets full of dusty piles of watermelons instead. The raspberries were barely in bud when I left and now people quietly rustled, harvesting in the leafy rows. I'd missed so much.

Equipped in my new summer walking outfit, merino wool tank top and swishy harem pants, I felt great. For half a day. In the afternoon fresh blisters bloomed on each heel this time, as well as the balls of my big toes.

It wasn't just the blisters; my feet were used to being encased in a padded leather shell and without ankle support I needed greater muscle strength to balance. Every part of my feet and ankles ached, my knees hurt as they took the strain of the new ways my body was wobbling, and my calves were painfully solid.

Muzafera ameliorated my strains. I passed through her village early in the morning, already hot and tired. It was at the head of a steep valley where I would climb up 500m from the main road into a few days' walking on top of a set of hills, and the heat made the gradient tough going. Her house was at the end of the tarmac, where a track led into the deep forest, and she called me in, alerted by her barking dog going crazy at the end of its chain. Muzafera was happy here, in her summer house with her two children, growing her vegetables. 'We have a guest,' she called to them, as she went into the house to fetch me dates and chocolate, water and coffee. The heat melts my brain, makes it difficult for me to make conversation, but we managed, as I sighed and cooled down slowly, pressing the refrigerated dates to my cheeks before eating them.

She tutted as I awkwardly hobbled to my bag and started to pluck leaves from a pot of succulents, telling me I should rub them on my feet. I did as I was told, stripping the skin to apply the juice to my soles. The only name she had for it translated as 'keeper of the house', although I later discovered it was a Balkan houseleek, a variety of sempervivum. Folklore in the Croatian area of Krajina, which was inhabited by Serbs from the 16th century until their expulsion in the 1990s, says that every house has three guardians – the snake, the houseleek and the gun.

Muzafera was one of a few hosts who called me over that week, curious about this strange passerby.

A man pulling a huge tree trunk behind a tractor stopped and beckoned me over, invited me for coffee. His wife had been dead five years, from breast cancer, and I sensed his eagerness to break from solitude. We sat on a rough wooden bench on his porch, looking down over rows of plum trees, dust blowing from the bare earth around the barns, all bright and yellow. 'Plums will be ready in two weeks,' he said, pouring me a shot of excellent *rakia*, aged to mellow smoothness. He was flirty, this pensioner, and liked it when I smiled back. Serbs are easy to be playful with; make a Serb laugh and you're in the gang.

'Bad place,' he said, when I told him I'd walked from Muslim majority town Novi Pazar, where bearded men and headscarfed women filled the streets, and I cocked an eyebrow, asked if he was a Serb. He was, yes. So was everyone in this hilltop village, a rarity in this Serbian Sandžak province of Tutin that was 90% Muslim. There was just one house where a Muslim family lived, he pointed to it, and in that casual identification I chilled to think of the vulnerability during conflict, how neighbours could be brought to turn on each other. The lines were already drawn, and just 80 miles to the west in Bosnia and 20 miles to the east in Kosovo it had meant historical violence and discrimination.

A Muslim family fed me *burek* and a teacup of fresh whey, sharp and lemony. I found them lolled on the grass in the shade of their fruit trees, watching with interest as I approached to ask for water. The eldest son, early 50s, was home from Germany for his annual visit and there was a sense of peaceful rest. Pet rabbits lolloped freely and there was a bullock tethered nearby. The youngest son pointed to my *burek* and looked at me with piercing blue eyes before his mother shushed him away. They asked me questions about my journey but I didn't have the language to ask my own in return, about how it is it to be a Muslim in Serbia. We took a ceremonial photograph and all shook hands.

After five days of walking, I was coming to the end of my hilltop route, with 3 miles to the border with Montenegro and I could see the mountains ahead. Here in Serbia I was walking at height; over 1,000m the land was gentle and forested and ahead lay steeper peaks, jagged and craggy. I descended to the main road on a long, slow, stony track, stepping carefully, and slept above the road, safely hidden on the stones of a building site, long abandoned and grassed over.

As I rubbed Muzafera's gifted leaves on my blisters twice a day, they calmed down and were no longer tender, what a relief. A new challenge faced me now, though, down on the main road. Once I crossed into Montenegro I had no route options, it was road walking or craggy cliffs.

The main road away from the border point was hot, narrow, fast and unrelenting, following a deep valley, running alongside a river some 100m below. It wound and wiggled to follow the curves of the water, the gorge so steep there were many tunnels through the mountainside, dark and intimidating, traffic roaring close to me. There was no escape from any of it. I couldn't climb into the hills and spend a pleasant three days getting to Rožaje. Instead, I had to take a day and a half of road walking and it was horrible. Not just in the ordinary, unpleasant way but because my feet started to hurt again. Accustomed to a padded insole, they weren't used to meeting the force of a hard, nubbly piece of plastic thudding down on unforgiving tarmac and were being mashed until they felt like tenderised steak. I felt like a squashed tomato with hamburger feet, almost sobbing with relief as I collapsed into the soft cushions of the first café at town edge. Inspecting the glowing pink soles of my feet, I was horrified to see new blisters showing white under peeling patches of skin.

The breaking in of these sandals was very hard work, but I could feel the muscles of my feet and ankles getting stronger, and the relief from the foot-sweltering summer heat of high ankle leather boots was worth it.

The first town in Montenegro was a scruffier place than Serbia, reminding me more of the wild feeling of Ukraine, the degraded quality to the pavements and buildings, not as tourist orientated as the southern coastal region.

I settled into a cheap hotel in Rožaje and messaged Martina, the hotel receptionist in Novi Pazar, to begin the package transfer. Days later, still packageless, after many hours spent waiting in the bus station, missed bus connections, drivers proclaiming ignorance, disappearing buses, confused phone calls, tears, wasted time and money waiting in a hotel, I gave up and travelled back to Novi Pazar by coach myself to collect the package and bring it back to a post office in Montenegro. There, they told me the cumbersome parcel would be €60 to send to the UK and, because the post office administration hadn't quite separated from its Yugoslavian history, they'd still have to send it for inspection in Belgrade.

I felt crushed. This could have been avoided if I'd ordered the sandals sooner and been able to test them back in the UK. Defeated,

I left the boots in the town square for some lucky passerby, and decided to trust that my feet would adjust to the sandals.

It was a very isolating feeling, being the only person who could fix this, being the only person it mattered to. I thought longingly of a personal assistant who I could simply hand problems over to and concentrate on walking. These logistic problems crumpled me. None of my procrastination would work, I was slapped against the brick wall of the problem and it wouldn't go away until I made the right decision.

Kale foraging in agricultural central Ukraine

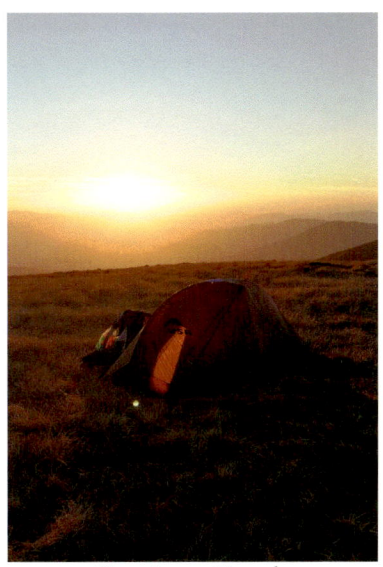

Camping at Hoverla, Ukrainian Carpathians

Wild camping on a road in Romanian Carpathians, the only vehicles were snowmobiles

Romania, Apuseni mountains Jan 2019

Bulgaria

Summertime kit,
base weight approx 12 kilos

Invited to watch the morning milking at a pensioners summer home, Montenegro

Wild camping in the summer, the standalone tent inner makes a great bug proof bivvy

Invited for coffee in Bosnia, a frequent occurrence September 2019

Waking up to a sea of cloud, looking down over Kobarid, Slovenia

Looking from Slovenia into Italy, Dolomites in the distance

Venice Jan 2020

3000 mile celebration, Italy January 2020

Sunflowers in Provence

Dusty feet in summertime Provence

Taking a break from the rain, Pyrenees
I love my wooden walking poles

Pyrenees, near Andorra

At 3000m in the Pyrenees

Port de Caldes after an intense snowstorm, Spanish Pyrenees

Going South around the heavy snow, wild camping Spanish Pyrenees

The thing I love about wild camping is making use of whatever comfy spot you find

Masked in public at all times throughout Spain

Wonderful wide open views in Navarra, Spain

The aftermath of Storm Philomena, it didn't rise above freezing temps for a week

Glorious arrival at Finisterre

7th pair of boots, worn to destruction

Finishline celebration

MONTENEGRO

It was hot, well over 30 degrees, and I felt fuzzy in the heat, a buzzing through every cell of my body, confusing and exhausting me as I tramped along. Fresh water helped, and this was where the sandals came into their own. Once I came to a spring, of which there were many on the roadside, I could sit for a while with my feet in the water, plunged straight in, and fully cool down, which also meant calming down. I could walk away with wet, refreshed feet, without having to don awkward socks and boots that had become clammy sweat buckets.

It was easy to leave the parcel stress behind in the town as I headed into the Montenegro heights for a week of mountain walking. It was blissfully beautiful up there, the scale making breath catch in my chest. Climbing up to where the breeze blew fresh and clear and my progress was measured in tiny steps on vast tracts of land.

I found people up there in their summer cabins, made of haphazard wooden planks or shiny metal panels, with high pointed roofs for the snow to slide off. People would usually come from May to September, bringing up their animals on roads called '*katun*'. As the sun was setting, I came to a high, open piece of land where I could see four or five houses decorously spaced from one another and three separate groups of sheep being walked home on the spreading green billows. Spiky, high fences surrounded each compound, protecting against wolf attack. There was nowhere I could camp without being seen, which made me nervous, so I walked through the grassland and back into the forest.

It was steep here and, tentative in the darkening twilight, I settled for an imperfect spot in the curve of a sidetrack. The long grasses were bent aside by wild animals, but the ground wasn't trampled, as it would be with the repeated press of hooves. It bothered me, to think of wolves coming out of the forest to find a tent in their path, but not enough to get up and move. It was almost dark and I was at the end of my tolerance. I didn't truly believe that I'd be attacked, but I didn't get a chance to test that theory as voices called out to me and used the words 'bear' and 'wolf'. They came down to talk to me, told me that there were dangerous animals in the forest and they wouldn't go away when I politely thanked them for the warnings.

The messages of caution had increased as I walked into the higher mountains of Serbia and Montenegro. Most villagers would tell me to be careful. These people lived with the constant threat of wild predators to their livestock, their income, but their realistic fear felt mythical to me. Bears and wolves are the great phantom creatures of Europe, the signifiers of wilderness, the inhabitants of the edges of human dominion. I didn't want to avoid the deep forest as so many village women did, but tried to balance the warnings with the chances that I would actually encounter something and then, should I actually see a beast, that it would threaten me rather than flee.

That night, given the markings near my choice of camp, I decided to trust my new friends and asked them if I could sleep in the compound. The girl shuffled a bit, said there were lots of people there, but I could camp outside. They were young, in their early twenties, with the darkened necks and thickened hands of farm life, a ten-year-old girl watching silently, breathy with excitement. As we walked back towards the dwellings, someone called out from above the track, curious. I was invited to stay the night with her and accepted.

This was Jivka, 65, widowed eleven years, living up here alone for two months of every summer with her four cows and two pigs. Her wooden cabin was uninsulated, carpet trodden thin over an uneven earth floor and a book-sized solar panel in the small window which charged a radio battery, and powered the light and her mobile phone. She fussed with elderflower cordial and a bowl of plums, then opened a box of chocolates white with age. She was a clumsy person, a little too loud, and the younger ones laughed at her a little as she asked questions about their families, probably getting the gossip from a captive audience; her snatching at passing moths made them giggle in particular. My saviours left, shaking hands in the light of the single bulb that hung naked from the rafters, and I was alone with Jivka. It was easier then, we could be calm and quiet with each other. She laid blankets on the sofa and we touched each other's arms in affection.

The next morning we drank coffee and talked about her four children. Her son helped her transport the animals up here at the beginning of the season, coming back to cut the grass that she'd use to feed the cows all winter. She'd sold the sheep once her husband died, too much work to shepherd them alone as well as tend to the cheesemaking.

She tied a cloth over her head, put on a jacket and was off to milk the cows. I asked if I could come and was rewarded with the experience of watching her sit squat on an upturned saucepan in the small dark barn, tucked against the cow's flank, her hands squeezing out thin jets of milk, expertly aiming into the bucket below. The cows were calm and gentle; the final one got up from seated as her time came, hooves sliding in the muck on the bare rock floor. Another ambled to the door for a long stare outside, the sun a pale ghostly disc in the misty morning, and I gave her a good scratch around the horns as she extended her neck to lean into me.

Back in the cabin I ate hot milk, bread and cheese as Jivka bustled with the cheesemaking. Without refrigeration or running water, she strained the milk through muslin then added a spoonful of liquid from a mysterious bottle, before leaving the bucket to sit in the corner. Turning to the previous few days' production, she unwrapped pressed slabs of crumbly white cheese which had been weighted down to squeeze out the whey, pouring that into a bucket for the pigs and salting down the cheese into a storage tub.

Jivka took the bucket of whey, apples, stale bread and crushed corn out to the pigs and pointed the way towards the spring for me to collect water. We parted with a hug and a kiss.

They're the best things, these unexpected connections, two strangers looking at each other with kindness. When I can do this, despite the lack of shared language, spirits speaking without tongues, it lifts my heart.

I got invited in for coffee and food four times that day; treated to bowls of bilberries, homemade sausage, cherry liqueur, *rakia*, cornbread. In some ways, Montenegrins felt more reticent than Serbs, quieter, calmer, less flirtatious and fiery. The men tended faintly to the sinewy, solid, square-jawed type. These were small, subtle differences between two countries which had been closely aligned for centuries; Slavs in mountain territory.

Water wasn't a problem for the first week, even up in the mountain tops at 2,000m. The cabins were mostly below me, tucked down to shelter from the wind, but I tended to pass three or four springs a day; usually a plastic pipe jutting out from the ground with water trickling into a carved wooden trough.

My feet were acclimatising to the sandals, although I could feel them stretching under the new effort of supporting themselves, twisting and flexing in the unaccustomed freedom, which hurt, but brought less pain day by day.

On the final day of walking I dropped down from 1,900m to

800m, making it into Mojkovac with aching knees, having covered 70 miles in six days; not a fast pace but that's mountain life.

I got into trouble about a day after I left Mojkovac, laden with the burden of six days' food that I needed to cross the high mountains of the Durmitor National Park. I had joined the Via Dinarica, an established route, stretching the length of the Balkans, along the Dinaric Alps from Slovenia to Macedonia. There were markings on the ground for me to follow, red-and-white flashes painted onto rocks and trees. I could even download a GPX route onto my map and know exactly where I was in relation to a thin black line, blindly follow along with someone else's planned routes for the first time on this journey.

At first there were the usual tiny settlements, I'm not sure they can even qualify as villages. Collections of triangular shacks, roofed in shiny tin or wooden shingles, weathered grey. One for the humans, one for the cows, one for storage, one for the hay. A small, square toilet cubicle a short walk away. Usually two or three would be together, spaced shouting distance away from one another. I knew that somewhere in that area would be water, a trough carved from a thick tree trunk, water dribbling in from a spout. The trough would be overflowing onto the ground, moss clinging on the wet wood, hoof prints grinding the earth to mud, butterflies gathering to drink at the damp edges.

I was carrying two litres but in the full August heat this was only about half a day's supply so I would top up at almost every source I came to, gulping as much as I could before refilling my bottles.

Each settlement had a name on the map – Pribranci, Okrugljak, Pašino Polje. I came to such a place towards the end of the first day, with less than a litre of water left, but the buildings were derelict and only a dip in the earth showed what had once been a stream running next to the road. Fortuitously, as I sat at a handy bench to consider my options, three huge lorries came roaring down the road and stopped next to me, the first man getting out to check his tyre. I asked him about water.

'There's none here,' he said.

'All the way to Zabljak?'

'You're going to Zabljak? Owwwww,' he said in that familiar noise of appreciation people make here. '*Bravo, svaka chasse.*' He handed me the water he had, to decant into my bottles, then called to the lorry behind him, who gave me more. After handshakes, they roared away, leaving me with three litres.

With the beginning of sunset, I made my camp on a flat piece of ground and watched an old woman walk down off the mountain with her thirty sheep. She was hunched, leaning on a stick, slow and awkward, but it didn't matter, she was faster than the sheep and felt no need to hurry them. There was a long period of time where the sheep nibbled, the woman sat and I waited, as the shadows lengthened and the sky over the faraway peaks turned lilac; then slowly, one by one, eight cows lumbered downhill, the bells around their necks softly clanging, adding to the music of the sheep in perfect discordance.

The gaps between settlements became bigger, and some were just rotting cabins and long grass where animals would have grazed. As I climbed higher, the sun became relentless; without clouds, the sky was a blaze of blue, the grasses and stones of the road reflecting white at me. I wore a cap and shades, lathered on suncream but it was no good, merely slowing down the roasting process. Sweat basted me, rolling down my arms, into my eyes, saturating my clothes. There was no escape; with no more trees up here, I would squeeze into thin lines of shade against heaps of stone, sometimes with the stomach to eat something and sometimes too jumbled by the heat to do anything but sit, sip water and wait for mental clarity to return.

I'd seen no springs for a while now. I had about a litre and a quarter left and ahead of me, there was wild, undulating land, pitted with bowls and lumps. There were no houses anymore, no road, just waving knee-high grasses, wildflowers and butterflies. The varied lumps and hollows of tussock and root made it incredibly slow to walk through, the path meandered around contours, climbing and dipping, barely there. I would have to scan the grass ahead to pick out a faint line catching the sunlight.

The map showed water just off the path, a detour wriggling down from the high plateau into a bowl of forest surrounding a spring-fed lake, but I wouldn't reach it until the following day so I rationed myself down to a mouthful every so often to keep my tongue wet.

Up early, I made it to the lake at 10am the next day, trying to walk as much as I could before the afternoon heat returned. It was beautiful there, surrounded by pine forest, pure clear water and small fish curling around each other, grouped in the shallows, coming in to taste the clouds of dirt that unfurled as I moved ankle deep. I filled my bottles from a trickling lakeside spring, drank and drank again. There was a family camping there and I watched as they took turns with an airgun, aiming it over the lake to make the pellets skip like curled stones.

I couldn't relax there too long; there was a walk ahead and nothing to do but tackle it. After the long climb back up to the plateau, it was only 7 miles to the next mountain but over the same pathless grassland as yesterday, very slow going. I was only covering about a mile an hour. At 1pm, I rested by a cowshed, only enough shade to cover my head, my chest sticking out into the light. A man appeared, surprised to see me there. We chatted a little and I asked about the water. He said they got their water from the same lake I'd come from, 3 miles away. The cows had a muddy pool to drink from.

'Is there water over there?' I asked him, pointing to the houses over at the base of the mountain.

'*Nema*,' he said. No water. No water on this whole plateau. He was kind enough to give me a litre, which I gulped down. I'd have to strictly ration it again, until I could get over the next mountain.

I didn't get much further that day; my period had started which means I suffer with a distinct lack of energy for the first day or two. The previous day I'd passed out in a patch of shade, thinking I was just sitting down for a momentary rest and then finding myself scrunching down, eyes closing all by themselves, lapsing into unconsciousness. That day, I stopped at 5pm, meaning only to pause for a snack outside a hay barn, but settled into blank immobility, utterly lacking any impulse to walk further. The barn was full of rubbish, the nearby house looked empty; with no water available for the stock perhaps the owners only came up here to harvest the grass. It was 5pm and I'd only pissed once that day, despite drinking three and a half litres.

Early again the next day, starting at 7am, all too aware of my dwindling supply. I drank small sips, motivating myself with water rewards. *I'll take a mouthful when I reach that mound. I'll take a mouthful after another kilometre.* There were bilberries to wet my mouth in small bursts of sweetness. After six hours of walking I made it over the mountain shoulder to the beginning of the next valley. There was a road only a few kilometres ahead and some houses I felt sure would have water. As I sat for a while to rest, watching the occasional cloud shadow move over the hillsides, somehow never blessing me with shade, I heard movement and looked over to see a man walking towards me in a yellow T-shirt.

We shook hands, his fingers and shirt all stained purple with bilberry smears. I found it difficult to make conversation, all I could think about was drinking, and once he realised, he pulled me up off the ground, shouldered my bag and we set off towards his house. This wasn't where he lived, he told me, his brother and mother lived here; he was in Podgorica, the capital city, just come back for part of the summer. He called out across the valley to where his brother stood, raking hay. Once the brother joined us, it was clear who was the awkward countryman and who was the suave city boy. The country brother didn't speak much, avoided eye contact and returned quickly to the hay, while we continued to the house where a mother waited, shuffling, paralysed down one side, with bright eyes and long white plaited hair sweeping over her shoulder.

It was one of the more bizarre encounters I've had. At first I couldn't speak, my throat choked until I'd had a drink. But then we ended up talking about whether I was single. It's a pretty typical conversation, but this one seemed to go further, until I realised that the mother was sizing me up for her youngest, the son who ran the farm.

I'd encountered a lot of matchmaking since entering Serbia; everyone seemed to have a single friend they must tell me about. 'He's got four cows,' they'd say, 'it's a friend of my brother's.' Women would tell me about their single sons, 'working in the ski resort,' they'd say. 'He speaks good English.'

'Oh, you want an English daughter-in-law?' '*Hochesh snaika Ingleska?*' and we'd laugh until the offer went away. There was an immediacy to the decision making here. 'Meet this man, he's single.'

But was Balkan love immediate or indiscriminate?

'I want you. Be my woman,' said the single men I met, with a quickness that felt false to my reserved British self.

The previous week I had been called off the path by Salvatore, a lean craggy man, with thick hands, missing teeth and a furrowed forehead. He had a jumpy energy, all sinew and jaw, trying to offer me beer until I insisted on coffee. I went over to his triangular cabin, where pigs padded around outside like farm dogs; inside, through the worn door, were two single beds tucked into the angle of the roof, a wood-stove with a big pan of milk on it, bare concrete floor and at the back of the room a filthy mess of bottles and tins. We talked a little about his life here: he'd worked abroad in electrical engineering, but for about ten years had been home in Montenegro, even staying in the hut through the previous winter, which was incredible in that small, uninsulated space, where sunlight shone in between roof and walls.

'I love the nature and the mountains,' he said, showing me bundles of chamomile he was drying to make tea. He bluntly propositioned me, 'Stay here and be my woman. We can live together, milk the cows and make cheese.'

I considered it, knowing that if I touched his body it would be solid with muscle. I imagined how his rough hands would graze my curves, how I could hold him, calm, in the nestled softness of a warm bed. Milk the cows. Be someone's woman. A position, ready-made, for me to fit into. But I knew that was not my true shape, that I'd always be crushing part of myself in order to try and complete the jigsaw.

The mother in this house though, she wouldn't leave the subject alone. 'How much money have you got? Where does it come from?'

'She could buy a house in Zabljak,' she said to the city son. She commented on my body, even asked if I had my own teeth, as I sat there, faintly incredulous, drinking glass after glass of delicious cool water.

'She's not wearing any nail varnish, that's good. No makeup. I can't stand women who wear makeup.'

I imagined the women that her city son had brought home. It was normal for town women here to be heavily made up, with acrylic fingernails. I couldn't help laughing. It was so strange to be lined up for someone I had only exchanged a hello with. They were laying out lunch and it was time for me to leave. In a final surreal twist, as I stood outside saying goodbye, the farm son came striding up towards the house, wearing a T-shirt and no trousers. Something to do with itchy hay. Everyone burst out laughing as he reached the outside shower and stripped down to his pants. City brother showed me the path down to the road and I looked back to see mother telling off farm brother as he hosed himself down, probably berating him for missing his chance.

BOSNIA and HERZEGOVINA

After a couple of nights in Plužine, the town at the edge of a great lake, dammed for energy in the 70s, I walked for two days around the eastern edge of the water, to enter Bosnia by an official border point.

Walking through Bosnia held a lot of apprehension for me – the war history, the ongoing political struggle of a country split in two, one half seeking missing relatives in hidden mass graves and the other denying genocide through gritted teeth. With peace imposed by NATO soldiers and forced external leadership in the form of an EU-appointed High Commissioner, the impasse manifested through administrative struggles over car number plates or birth registrations, each side pushing papers back and forth over the negotiating table, always tensed for the other to break.

After walking from the border crossing to Tjentište and rejoining the Via Dinarica, I faced a full week high up in the Zelengora mountains without passing a single village.

'Be careful,' said Nils, the cross-Europe mountain walker, when we discussed my upcoming route. 'There's a long stretch with very little water.'

The border crossing was a narrow wooden bridge across what seemed like a perfectly ordinary river, but as I followed the road north-west the land rose up to form a huge canyon, one of the longest and deepest in Europe.

Although Tjentište was only a few miles across the water, the only way to walk there was via 30 unnecessary miles up to the next bridge at Foča. The road wound above the bright blue ribbon, below the sheer forested banks, studded with advertisements for rafting and camping. There were occasional ziplines strung across the canyon, bored workers watched cars pass, awaiting tourists looking for spontaneous excitement. After a couple of hours of tedious tarmac, I had the bright idea of taking a zipline across the gorge as a shortcut, and asked, to some amusement, for a one-way ticket for me and my rucksack. They sent the baggage first and I couldn't keep from squealing in fear as I watched all I possessed swaying on a metal rope 100m above the water.

I spent a blissful night in fields, feeling very pleased with my shortcut, then climbed up out of the canyon to Tjentište, which turned out to be a tiny village with no cashpoint and only a few small shops and restaurants, catering mainly to the tourist crowd who'd come to see the Battle of the Sutjeska WWII memorial. It was made up of two angular blocks of pale concrete arrowed against each other in an explosion of force, marking the resistance of the Yugoslav Partisans against the outnumbering might of the Nazi-led Axis powers of Germany, Italy, Croatia and Bulgaria. The Partisans' success led to the creation of Yugoslavia.

With the knowledge that when I set out up the first slope, I was committing myself to days of remote walking with limited water sources, I found myself procrastinating, heading into a restaurant for an unnecessary bowl of watery noodle broth, then a mere mile later, another pause for coffee.

When I'm not actually climbing mountains, I'm not all that fond of the idea – it just feels like a lot of unnecessary effort. There may be wonderful views and a euphoric experience, but it comes with hours of pain. Pain and sweat and nothing but the brute force of your meagre muscles to get you through.

Going alone to remote places contains the danger of injury somewhere far from human help. A chance twist of an ankle could turn into a confused descent of the wrong side of a hill, could turn to an isolated death, a crumpled body in the wilderness, alone and undiscovered.

As I drained my coffee cup, I told myself to cut the mental chatter; it was time to push aside fearful anticipation and get on with it.

So I pushed myself up from the table and shouldered my pack. The first climb was a big one; 864 metres of ascent in 2 miles, directly up from the road, through a forest thick with fallen trees, on small footholds worn into slippery bare earth. I was aiming to camp up at the top by the first water source, but couldn't make it, my legs feeling empty, hollow. *That's OK*, I thought, *I'm out of energy, it happens.* Although the path was on a steep slope I found an outcrop big enough to fit my tent, spending the night with a pair of curious wild goats in the vicinity, intrigued enough to creep forward, before snorting in fear and crashing away into the trees whenever I rustled my bedclothes. Late in the night I awoke to the sway of an owl landing on the crossbar of my tent but as I turned in surprise it opened its wings wide, and silently took flight, less than a metre from my face, leaving me peaceful in the wake of such deep night magic.

The next morning I set off fresh but my usual early burst of energy quickly drained away to heavy limbs and it became an effort to heave myself up the slope. A little demon of doubt started speaking. *This is too hard. Maybe I should go back down again.* The mountainous days to come felt incredibly intimidating and as I reached the lake, after searching for it through grasslands, and crouched at the spring, holding my bottle under the trickle of water, I found myself lost in stressful thoughts of hard times ahead. What was this? *Stop, Ursula, don't let the fear overwhelm you. You are walking through spectacular mountains, this may be the only time in your life you will be here. Why are you poisoning it, wishing it over?*

There was a hunting lodge at the lake edge, all doors shuttered and locked but with a verandah containing wooden tables and benches where I could rest. I ate some breakfast – oats, banana, jam, raisins and pumpkin seeds – and shortly afterwards realised that this low energy was illness. Diarrhea came on and I felt limp, drowsy and weakened. All I could do was doze on the bench, read my book, doze again. At 2pm, once the bad bowels hadn't stopped, I realised that I needed to stay at the lodge overnight without eating or drinking so that, if I was no better the next morning, I would be able to descend to safety on the nearby road. This was my final escape option before miles of waterless mountain walking and I had to be fully capable before I went any further.

I dozed groggily on and off all day, wondering what I should do, battling against self-judgement.

Turning downhill and giving up felt like a confirmation of weakness. All this way across Europe, I constantly felt like I had taken the easy choices: I didn't buy snowshoes and climb the snowy mountains in Romania, I chose to take the low-level route across the top of Bulgaria in the spring, as the snowy Stara Planina glistened to the south of me. Now, here in Bosnia, I was finally following the challenging route and it would be so easy to bow out, pretending it was for my own safety. There was no firm decision to make, I could only see if the sickness continued the following morning. If it did, then how could I go on?

With relief, I woke up feeling calm in mind and body. Quitting was immediately unthinkable again and I realised just how much of my mental uncertainty had stemmed from physical weakness, something I'd never connected so clearly before.

I ate a plain breakfast of oats in water – my first food in twenty-one hours and my first water in seventeen – then waited a final two hours at the cabin to see how it sat in my body, sipping three litres of water like a camel, needing to fully hydrate before I left the water source.

The sun shone, as it had almost constantly for the last month, and I set about the task, slowly and carefully. Every section took longer than expected, edging down sheer drops, feet twisting sideways on the lumpy grass. There were grassy meadows and cool woods, the path skirting around a huge forest basin, miles wide. The only other humans I met were a group of five bilberry pickers, sweating under huge packs, spiked berry-pickers strapped to the sides. 30 kilos in each pack, they told me. At €5 a kilo that's a good income for the few weeks of the harvest. We squatted together in the forest as they smoked, passing a bottle of *rakia* between purple hands and expressing the usual shock at my being alone. 'There are bears here,' they told me, showing me a photograph of them on a steep slope above one, busily employed in its own bilberry harvest far below.

Bear chat set me up for an unsettled sleep, once I'd negotiated the final climb of the day, a thin strip of trodden ground curving up a huge slope into a scramble through sheer rocks.

There was a light wind up on the ridge where I made camp, and I pulled my silk sleeping bag liner over my head to keep the chill off. It meant my hearing was blocked, a key sense at night, and my nerves turned the rustles of my tent to the noise of predators, leaving me alert and sleepless. I rolled over onto my back and, with only the tent mesh between me and the night sky, lay under a benevolence of stars, the ethereal dust of the milky way. Starlit grasshoppers climbed the tent mesh, swaying with the wind as if on grass stalks. The stars' magnitude made me a tiny thing whose worries meant nothing, and I watched the sky until the thought of bears was very far away, and I slept, comforted.

The next day was longer and harder. First I descended down to Orlovačko lake, two hours of gentle steps, where I was welcomed by a German couple who offered me breakfast from their campervan, permitting me a genteel forty-five minutes of recovery in a folding chair, sipping their black tea, nibbling bread and butter, and surreptitiously gulping two litres of spring water.

It was 26km to the next water source, which I hoped to reach by the end of the following day. First though, the 6km to the valley head took me four hours. After a climb through rocky forest, pulling myself up on tree roots, levering myself using my walking poles in a full body effort, I found myself in a wide flat valley, rocks high on either side and a swathe of thick yellow grasses ahead. It was the kind of place where I feel the roaring spirit of wild nature, bursting and unquenchable. There was an immensity here, that I sensed merely the faintest trace of.

I stopped for a late lunch, comfortably isolated in the half shade of a boulder. Targets disappeared in a place like this – it no longer mattered when I would reach Sarajevo, or home. The future did not exist, only me and my footsteps, me and this bilberry bush, me and the rough surface of the boulder against my back, the endless waving grasses, me and the butterfly on my hand, me and the eternal sunshine, the sweat on my skin, the itching of the bite on my foot, the smell of my body, the breeze brushing hair against my cheek, my certainty that in my rooted strength I could exist here in this wild place. It was mindfulness made manifest in the animalistic immediacy of immersion in wilderness.

The final climb of the day took me up to 1,900m altitude in a rough landscape of boulders and stunted pine forest, where the trees grew to head height, bushing out horizontally, sending out a fresh pine smell in the hot air. It was an undulating landscape, full of small hollows and rises where snow collected and water drained into the ground.

With an hour until darkness, my tent was set up, bed inflated, and I was tidying the final pieces of kit when I heard a clicking noise. There's a reason I don't listen to music while I'm walking: my hearing is usually my primary sense of change in my surroundings. As I straightened up and looked around, there on a nearby rise was a bear. Smooth and sleek, with a sheen of gloss on her brown coat, the animal stood on her hind legs surveying the view away to the west, maybe 25 metres away from me. In the immediate shock, I responded with what I had read on the internet about meeting bears. 'Calmly let the bear know that you are there.'

I called out gently and waved. 'Hey, hey, bear, a human is here.' As her head turned towards me, she dropped to the ground and bustled out of view, followed seconds later by inquisitive twin cubs who mirrored her movements in seeing me and then turning to leave, a waveform of sequential motion.

A bear. A bear was here. *Well,* I said to myself, *this is really it now, this really is your test.* It was 7pm, I was alone in the mountains and I had seen a bear close to my sleeping spot.

I realised I was standing frozen outside the tent and began to talk myself through the paralysis.

Can you walk away from here to where there are no bears?

No, it's too far to manage in the remaining daylight and if you walk in the dark the risk of falling is very high.

Then you must make camp in these mountains, in bear territory. Can you stay where you are?

A bear knows where I am. Even if it looked scared and ran away, maybe I shouldn't stay where it could easily find me.

Then go somewhere else.

Action decided, I packed up quickly and began to make my way further down the mountain, telling myself I was calm and under control but aware that I was jerky with adrenaline, eyes wide.

'Aren't you scared?' The question would come repeatedly, both online and in person, and I never really knew how to answer. I've spent many nights in fear, listening hard to what might be rustling outside my tent. I am still jolted from sleep by the noises of the night, my heart a flurry of adrenaline-fuelled beats.

I don't feel like I am brave or capable, more that I am drawn to excitement and don't like being told no. I was squashed, restricted and controlled when I was young, beyond all sense of fairness or reasonable explanation, only told that I was wrong, or that I shouldn't, and that meant that I was bad. Starting serious travelling in my twenties, I set out with a burning desire to do exciting things, to hitch-hike across Spain or to kayak the Danube, and I mostly learnt how to recognise and navigate danger as I went. When all you ever are is wrong, it leaves you with no accurate sense of your own abilities. I had to show myself who I am, define myself through action, take myself to my edges in order to see them. And the more I did, the more I realised what I was capable of.

Through my travelling and wild camping I have realised that any given animal which has happened to unknowingly venture near my bed is not necessarily interested in attacking me; that most people who warn me of dangers have never actually had those experiences, and are talking about the fearful myths rather than the realities.

Seeing a wolf in the woods is not the same as getting eaten, risk is not the same as certainty, danger is not the same as death, but when we're feeling vulnerable we don't recognise the space between those opposing concepts. However, that space is exactly where our ability to affect the situation lies. We can't choose not to feel fear but we can learn how to manage fear until it reduces; become comfortable in the gap between threat and assault.

Balancing myself in that metaphorical gap, trying to keep away from nervous overwhelm, I picked my way down a steep tumble of rough limestone towards an open valley. The nearest road was 5 miles away, it would take me hours to walk there and I'd still be in the middle of the forest.

I twisted my body around the sharp corners of the path, catching on low pine bushes, balancing myself to lower between boulders. 'I am not bear food.' I'd been using that flippant phrase whenever people warned me about going alone into the wilderness and now I had to start believing it. *What did that bear do when it saw you? It turned and left. A bear will only attack if it is surprised or scared.* I repeated these things a few times, trying to calm myself.

The sun had set and I had to stop somewhere and sleep. I'd walked for forty-five minutes and descended 60m down the mountain. It would have to do. I paced around for a while, unable to settle, scanning the shadowed rocks for predatory shapes, before firmly telling myself there was no option, I had to put the tent up. After an hour of wakefulness, listening to the plastic rustles of my tent in the wind, I finally slept and I didn't dream of bears. In the morning, my foodbag was untouched on the nearby boulder, the valley was full of damp mist for the first hour of sunlight and I made my way down off the mountain, into the forest and towards Kalinovik.

As my first experience of Republika Srpska, the Serbian controlled part of Bosnia and Herzegovina, whose breakaway creation in 1992 had triggered the most recent Balkan War, Kalinovik confirmed all the fear and anticipation I had about the continued presence of conflict in modern Bosnia.

At a glance it was a poor and unfriendly place, with broken-down buildings, and more suspicious sideways glances and stray dogs than usual. There was an army barracks here before the war; there had been 2,826 Serbs and 1,716 Bosniaks (Bosnian Muslims) living in the municipality. Now there were 1,947 Serbs and 57 Bosniaks, and the barracks were derelict.

I walked through the barracks on the way into town, large buildings crumbling to bare concrete boxes with doors and windows long gone, open for cows to walk in and shelter from the sun. There were names and dates scratched into the sentry boxes. 'JM 14 XII 93.' The Bosniaks were already gone by then, forced from their homes into death, detainment and deportation. War crimes were committed in this community, incidences of rape and torture by Serbs on Bosniaks successfully prosecuted in the Hague seventeen years later. Ratko Mladić, the Republika Srpska army leader, was born in this area, and defended and protected here long after genocide charges were made and international authorities sought him.

I found a shabby bar that kept rooms where I could sleep for €5 a night. There were no curtains or toilet seats, and the shower was a mess of cracked tiles and dripping pipes, but the owners were friendly and every time I went downstairs I was plied with coffee and *rakia*. People kept discussing me, the woman who had burst in, sweaty and tired under a huge rucksack, claiming to have walked here from Kyiv. All seemed cheerful on the surface, but when conversation moved on from me and I listened a while, I could pick out sparse words like 'Muslims' or 'bombs' or 'corruption'; ugly opinions bubbling to the surface. It was twenty-seven years since the outbreak of the Bosnian war, which meant that every man over 45 I encountered had either fought or fled. They were there in the bar, older Bosnian Serbs, day drinking and chewing over their bitterness, like Brexiteers in a Wetherspoons.

I felt the depressive energy of the place and turned away to talk to barman Darko, a young student back for the summer holidays. 'All the young people have gone to Foča or Sarajevo, only the old ones left here.'

I made a mistake with him and asked how he felt about the ethnic cleansing committed here. The sense of this town living with the memories of violence carried out in its name, actually in the lived experience of the men sitting in the bar with us, was overwhelming to me, and my misjudged question reflected that.

It made him angry and he responded through clenched teeth, saying that all sides did bad things. 'Serbia lost the media war.' He meant that my media story was wrong because it only said that Serbia were monsters, his was right because it said that all three sides, Serbians, Croatians and Bosniaks, were culpable. The men of this bar were not embittered genocide supporters, they were his heroic war fighters.

But the shared culpability argument misses the point that Serbs responded to a perceived threat; the severance of links with Serbia/Yugoslavia when Croatia, with German support, voted to leave the Yugoslavian union. Croats and Bosniaks responded to an actual threat; violence initiated by Serbs.

Darko dissolved responsibility for the 1992-1995 genocide committed by Bosnian Serbs by talking about Jasenovac, the Croatian Ustaše WWII concentration camp run in collaboration with the Nazis, where up to 100,000 people were killed, about half Serbs, then Roma and Jews; then the fact that Kosovo was inhabited by Serbs until the Ottoman Conquests began in the 14th century and forced a series of northern migrations in the 17th and 18th centuries to the safety of the Hapsburg Empire. The 13th century Serbian Orthodox Church was founded on the land now called Kosovo and when he showed me YouTube videos of Kosovo Albanians on church roofs pulling down crosses, it was no use saying that Kosovo has been majority Albanian for over a century or discussing years of oppressive policy against Kosovo Albanians under Serbian governance.

He was right about the media war.

'Serbs have always taken land that doesn't belong to them,' says a Frenchman when we're discussing my decision to walk through Bosnia.

'Tell them Serbs are good people,' says a Kosovo Serb when she learns I'm British, herself fled from her Kosovan homeland and resettled in Southern Serbia.

The Balkan Wars were layered upon centuries of grievance and attributing fault based on actions taken during the last conflict was a massive oversimplification.

I was getting it wrong, talking to 25-year-old Darko about what happened before he was born. I should have been asking him about Bosnia now, about his experience of government decisions and political tensions. Darko told me about his friends of all nationalities at university in Sarajevo, said that he didn't want to think of those days, the photographs he'd seen.

It was me, the gauche tourist, who was 12 years old in 1992 and knew nothing of the Balkans, who received the body blow of all this sadness at once, the shock of the violence that Bosnians have been holding for a generation, in order to pass through the country with greater understanding and without ignorant mistakes.

They were friendly to me, these Bosnian Serbs, just as much as they kept the embers of bitter grievance glowing deep within themselves. Two of the bar customers, Lyuba and Zbigniew, were keen to invite me over for a meal, with much love and tenderness. Zbigniew was a transplant from Poland, having arrived here thirty years ago as a military transfer; he was an emotional man who felt the loneliness of always being a stranger. They fed me *pita*; oven-baked meat and potato wrapped in thin pastry, with a tall glass of yoghurt to drink.

Lyuba packed me an ice cream tub full of juicy pieces of *pita* that I knew I'd have to eat swiftly before it spoiled. They'd also given me a bag the night I met them, with apples, tomatoes, nectarines and chocolate. The bulk of these fresh foods meant that I couldn't stock up with any of my usual dried provisions.

I'd seen villages marked on my route but didn't know whether they'd have shops and restaurants, or were simply small clusters of farmhouses. In the end, I didn't see a shop for six days.

As I made the first climb up the bare mountainside out of Kalinovik, the love I'd felt from Lyuba and Zbigniew chilled when I saw the symbol of the four Cyrillic Cs on the Serbian cross daubed onto a boulder, a reminder of Bosnian Serb violence. '*Samo Sloga Srbina Spasava*' (Only Unity Saves the Serbs), a centuries old rallying cry against Ottoman colonisation, turned nationalist slogan in the 80s and scrawled onto Bosniak houses in towns captured by Serb forces.

There was no escaping war. Indeed, it had been fought all over this mountain, 'a frontier line' said a man cleaning his chainsaw by the trackside, crooking a finger to denote gunshots as he told me he'd fought here.

As I came down off the mountain, I'd looked for a flat spot to camp but it was very steep either side of the stone track and then I'd spotted the red skull and crossbones signs: 'Danger. Landmines'. At that time, 2019, Bosnia still had $1,000^2$ km of uncleared mines, decades after enemies dug bundles of death into the ground. Steep, forested mountainside was the most difficult and last to be cleared. I would be safe, as long as I stuck to clear paths and slept on cultivated land where tractors had already pressed and grazing cows lain down to chew cud.

Over the following days I slowly followed the trail as it wound through the area of the Treskavica mountain. I'd come over its shoulder on the first day, climbing the peak of Lukavac and then following the valley as the land turned from Republika Srpska to Bosnian Federation territory. The mountain stayed within view for the entire week, as I passed from east to west along its southern side, making steep climbs to ridgeway walks, through deep forest where large animals growled and cracked sticks as they fled, unseen, from the sound of my passing. The path had me negotiating landslides, sheer slopes, pressed gravel roads and bilberry patches.

As I walked the ridgeway, the mountain falling sharply away on my left side, 1,000m down into the depths of Rakitnica canyon, I could see the village I was heading for, away over the other side of the deep crevice. Lukomir, the highest village in Bosnia, so remote that the fighting hadn't touched it, had become a tourist destination, showing off untouched old style Bosnian houses. There was a restaurant there, apparently, and I'd reach it the next day.

A final meal of potato, rice and pâté, churned into a bowlful of salmon-coloured mush. Calories, that's all it was, a bowlful of calories. I spooned it in beside a fountain at the village of Bobovica, a collection of ramshackle houses and barns with tin walls hammered out from flattened metal barrels, as a dog came to sit beside me, giving some serious side-eye as forty small squat sheep filtered past, followed by a man in a ragged woollen hat, trousers tucked into home-knit socks and rubber clogs. Shepherds, the toughest of the lot, repeating daily my once-in-a-lifetime experience. After three squares of chocolate I walked further into the canyon below, eventually finding a place to sleep in a long abandoned barn.

Chewing on the handfuls of peanuts left in my food bag. I followed 8 miles of a steep and winding path up out of the canyon to Lukomir, where women in white hair-coverings were setting out trays of onions to dry in the sun, waving me over to inspect the knitting they'd draped over the fence to attract tourists. There were traditional thick woollen socks and jumpers in plain cream, browns and greys, alongside brighter, acrylic, long socks with intricate repeated designs of checks or pixelated curlicues.

The restaurant was calm, only a solitary couple eating at the outside wooden shelter, open to the sunshine and the gentle breeze. Hunger hollowed me and I ordered soup and *uštipici,* not really knowing what size of dish would come.

In the end, I filled myself with thick chicken soup and bread, eyeing the plate of *uštipici* nervously as it came towards me. Bloated pillows of herby fried dough, served with cream and cheese. I ate almost half, wiping up the thick cream, then packed away the remaining five pieces with the homemade cheese. It was all I had to eat the next day, while walking 25 miles to Sarajevo.

I thought I might find a shop or bar but all the villages named on the map turned out to be empty road and I faced down hours of painful tarmac in the unrelenting heat.

Finally reaching a cheap hotel on the side of the busy main road, I went to bed hungry, unable to sleep and staring at food recipes online as my stomach growled, but the next morning I was only 500 metres from a popular bakery and could fill my stomach with *pita* and yoghurt, priming myself to walk the final miles into the centre of Sarajevo and food abundance.

It was impossible to visit Sarajevo and ignore the bullet holes; they spattered older buildings like thrown paint. This city was besieged for almost four years from the hills that can be seen through every gap between buildings and it was a stark shock to realise the extent to which every single building took fire. As I waited to cross the road by the post office, I thought of the grainy camera footage of people trying to navigate the city while under constant threat of snipers, peering around corners as they plucked up the courage to cross the open spaces, older women shuffle-trotting as quickly as their hips would let them. There are blast marks of mortars on the pavements, becoming slowly blurred by the repeated pass of feet.

I stayed for a rest day and slept deeply, exhausted by the mountains. To leave the city I climbed up stone steps that slunk between the closely packed houses, cats prowling over layers of red roof tiles. Passing the cemeteries which forest the north eastern hillside with the bare trunks of thousands of white gravestones, I ascended beyond the suburbs and into the forest where a big, white hunting lodge nestled at the valley head.

I couldn't stay there; it was only open on weekends, said the old owner in a creaky voice, as he made me a mug of sweet fruit tea. He had a few friends come in and join him, pensioners all, with the camaraderie of old friends. One of them groaned in pain as he got up, holding his knee as it made an unexpected grating noise. I knocked on the table to show that I understood the leg was fake. He nodded, and mimed a machine gun to show me how he'd lost it.

I'd told a girl I met in Sarajevo how shocking it was to see the traces of the siege. 'When new buildings are put up, they get graffitied to say, "Where are the bullet holes?"' she replied, showing me something of the effect of a besieged experience. Bullet holes can be mended, missing legs cannot, and Sarajevo manifests as a visible scar of the war history that all Bosnian people hold within them.

Leaving the city I joined the Via Dinarica Green trail, which promised to be an easier, low level route than the White mountain trail I'd left behind. I'd enjoyed the high mountain territory but the White trail went west towards Mostar for only 126 miles before crossing the border into Croatia, whereas the Green route meandered through the centre of Bosnia, leaving in the far north-west at Bihać, 410 miles on.

My first target, before the end of Bosnia, was a rest week in Zenica, 140 miles away. I gave myself twelve days to get there, perfectly achievable, yet somehow I struggled the entire time. The walking was never smooth and unruffled. Storm clouds glowered, mud held me, tarmac ached and hills were an endless clamber.

The Via Dinarica trails were a major EU investment in Bosnian tourism and rural development; the White trail widely advertised, but the Green trail was a later addition, still in development. The Green trail was a mixture of back roads and forestry tracks, taking anything but a straight line, curving in repeated semicircles to follow hill ridges, high up at above 1,000m but formed as gentle rumps of land, forested and inhabited. I was using a GPS track uploaded by one of the researchers who had walked the path two years previously, meaning that it wasn't an easy path to walk and it wasn't a coherent one either, created as a way to cross large amounts of land between interesting touristic points, researched using satellite imagery, then walked once before being made public. I spent far too much energy losing the unmarked path in deep forest, fighting through nettles, bracken and brambles.

People were the bright points in my gloom, along with plunges into the deep forest, an endless source of joy and satisfaction. The sudden chatter of wind in beech leaves, the placid moss patches, the mushrooms unfurling like surprise party guests.

There were sunny days and there were looming clouds. Autumn is the time of cloud inversions in Bosnia, the country of constant slopes. There were misty mornings, where the valleys were full of swirling droplets, wet grass and spiderwebs coated with a thousand white beads. I climbed through it to the brittle brilliance of blue sky, eventually looking back to see a bowl of cloud soup below me, cupped in the hollows of the hilltops. The day after I left Sarajevo, I turned back to a sea of white covering the valleys, at a full three points of the compass. *That's Sarajevo under there*, I thought, *they're looking at the sky and thinking what a grey day it is*, and I continued on, sweating my way along a dirt track, squinting in the sunshine.

There came a few days of stormy forecasts, sunshine dimmed by afternoon thunder, and one afternoon I found myself on a long ridge wondering whether I should camp up before starting the steep descent to the road. A locked barn offered shelter under its overhanging top storey and I sat for a while, pondering whether I could accept an early finish, as I watched the faraway hills disappear behind a white gauze of rain. As I was slowly concluding that a storm was coming, a jeep stopped by the gate.

I said hello, embarrassed to be caught there, but the man didn't seem to care at all.

'*Sestra moya!*' (My sister!) he exclaimed, when he saw my plans to camp, and I knew I was safe with him.

We sat together under the barn roof as rain began to fall; there were a few faint growls of thunder and he called the sheep repeatedly, the same sound rising and falling. They moved, bunched together, slowly coming closer to us. He said he had a house in the village that he didn't sleep in, and I could stay there, while he went back to the town.

At first I declined, ever uncertain of solo men, not wanting to retrace my steps, thinking the tent would be fine. But as the rain came more heavily still, and the thunder crashed, I accepted. It started to hail huge chunks of ice as I was rolling up my kit, Sabit calling for his sheep, who were no longer listening, and we ran for the jeep. The track turned to a delta of rushing streams, the sheep clustered under bushes and hail assaulted the roof, banging like bullets as the vehicle swayed along through the torrent. Thunder boomed right above us and we waited in the house for an hour, marvelling at the endless rain. '*Opresno vreme,*' said Sabit, 'dangerous time.' He told me about his wife and children, how they'd fled to safety in Germany when war broke out, while he stayed to fight. His house had been damaged and he'd rebuilt it himself. The frontier was not far from here, he said.

'Were there Serbs in this village?'

'Yes, it was mixed, now only Muslims. There were three Serb houses near this one.'

'And where are they now?'

'Republika Srpska,' he said, indistinctly.

They were gone, really that's all he knew. Multiethnic villages made mono, all over the country. Now his daughter remains abroad, his son works in Sarajevo and his wife goes regularly to Germany for work, three months there and three months here.

I went to leave the key with neighbours the next day and got invited in for a second breakfast. My solitary bowl of water-soaked oats, seeds, dried coconut and raisins was surpassed by polenta fried with bacon, a platter of meat and cheese, fresh tomatoes, roasted peppers, yoghurt, milk, bread, coffee and blackcurrant juice. These neighbours were visiting from Austria, the place they'd fled to as refugees twenty-seven years ago and where they still worked, waiting to become pensioners when they could permanently return home.

Before I left, as I unpacked my bag to fit in the bread and cheese they'd pressed on me, someone picked up the book I'd bought in Sarajevo. Books were my luxury item, I'd get them sent to me in my supply packages, usually about the history of each country I was walking through. This one, *Bosnia's Paralysed Peace*, was an academic text about the failures of the peace process and methods of international reform making. All I could tell the interested host was 'Bosnia *politick*' and wish I had the language to discuss how this lovely family felt about their fractured country being sewn back together by external governance, international powers forcing the opposed entities that formed Bosnia and Herzegovina to stay as one, like holding two dolls together and making them kiss. I would have loved to hear these people's opinions on power being released from the political authority of the EU-appointed High Commissioner back to Bosnian government piece by piece, on an irregular timescale inconsistently applied, about recriminations, corruption, electoral manipulation, non-cooperation, sabotage and subversion. Without the language skills to get into it, I just thanked them for their kindness and we took a selfie in their abundant garden.

It was a phenomenally lucky meeting, to get me out of that colossal storm, the hail could well have ripped my tent apart. As I left the village, it was as if nothing had happened, the rushing brown water that covered the roads had disappeared and I descended into a cloud inversion as I walked down to the next valley bottom, wisps reaching out to me as if I walked into a cauldron.

One storm remnant was wet earth, and I realised that my summer sandals were no longer viable footwear as I squelched through the forest, following earthen tracks that had been turned to filthy trenches by the heavy machinery that shuttled felled trunks down to tarmac and logging lorries.

Bosnia is almost 50% forest and logging operations were a constant companion here, huge lorries shaking their way delicately along thin tracks as I shrank into the bushes, saluting the driver to make sure he'd seen me. The background village noises were the clinking of cowbells and the buzz of a chainsaw. I saw bear prints in the mud, as I squelched through the forest. I thought I heard wolves one night, awaking to beautiful howls that echoed to the stars.

Finally at Zenica to begin my rest week, the apartment owner picked me up from the town centre in a yellow Skoda Fabia. He spoke good German, worked as the sales rep for an Austrian company and travelled all over the country. His Bosniak family had escaped from Banja Luka (now the capital of Republika Srpska) to Germany in 1992 and, to be able to return to Bosnia, they swapped their apartment in Banja Luka with a Serb family from Zenica (Bosniak majority city in the Federation). Apartment swapping was common in that era, he said, you'd get them advertised in the papers. In this way, post-conflict, Serbs concentrated in Republika Srpska, Bosniaks escaped to the Federation and the division of the country became complete; neighbours made enemies and driven out during war and then the enmity underlined by permanent ethnic separation during peacetime. Separate education systems, separate political representation, separate courts. Bosnia is a country torn apart and sewn back together with thorns that prick at every laboured heartbeat.

Planning this journey, I had promised myself that I'd take a full week break every couple of months, for the chance to sleep deeply and drop the tension from my body.

I'd done it three times so far – in a hostel in Ukraine, Christmas in Bucharest with my brother and early March with friends in a house in Bulgaria – but this was the first break that I spent completely alone, nestled in an Airbnb apartment in an unattractive town that seemed no more than a cluster of tower blocks around factories that released a diffuse yellow haze into the air. I didn't care about tourism, I was there to do nothing and I slept for most of the first two days. Stretch, eat, write, read, watch TV. Condition my hair rather than washing it in hand soap, moisturise my body. I washed my clothes in a machine rather than unsatisfactorily in a bathroom sink with a plastic bag as a makeshift plug. It was important to replace the nutrients I'd been lacking, give myself some relief from the dried carbohydrates and preserved protein that I ate cold on the road.

I spent hours plugged into social media, trying to feel connected to my other life. The world of Brexit and Extinction Rebellion, children's photographs and family birthdays, of silly dog videos and edgy tweets. The world where we all share with each other how we are, while keeping a constant distance.

I was realising that I felt lonely on all my days off. Out there struggling with wind and hills, the balancing of body temperature and calories and hydration, the glorious immersion in nature, the language difficulties and stimulation of a new country was so all-consuming that I didn't miss anything at all. But when I returned to see that the internet had continued chattering without me, that some friends might have been in contact but most had not, I felt small and sad and forgotten about. The first time in all my adventures that I'd felt this way. Maybe I was getting less and less ready to leave home. Leaving Llanidloes felt like leaving home. For the first time in my life I wasn't escaping from something, or running to something better. Maybe this was homesickness. I tried to look at it as positive, that I had a lovely hometown to miss. That hadn't always been the case, rootless, flitting, traumatised beast that I am.

At the end of the rest week I was loath to leave my little cocoon. It all seemed so impossible, to pack everything together, heave it onto my back and set foot outside with absolutely no idea where I would sleep that night. As soon as I found my rhythm, tarmac giving way to packed stone, sure enough, it was normal again and I was in fields, turning aside to pee under fruit trees, assessing the route ahead for level ground to sleep on.

Physically, I struggled a little, coming back from the week off. I had a lot of hip pain the first few days, stabbing up into my lower back as I was walking, and radiating a deep, unavoidable ache at night, no matter how often I switched position.

I'd been scared of the weather changing; the dampness of autumn showed I was losing the light, I was losing the heat of the sun and soon the night would come at 5pm and there would be ice in the darkness. But as it happened I adapted to it with pleasure. Leaves rattled in the wind, scraped along the tracks, landing in the troughs of the springs where water came from the ground, sometimes in trickles, sometimes gushing, sometimes falling into hollowed-out tree trunks, sometimes ornamental stone in remembrance of a loved one. Springs where the travellers and the cows quench thirst equally.

There was a brown tinge to the grasses, yellow tips on the leaves. People were out gathering rosehips, all at once, as if the signal was broadcast that this was the week to go forth with plastic bags and rakes to pull the spiky branches down towards you. It was the season of harvest, of preservation, of preparation for the hard times, just like Ukraine. I saw corn drying, strings of onions hanging in eaves. The difference to Ukraine was that not everything was carefully collected; as in the UK, Bosnians would leave fruit to fall and rot. Nobody offered me carefully treasured apples here, as they had so often a year ago.

Here they offered me cigarettes and *rakia*. Small cakes. Meals and beds. It all contained the same love and tenderness as Ukraine, just differently manifested.

Walking downhill along a clear stream that swelled to a thin river as the contours of the steep valley sides smoothed out, I came to small villages where neighbours called to one another across the river, where cows were brought out to graze and taken home again at night by patient people pacing along with them, and where every house had a vegetable patch – onions, potatoes, peppers, beans.

Two women stopped to look at me as they locked the car in the garage, draped in the elegant headscarves and flowing clothing that characterises devout Muslim dress. I grinned as I walked towards them, my difference so obvious in my grubby leggings and stumpy sweatiness. They invited me in and I found myself having a conversation in excellent English with an intelligent woman,

Dženana, the 21-year-old daughter of the house. I could finally ask all the questions that had been hampered by language barriers; about how she felt about the state of Bosnia, her hopes for change. She talked about the lethargy, the futility that weighted people down.

War was long gone and war was still present. The sheep grazed as the houses decayed; many people had fled elsewhere, their children growing up speaking new languages. There were nice cafés, the shops were well stocked, the roads were busy. Bosnia was alive but choking in a slow death of antagonistic, administrative asphyxiation. When I asked what the problems were or what should be done, people would gesture in the air, huff and say nothing. It was beyond simple statements such as an ineffectual opposition leader or underfunding of public services in artificial austerity. Bosnia is terminally, congenitally divided, and nothing beyond complete systemic overhaul and an extensive reconciliation process could change that.

It felt like a ghoulish conversation to get into, the pain of a badly performing country haunted by the spectre of its most recent war, and I asked Dženana if this was a normal conversation among friends. 'Yes, when Bosnians get together, they'll talk about it sooner or later.'

I slept well that night, a part of me restored by this family's love and tenderness, which hadn't been fulfilled by the solitary week in Zenica. We hugged goodbyes and I left, walking through the misty village and out towards the forest track that would take me over the hills to the next valley.

I didn't make it that far though. There was a huge black metal stove sitting in a front garden with a fire at the base of it, wheels turning on the sides and a pipe leading to another container of water. I stopped and stared for so long that the men sitting in the garage beckoned me over. It was a huge still and they were gathered there to make *rakia*. Empty buckets of fermented plum mash stood by the stove and down at the base of the water barrel poked a pipe which dripped the beginnings of distillation while the contraption came to temperature. They sat me down at the table in the garage, buckets of rosehips and sacks of corn stacked around us, and poured me shots. It was good.

Rakia can be nothing but firewater, but at its best it slips easy down the throat, sharp and smooth, starting embers glowing that spread a pleasant warmth from the belly outwards.

I sat there tingling – 10.30am and I was three shots in. When one of the guys invited me to see his sheep (not a euphemism), I thought sure, why not? We collected them from an enclosure up the hill then walked them through an orchard and further into the forest. Dalibor, a Bosnian Croat, who'd left the village at 17 and spent thirty years in Germany, returning home with a small pension, kept asking me if I had time to spare. I didn't know what to say. I had infinite amounts of time, there was no deadline for me to be back in the UK, but I also had no time at all; if I wasn't walking then I wasn't making progress and if I didn't make progress then I'd never get home. Dalibor preferred life here, he said, nobody stressed about time; people were busy in Germany, focused on schedules and efficient logistics. I sensed something I'd been unable to see before, so deeply entrenched in my days measured by miles per hour: an economically inefficient system means time for spontaneous enjoyment.

He carried a pistol, this Dalibor, a Glock in a bag around his waist, and asked if I wanted to go and shoot it. We put a piece of wood and an empty beer can in a tree and took turns. As we walked through the forest, he pointed to the way that the ground curved strangely, unnatural dips and lumps. He crooked a finger, mimed gunshots and I chilled to realise that we were up in the Croat emplacements, the sniper points where they shot down into the village, attacking their Bosniak neighbours.

The previous night, through Dženana, I had listened to her mother Sedina's war story, of how the villagers were friends before 1992, that it didn't matter who was Muslim and who was Croat. One night her Croatian best friend came to her, desperately offering her money to leave the village but wouldn't explain why. The next day the firing started, Croats attacking Bosniaks. Sedina fled to Zenica and her husband stayed to fight. Now Sedina lives again with the people who once shot at her, but there's an uneasy gap between them, friendships betrayed in favour of tribal affiliations. She did an impression of waving uneasily to someone, sneering a smile while fully aware of the emptiness of the gesture. Twenty-four years of false politeness to a neighbour who would have been happy to kill you and you both know it.

I was the rare tourist, a neutral person able to be invited into both houses and experience the dissonance of two sides of a village where people are humane to strangers and shun their neighbours.

The next few weeks seemed to pass in a flit; 150 miles blurred together in a smooth progression of days in forests and nights in damp tents. Villages were clusters of red-roofed houses in the bottom of valleys. If they were inhabited, I would arrive at a pecking of chickens, sheds carefully stocked with ancient tools. Every house had an aspirational wood pile, the kind that British people buy books about. The buzz of chainsaws was as familiar as the discordant croak of the jaybird, which I seemed to see regularly on this journey, the flicker of their striped wings showing quick blue under the grey body as they flitted away from me. Tractors rumbled along the lanes, there were horses picketed in the fields, cow shit on the tarmac. If it was a Serb or Croat village there'd be the smell of pigs coming from a dark enclosure where hogs live out their enforced inactivity.

Sometimes the settlements were no more than names on the map, trees grown over where humans once wore paths, houses left to crumble in the gentle force of rain and sunshine. I would check the graveyards for crosses or crescents, to see if it was a Bosniak or Croat or Serb village.

In between, I walked the forest, admiring the silence and the shifting colours of autumn's full fire brightness. My breath was the loudest sound. My footsteps crunched until I stopped and tuned in to the falling leaves, the flutters of birds and, occasionally, the growl or bark of a larger beast, breaking sticks as they crashed away from me into solitude.

Most of my time was spent sweating and stepping. I would heave myself slowly up the side of valleys that I'd just descended to cross a river and now had to climb unwillingly back again. I followed paths that wriggled, bending to take account of trees and hollows and streams. Paths that became thinner and thinner until they suddenly disappeared and I realised that I was following the traces of animals and I was doomed to crash through grasping undergrowth, clinging to branches, kicking my toes into slippery leaf mulch to find footholds of rock or earth and return to the route.

The villages were changing around me, extremely poor farmhouses now a rarity rather than the norm. There was no more wood worn to smoothness by decades of handling, flaking lime wash revealing packed earth around wooden lath walls. It was concrete blocks and clean sharp corners now, the blank, plastered face of modernity. Cheap plastic disposable ornaments were making a comeback. I saw a string of fairy lights along the edge of a porch. I saw a plastic solar light stuck on a spike into the ground. The con trick of accessible luxury with secret obsolescence built in. I was almost back in the EU.

Walking through my second autumn, I kept remembering my first one in Ukraine. I kept thinking of fallen leaves in the forest and the search for places to sleep off quiet tracks where no one ever drove. I kept thinking of pulling water from wells, the way each village was a cluster of houses along a few wide roads, with long distances of field and forest in between. I missed the geese being ushered out onto the street in the morning, the sacks of apples waiting for collection. I missed the way everything was old and richly patinated. I missed the worn and mended clothing, the flowery prints, the home-knitted woollen jumpers, the scars and the gold teeth, the way people marvelled at me. It was a year ago that I was there, walking across the flatness of the centre of the country, eyes wide in discovery as the season of warm gold changed to frosty silver.

Maybe this walk would become an endless loop of associating emotions with the growing and falling of leaves.

Maybe that's all life is anyway.

ENTERING THE EU

I was warned about Bihać, the final canton in the north-west corner of Bosnia, tucked in against the curve of Croatia. Newspaper stories talked about an overwhelming number of refugees stuck there, funnelled up from Sarajevo and prevented from entering the EU by aggressive border patrols and violent illegal pushbacks. 'Be careful of the migrants,' said other travellers, 'they are dangerous, they are desperate, they will take everything from you, just as it has been taken from them.'

In fact, the people I saw on the streets were separate, in their own world, politely ignored and rarely making eye contact. They were scruffy humans in grimy tracksuits, thin ankles above ill-fitting sandals, heels slipping out of the back. There was a scavenged feeling to clothing, as if they'd pulled anything from donation piles that would vaguely fit. People with bags on their back and front, carrying their entire lives with them. I saw mostly men, mostly under 30, but there were women and babies too. Humans drifted along the streets, coming out of the makeshift camp on the edge of the town to sit in the shade of trees, on benches or just walk endlessly.

Everywhere in this town I saw displaced people; they seemed in constant motion but their lives were on pause, no forward progress.

This wasn't just a refugee situation, this was a Bosnia situation. The forests contained mass graves. There were minefields. Townspeople and migrants all shared the trauma of persecution and ongoing helplessness in the face of international power politics.

I read news stories of how the Bosniaks had helped these people, fresh with their own memories of being made refugees, but I also read of how protests in the town of Bihać earlier in the summer had led to the official camp being moved further north, near to the town of Velika Kladuša. The people in Bihać were the remnants, the unofficial squatters.

Actually, I had no real idea of the actual situation of these people – their nationality, finances, income, whether or how they were fed, clothed, housed, what happened with an asylum claim, how they got here, what their prospects were, how they would get into the EU, what would happen next. They were a mystery, a blank. I couldn't place them, I couldn't fit them into this landscape.

I stayed in Bihać for a few days' rest, went to the same café every day, and as I watched the stream of refugees passing on the road, slowly I recognised the same faces. I realised a man I'd seen each day was sitting at the next table and decided to smoke a cigarette and ask him for a light.

He was Iranian, fleeing repeated prison sentences for protesting against the government, starting when they made his young daughter wear a hijab to primary school. The family boarded a flight to Serbia five years ago on the rare occasion that it offered Iranian visas. Now they were separated – mother and daughter had made it to Germany and he had been stuck in Bosnia for three years, suffering repeated violence during pushbacks, slowly weakening. He showed me photos from his arrival in Bosnia, a full-faced, healthier man; now he was thin and drawn. His slender frame leaned back in the chair and stared out of the window, his stillness framed by wisps of cigarette smoke. I watched his lips during the silence, pressing and moving on the emotions he wasn't expressing.

'I feel like a bird in a cage. I have to get out of Bosnia and continue with my life but I am out of resources, all of them.'

It was shocking to poke my head out from my velvet nest of UK life and see real hardship. I felt ashamed of the heroic validation my journey received at home, compared against the unacknowledged struggles of these people fleeing conflict, oppression and poverty.

They too had walked long distances, in ill-fitting trainers that rubbed open their heels or popped off their toenails. They had slept outside without the benefit of expensive equipment. Nobody subscribed to support them online. I would hopefully finish my journey to cheering crowds. They were heading for rich, selfish Europe where every scrap of survival is given begrudgingly; the so-called safe haven that will always present racism, rejection and barriers.

As I walked the 15km towards the Croatian border, I passed a roadside bakery. A man sat outside, staring towards the border point, the mark of the invisible line on land that he could not cross over. I felt shame as I crossed the border, so easy for me to wave my passport and walk through into Croatia, underneath the metal archway that forms the checkpoint. Shame that I was selfish, that I put my own journey first, instead of staying to join the local charities that were working so hard to help the influx of desperate people that unaddressed global inequality ensured would never cease.

CROATIA and SLOVENIA

It was sunny again as I entered Croatia, as it had been for months. Only the heavy evening dew was a sign of the seasonal change; the winds were getting colder, with ice in the shadows. The trees reacted to the changing light and shed their leaves, the world turning brown around me in the final fire of dying. I knew that winter was coming, I knew that life would soon become much more difficult but still relished the nights under my tent mesh. When I woke to morning dew on my kit, moisture on my sleeping bag and a wrinkled book cover, I would mildly scold myself for not fully putting up the tent. But then, at night, I would do it over again; leaving the cover off so I lay there under mesh as the light faded, admiring the patterns of grass pressed against my nomad's bedroom, watching as the stars came out, the airplanes twinkled and shooting stars soared at the edge of vision.

I felt grumpy and sad to be leaving Bosnia, a country whose people I had loved connecting with, an irritation exacerbated by a lack of food. My energy levels were concerning; it was a struggle to walk 15 miles a day. I felt as if I should be easily able to manage 18 miles, even the occasional 25. I was in condition, I could feel my strong muscles working as I climbed hills, and yet I seemed to run out of impetus, found myself taking long breaks. I vowed to eat more, up my protein intake, and so it was a shock to set out into Croatia with good intentions and find myself in a dearth of shops.

The first village I came to was full of tourist accommodation. Every house had a board outside it, 'apartman Maria', 'apartman Korina', 'apartman Nina'. I'd hardly slept the night before, tossing and turning in my hotel bed in Bihać and decided to pay for another night's sleep rather than an uncomfortable night in a tent. The price was €30, with another €12 for breakfast – this was another change on my entry to Croatia. EU money meant increased prices.

I don't want to labour the point about money but spending it was stressful. As I started walking to Ukraine, I could live on £42 a week – all my food plus two nights in a hotel. Now in Croatia I'd be lucky if the same expenses cost less than £100 and it was only going to get more expensive further west. For all the ways in which I have lived close to the edge of life's comfortable limits, I have never truly had no money. Even when I was diagnosed with cancer while technically homeless and spent the following year living on benefits, I began my cancer experience with a thousand pounds in savings and, as that trickled away, I had the security of a rented home and small income to offset it.

Being hundreds of miles from your community, with absolutely no access to the funds to get you a warm bed or food to eat, is a deep dark fear of mine – I guess because I have chosen a lifestyle which brings me precariously close to that. Just another limit for me to explore? Perhaps. I have broken myself down in many ways over the last fifteen years, breached the boundaries of my contained, frightened self, shown myself some of my cultural or childhood-imposed behaviours and beliefs, and become a better person for it, freed myself from limitations. Maybe the deepest power can be found in launching yourself into the world with absolutely nothing; the strength of stripping yourself down, following the ascetic pilgrim tradition.

***

Croatia was strange. The bullet holes continued across the border, albeit with decreasing frequency. The memorials carried death dates of 1991 now. I checked a map and saw that my first week of Croatia passed through the territory taken over by the Croatian Serbs during 1991, making this a place of log barricades across roads, of roaming militia groups, vicious killings and equal reprisals.

I knew I wouldn't be in this country long enough to get to know the people; they looked through me. Tourism was normal and I was no longer an oddity worth calling out to. Things were cleaner. The houses felt more withdrawn, shutters half closed like sleepy eyes, often standing isolated in pools of cropped grass inside boundary fences. It reminded me of the sterility of the German suburb when I hitch-hiked home from Serbia last June. This was very clearly Austro-Hungarian territory now, with a completely different heritage. The exuberant messiness that I associated with Serbia was gone. Nature's glorious tangles were tamed to neatness, leaving sterile luxury.

I didn't feel halfway through the journey, but this was a significant milestone. I was taking the shortest possible route through Croatia, 120 miles across the corner of the country, a mere week or two of walking. It would have been straightforward but I was already struggling with low energy and then I started having kit problems.

I'd decided against getting a supply package in Bosnia and gambled on waiting for cheaper, faster courier delivery to Slovenia. My luck ran out. Weeks of autumnal sunshine turned to rain. Late summer temperatures shifted to early winter, and, practically overnight, much of what I was carrying was unsuitable. Juggling the receipt of specialist kit from the UK that I couldn't source locally, in the dearth of outdoor shops in rural places, was sometimes a logistical nightmare, especially to time one package receipt and minimise having to spend money waiting in hotels.

Sarajevo had a single outdoor shop which didn't stock clothing in my size. I'd met a woman leading an outdoor events group who'd told me to try secondhand shops, as most Bosnian people couldn't afford expensive outdoor gear. The secondhand walking shoes I bought in Sarajevo could handle the odd splash in a puddle but when they brushed against overhanging wet grass as I climbed a thin path leading up a mountain, I felt the slow seep of wetness creeping through the sodden fabric. My secondhand long-sleeved top was cotton and didn't retain warmth, but it was all I'd been able to find to fit me.

The rain didn't stop for days. From drizzle to downpour, it just kept coming. I climbed a mountain, up a thin grassy path – wet leaves on clear trodden earth meant treachery underfoot – clinging to branches, my feet sliding uncontrollably. It started hailing near the summit, thin pellets stinging as I navigated a rocky descent that came as an unpleasant surprise in the mist. My wet gloves soaked into my sleeves, another bad purchase in a cheap shop in Bosnia. Nothing was holding heat. I was wearing the wrong fabrics, which meant I couldn't stop walking for long before I got cold, leaving my legs less time to recover.

I can handle being cold. I can handle being wet. I can handle being achy. I can handle being tired. I can handle the conflagration of all those things at once. What finally broke me was to experience all of those things while trying to spend night after night on a slowly deflating air mattress. It flipped me over the edge.

The mattress started leaking as I crossed into Croatia, a very small, slow leak which meant I dozed into sleep on a comfortable bed only to wake several hours later with cold feet and blunt hip pain where my bones were pressing against the ground.

The great frustration was that I needed to pay for a hotel in order to fix it: get in the shower, immerse the mat under soapy running water and watch for the tiny bubbles to show the escaping air. Patch it up and off you go, back to comfy camping. Except that it failed.

Twice. I would fix the leak, successfully test the mattress in the hotel room, and then find myself dismally sinking onto the cold ground the following night, trapped in hours of discomfort and with a couple of days' walk to the next cheap hotel because I refused to walk back on myself.

It took a week to give up. My spirits slowly deflated. I couldn't keep walking if I was going to sleep on the cold, hard ground every night. The forecast showed nothing but rain ahead.

With wrong kit and now broken kit, it was time to stop. I had been hoping to walk another month before taking a break to receive a supply package but it had to come now.

I checked out the cheapest bed in the area and arranged for my friend to send the package from my supply dump, a heap of boxes piled in the corner of her art room.

I had to wait, alone in a quiet village, in the cheapest Airbnb I could find, feeling sad. When I looked out of the window, I saw that the rain had flooded the vegetable patch between the house and the road, leaving occasional green shoots poking out from a square of brown water. I was in courier limbo, having tried to book this pause for the minimum of delays but the package had disappeared, passed on by DHL to Croatia Post, the tracking last updated three days ago. I couldn't leave without it and there was absolutely nothing to do in the meantime but stare aimlessly at the internet.

I was used to being alone; this was a very solitary journey. But the solitude of a mountain is different to that of a kitchen. Small voices of doubt started sneering – *Is this really a good life?*

Every urge in me pushed to shy away and hide from how hard this was. I've always been an avoider, a procrastinator and learning to be different was difficult, but beating back negativity was part of the adventure too, not just navigating across mountains or doing the right things when you see a bear. It was continuing to do the right things to look after yourself and stay strong enough to complete the challenge, even when you were tired and sad. It all felt a bit much, coming out of that solitary week in rural Croatia, looking ahead at the forecast to a full ten days of rain.

I felt so alone sometimes, setting out with my pack to walk by myself, not just for weeks at a time but months, years. Just little me and the whole big world of uncertainty, not knowing where I'd sleep or what would happen to me, only that it would be vaguely uncomfortable, even while I was enjoying it.

Here came Slovenia; the first day was a full march on road, down to the border from Delnice, rain pelting at me nonstop. I focused on the edge of the road, marking where to step aside when traffic came rushing towards me, ducking into bus shelters in silent villages to breathe for a while, check my progress, shake the droplets from my clothing.

Welcome to the Schengen Zone and freedom of movement, there would be no more immigration control until the English Channel, and I was free to cross ethereal borders up high on mountain tops instead of having to descend for dreary road miles and official passport stamps.

The rain continued, dripping, endless, as I trudged along a back road beside the river that formed the border, a fresh green fence alongside it, topped with razor wire. I may have been free to pass but refugees were unwanted. I'd been following the migrant trail since Bosnia, where hundreds of desperate people wait for their opportunity to climb fences, dodge patrols and make it to the hidden parts of cities, the shared rooms, the illegal working; or declare themselves and wait for administrative asylum application processing that could be years in the churning, living on the scraps that rich people let fall to the bottom of society. What have they left behind that makes this worthwhile? They must hide in the shadows while I walk in full view. When I was stopped by police in Croatia, once they saw my passport, they asked if they could help me, they took photos with my heroism, because I am a part of the first world system that has created the mess that refugees are escaping from. It protects me because I am white, I am well dressed, I am one of its own.

I spent one night sleeping in a summer shelter, four uprights supporting a roof over a wooden table and benches, wood-fired barbecue nearby. It was very near to a village and, judging it public space, I sat at the bench to eat, watching the dog walkers as they patrolled the road up and down, turning umbrella shells towards each other for short chats. Dog walkers were new, I hadn't seen them outside of cities since I left the UK. Dogs were becoming house pets again as I walked west, rather than chained forever on short leashes to tiny kennels, or left to roam loose.

Ahead on the map, I saw that my chosen route climbed from the border up into a high ridge of mountains that curved away to the north-west, around an outstretched tip of Croatian territory. There were towns down in the valleys but up where my route trailed, there was unbroken green forest.

What I didn't expect in all this rain was a lack of water. Back in Bosnia, there had been springs everywhere, stone spouts installed to provide water for animal care or the possibility of roadside prayer. Here, nothing. Just thick forest, no cleared spaces for grazing. Strangely though, there were no streams. Karstic rock forms the Dinaric alps; it's limestone based and very porous, meaning there were often strange circular dips where the water had sunk into the ground.

For days the sun hid behind drab, grey cloud covering, sometimes far above, sometimes all around me as I walked on high hills where sky came to ground. The air was full of water, cloudmist hanging between the trees, every leaf dripping. My body was wet with rain, while my water bottles were empty.

I dropped down from the ridge to ask for water at a small cluster of houses, heading for the one with a smoking chimney as the others showed few signs of life. People had gone to winter in towns and closed up their summer houses; plucked vegetables from gardens, shut windows and drawn curtains. When I knocked, I was welcomed into a warm kitchen where cats dozed and there was a carafe of herbal tea cooling. This was Aprilija, an artist, spilling her words all over me as she wiped scattered tobacco shreds from the shining wooden tabletop. She offered me tea, coffee, a banana, a bed for the night, she just had to leave for an hour, right now, she was late. I said yes to all the things, and sat alone by the warmth of the wood fire, letting it seep into me in silence, touching the infinite softness of cat fur and wondering how I came to be here, whirled from forest life into a home.

Sometimes connections seem natural and Aprilija and I talked our stories across the table – cancer, feminism, activism, sexual assault, astrology, fear, recovery. She made an important piece of art in the late 90s, recording women speaking openly about rape, of having their lives changed against their will, yet rejecting the label of victimhood, taking back dignity by telling their own stories. We discussed the healing power of talking about trauma, purging yourself of hidden poison, freeing yourself of silencing shame.

She gave me a carved bear to wear around my neck, a little lump of wooden body, blunt muzzle crudely sliced, just large enough to feel solid in a clenched fist. I took it as a talisman, a reminder of the strength that comes from accepting vulnerability.

We walked through the village to say goodbye, then I trundled away into the mist, heading for more forests, more silence. The summer hum of insects and morning birdsong gave way, as the seasons turned, to the deep, damp, drenching silence of a winter forest. When I stopped, sound stopped; the rustle of my clothing, creaking of rucksack and crunching steps. I was the noise pollution in this place where beetles nibble inside tree trunks and the loudest sounds were droplets falling from leaves.

I found no water for the rest of the day but I'd taken enough from Aprilija and, as I camped in a thunderstorm, listening to wind roaring above me and counting the seconds between flash and rumble, I was happy and secure in the wild forest, sleeping on the pine needles that blanketed the ground, green moss squelching like plumped pillows.

It was a night where I felt at peace in the depth of darkness, listening to the slow clatter of single leaves falling.

I was complete; both dissolved into the land and whole upon its surface. The trees gave me no definition, I was solely and completely myself there. This was how I could best come to understand myself, by going out alone in nature, to places with no human eyes to reflect their version of myself back towards me.

Aprilija told me that her village had been a closed military zone since the second World War, only opened up to civilian settlement in the last twenty years. Before WWII this area of Slovenia was full of German settlers, who spent six hundred years in the region before being moved back to Germany by Nazi occupying government, or exiled by the subsequent Yugoslav administration. Almost half the villages in the Kočevsko region were left empty, for forest to grow into them.

Empty villages meant ... no water, and when a car came winding along the forestry track as I was walking desperately away from yet another cluster of empty, shuttered houses, I flagged it down and showed them my empty bottle. They were the first people I'd seen in over twenty-four hours. Father and son, Vinko and Samo, had come to the forest to give Samo driving practice. We chatted for a while; they told me that 3 miles west I'd be out of the forest and down in the valley where the people lived, but following my route north it was 12 miles to the first populated village. I didn't have enough water to walk 12 miles and as I was trying to decide what to do, Vinko offered to drive me down to the village, then, once we were there, said I should come and stay the night. They had a calm family home of grown-up children, pans of food left on the stove for people to help themselves. Vinko settled back on the sofa with the grunt of a hard-working man. He couldn't leave me in the forest, he said, knowing that there are bears around. I protested my capabilities but gently – it's OK to be looked after, to be cared for.

I found myself chatting with Samo while Vinko went into the garage to butcher the deer carcass that had been in the boot the whole time. Samo was 19 and studying web design in Ljubljana, uncertain that this was exactly what he wanted out of life. Most college students in Slovakia study in the capital, only returning home at weekends.

'How is Wales?' said Samo. He thought of it as a place where it rained, populated mainly by old people, like the cute villages where mysterious crimes happen on Sunday night TV. It led to a conversation about city vs rural life, what Samo considered the future, what he considered progress. I told him that I thought people have so much there that the basic standards of living I'd seen in the Balkans are viewed as unthinkable poverty in Britain. That people are less connected to the land, in just a few generations we have lost much of our knowledge of how to live in harmony with the natural world and now, people are struggling to get it back, to relearn traditional wisdom, or to create a food chain that doesn't involve mass production or adulteration of ingredients.

On the table, next to a carton of fruit juice, was a carafe of rosehips and wheat grain, soaking in water. Vinko had made it, picking the rosehips himself.

'Imagine you moved to Ljubljana and became an app developer, Samo, imagine you only bought your drinks in plastic cartons. Your city children might remember the drink that Grandpa Vinko made but their children would have to look it up in books. It only takes a couple of distracted generations for traditional culture to disappear.'

I gestured to the two drinks. 'Which contains spiritual nourishment?' It was missing from modern life and we didn't even realise it. Corporations tried to replicate this by giving their products personalities. 'Hi, I'm made of eco-friendly packaging, so after you've finished consuming my delicious contents, make sure you put me in the recycling bin!'

Samo nodded, hearing me. We talked in English, as Vinko sat at the end of the table, not understanding, wondering why we were talking so intensely about his drink.

It's wrong to say that Wales is awful, but I think the idea that Britain is at the forefront of how life should be lived is completely misguided. We're wrecking the planet, deludedly chasing the spiral of ever more luxurious concepts of a basic standard of living. We're manipulating global economics, causing and interfering in conflicts, then voting to keep foreigners out when they come to us in desperation.

The rising floodwaters of the messes we ignored because they were at the other end of the world, are beginning to lap at the end of our gardens and we're afraid. A houseful of plastic tat provides no security, no emotional grounding. Without a sense of functional community, it's time to look after our own, every man for himself. Climate fear affects every vote. Bring up the drawbridge, there's no room for compassion.

We hugged as they left me in the forest the next morning. I wished Samo good luck with university and I hoped he managed to sell all that green tea he bought cheap from China in a typical misguided teenage business idea. I continued on the remote ridge, up and over the mountain shoulder and around to the beginning of '*civilisatsija*', as Vinko called it. These were my final days of walking in the '*vuko jebina*', the 'place where wolves fuck', this amusing slang phrase I'd been hearing since Serbia, meaning the remote, wild places, that would become ever rarer as I headed west.

ITALY

To leave Slovenia I chose an easy, comfortable ridgewalk, 30km and two nights without water sources, high above the Natisone river valley to the south and alongside the Julian Alps to the north. Once I'd toiled to Stol, the highest peak at 1,673m, a stupendous view opened up ahead: the thousand licks of cream that formed the snowy Italian Dolomites and a tissue of cloud haze over the deep blue plains down towards Udine and Venice. I shouted with joy to see it all before me, my first view of Italy, the reward for all this effort.

I slept warm and deep that night, cuddled up under blankets in a tiny triangular cabin wedged at ridge edge above the sheer mountainside.

Overnight, the cloud smoothed and calmed, lying gently below me in a pool that stretched white to the horizon. The sky was yellow at the sun's entry and pale over to the west, where the snowy Dolomites gleamed faintly. My pointed ridge had become an island in a cloud sea, which gently undulated over slumbering towns beneath. I was alone amongst the frozen peaks in the crisp, fresh dawn, just me and the chamois goats here to witness this beginning light, the birth of day.

It took a full day to achieve 5km, climbing five peaks on a thin footpath that snaked along the ridgeline, sheer descents either side of me. Every step was a balance or a scramble on tree roots and boulders. Every time I dragged my attention away from my tentative foot placements, I was in awe at the stupendous view; the mighty brawn of the rocky Polovnik ridge directly across the cloud-filled valley to the north; the Dolomites further ahead, dozens of peaks, all snow gilded. To be so high on a mountain was to crawl over solid power; this was no conquering. Mist came lapping from the cloud pool to pour over the ridge, covering me, icy and dim, as I dropped between peaks. Finally, as the sky darkened, I descended into Italy, making a hasty bed in the forest. In early morning, I walked through damp mists into my first Italian village, noting the shutters at the windows, the solidity of the square church tower, the modern cars in every driveway.

I stopped for a celebratory restaurant meal the next day, soaking wet in the dribbling rain, stumbling over Italian words to access a fizzy red wine and plate of pasta, choked by the significance of where I was. Entering Italy was a huge milestone, a complete change of language, culture and history. My Spanish knowledge meant that Italian would eventually come easily, but right now Serbian words were invading – after a summer spent working my way into angular Slavic communication, the flow of a Latin language felt mushy in my mouth.

Crossing west through Italy to head for France, I had a choice of routes ahead: I could trek through the snowy Dolomites and Alps or descend to the flatter, easier Po Valley river plain, with a short detour to visit Venice, somewhere I'd never been. After a difficult, low energy autumn in Croatia and Slovenia, I didn't feel ready for a second snowy winter struggling in mountains and chose the lowland option.

The snowy mountains were always there, a floating sky wall glowing pink at dawn and dusk. I looked back at them, often imagined myself struggling through the snow, taking hours to walk scant miles, on the edge of survival the whole time. It was easier down in the water channels and vineyards, treading the land reclaimed from water.

I reached Italy at the beginning of December and, in the progression towards Christmas, everything felt rich. I had battled through the Balkan desert and reached an Italian oasis. Fountain spouts came carved in scrolls and dragon mouths. The streets were stone cobbles laid in patterned arches, shining with decades of use. There were window displays of beribboned hampers, pasta makers gleaming with the clean precision of worked metal, glowing chocolate wrappings nestled in tinsel. People carried huge ceremonial cake boxes through the streets. The supermarkets piled vegetables in bountiful displays. All the sandwiches were made with good bread; there were a thousand varieties of cheese. Cups of hot chocolate were thick with starch, a chocolate soup that I spooned in like liquid mousse, shivering in bars, sheltering from the rain.

I was overwhelmed by the sense of luxury. Grandeur was universal. Everything was a castle. Men were more awake to women, I felt less innocence here. Young men moved and I sensed a pack. Northeast Italy was ornate. Precise. Glossy haired and sharply tailored.

After experiencing a year of sparse rural poverty from Ukraine to Bosnia, I was shown, in stark relief, that I had walked into the lands of the colonisers; those who have historically accumulated wealth and power at the expense of much of the rest of the world. I struggled to absorb this complex, ornate antiquity, centuries of money, attitude and architecture condensed down to a thick, rich, cultural oil.

Having chosen the Po Valley over the Dolomites, I was walking through rain rather than snow. Having left the Balkans, the buildings no longer had bullet holes, the forests had almost no bears. Italy's war was seventy years ago. It was a wonderful relief to return to first world problems. I needed this. I was tired and needed life to be easy for a while.

I wanted Italian warmth and splendour to infuse every part of me. I wanted to fill a bath with chocolate soup, and lie there for an hour, conditioning my hair, drinking Prosecco and eating good cheese. The deep winter was approaching and, like a bear slowing into hibernation, I felt in need of a burrow.

Two weeks passed as I progressed towards Venice, including a dismal Christmas break housesitting for a kind couple who'd been introduced to me through a Welsh connection. No matter how much I tried to rationalise that it was my choice to remain alone in the journey, it was still hard not to wallow in misery when I woke to spend Christmas Day by myself. I felt a hollowness in my chest that my life was this way, no children, no partner, nobody I'd ever made a home with. The comparison with glowing faces around full dinner tables was hard to shut out. I had blocked my lover by now, but he got around it by emailing me, which made me swear and then cry. It was the usual garbled message which reflected my own journey back to me while saying nothing about himself. Painful to experience but easy to ignore, now I'd chosen to stop chasing his scraps of affection.

Post Christmas and back in the daily grind, I approached Venice along the spit of land that forms the north-eastern side of the lagoon. The human-planted forest was behind a high fence, a thin strip of trees, difficult to hide in, so I chose the verandah of a fishing cabin and enjoyed a glorious pink sunset and golden dawn, a dew-wettened sleeping bag and a cold nose, herons and cormorants flapping solemnly away from me through the high reeds.

It took four hours along a straight road to get to the tip of the peninsula, focusing on a distant fragment of white light at the end, which swelled and grew into the first piece of open water on my route, after a year of inland walking.

The boat journey took thirty minutes over the open bay to Venice and the water was gentle blue, limpid and swaying. I stood on deck as the black flash of a cormorant flew alongside us for a few masterful seconds before fluttering to a stop at a wooden piling.

Water and air felt melded, blurred together and I floated on the wind, turning my head through a range of colours from the gentle pink of the mountains behind me, a misty rose haze, to the teal, turquoise and green water, and as I looked towards the islands, the colours paled and whitened into tissue blue, the sun dappling a golden path ahead. There were layers of islands, thin silhouettes of church spires and defensive towers. Boats of varying sizes carved perfectly aligned paths around one another.

I was arriving in Venice on New Year's Eve 2019, skimming over the water to a fantasy island. Look at where I am, look at what I've done. How incredible that this is my life. A sudden spurt of tears flashed hot into my eyes.

We have created homes based firmly in fire and earth for so long and Venice is the opposite, a place of water and light, the strangest of human habitations, a pinnacle of achievement. It's an endless set of corners and small bridges, a million shuttered windows. A city of hidden places, of unknown lives.

I walked and trailed my hand along stone balustrades worn to a gleaming patina. There were small doorways set directly onto the water where you could imagine secret escapes, slipping out in darkness to silent waiting boats. Venice is a shifting place of alleyways, rarely leading in a straight line, built on tree trunks hammered down into mud and slowly, inevitably sinking. Every time I walked for a few hours, I felt off balance, as if the whole island was buoyant beneath me.

After the glorious fireworks of New Year's Eve and two days of wandering a thousand tiny alleyways, peeking around corners that only led to dead ends and closed doors, silent water and occasional gondolas, suddenly it felt boring. Nobody seemed to live anywhere. The street traders opened their wooden shacks and hung out boards covered with gondola magnets, glittering masks, jester faces, hats, aprons, hoodies, a thousand souvenirs made thousands of miles away and brought here for export home. This is a place designed, like Barcelona, like London, like Paris, to siphon money from the large numbers of visitors who insist on coming.

As I crossed the main road bridge off the island cluster, I was dizzy and uncertain, wanting to hold the railings as the bridge rocked back and forth, my head stuffy and congested. Sharing a cheap hostel dorm with heaters blowing hot electric air and fifteen other people who didn't like open windows had left me with a feverish cold.

A woman named Mirca messaged, offering me a bed; she was slightly to the north of my route so I'd said probably not, not wanting to ask her for a lift to get there – the extra favour she might not be offering. It's a difficult thing, trying to gauge how much somebody is offering you, how out of their way they're prepared to go to help. It may sound selfish, to refuse offers that aren't useful enough but, having wasted many half days trying to transport myself backwards and forwards from my walking path just to take up the promise of a bed when I'd have slept just as well in a tent, unless it actually works for me I might as well not bother.

But I also felt nervous about asking for more than people were offering. It's hard to gauge when I've crossed the line into unacceptability. Mirca was strangely insistent though, and came out to find me for a coffee.

I'd put trust in strangers so often on this journey, stepped into so many cars, crossed so many thresholds. *Who is this woman?* I wondered, as she rushed out of her car to fling her arms around me and pinch my cheeks.

'What do you need?' she kept saying, as she took me to a restaurant, wanting to buy me food, clothes, shoes.

I realised that I needed a bed. My head was swimming with fever and I couldn't think straight anymore. 'Right then,' said this lovely little fairy woman and took me back to her house where I collapsed into her boudoir of a bedroom, all red walls and mirrors and four poster bed.

We looked at each other across the breakfast table, two humans with no idea of who the other was, only predisposed to like each other. Spinning webs around each other, we shared our stories, connecting ourselves detail by detail.

I slept most of the day in a deep, sweaty, feverish unconsciousness and, late afternoon, when I finally got up, said yes to another invitation. It was the 6th of January, the night of Epiphany when Italians burn bonfires. Their peasant tradition is to watch the way the smoke is blowing and predict the harvest for the summer ahead. West good, east bad. They put a *nonna* on top, white apron and pumpkin head. 'Burn the witch,' they say. But it's the witches who knew. 'My grandmother knew the meaning of every single wind direction,' said one woman. Now they clustered together using Google to fill the generational wisdom gap.

People crowded around the food table, insulated in thick coats and woollen hats. Children were given stockings full of sweet fake coal, in black sugary lumps. We ate *pinza*, a sweet, spiced polenta cake with sultanas, poured cups of mulled wine. It was really nice to feel something more real and culturally grounded, after the hollow splendour of Venice. We clustered around an open-sided marquee on a back road in the flat grid canal system in the countryside between Venice and Padua.

The pile of pallets in the nearest field was set alight and it burnt up hot and quick, the witch's white apron flapping in the heat and ten thousand sparks flying up above her head to swirl in the cold air, like goldfish circling a pool.

The plume of smoke streamed away to the south-west and the crowd muttered predictions. 'It's going to be a good year, six months of warm weather.' Not that our lives depend on this anymore, disconnected as we are from living with the rhythm of the earth.

I stared up at the sparks and smoke, watching the golden goldfish swim, and thought about all that lay ahead of me, away to the west: France, the Pyrenees, the Camino de Santiago, all before the far distant finish line. What would this season bring for me?

***

Leaving Mirca with a grateful hug and walking away west of Venice, my illness continued. After another rest stop, where I slept all day, I could just about keep going, but I suffered with low energy and struggled to make even 10 miles a day, feeling drained and sad.

At first, I passed through the Prosecco region, seeing single workers tiny in huge fields, moving slowly from plant to plant, up and down the acres of rows, clipping down last year's growth into two whips, twisting them into the grey wires that held vines captive while they obediently bore fruit.

Beyond the vineyards of the Berici hills west of Padua, I walked onto the Po Valley river plain. I hadn't been anywhere so completely horizontal since the Romanian Danube floodplain. The white snow-covered peaks of the Alps hovered in the far distance like marvellous apparitions; ancestors watching from the mantelpiece, as I tracked parallel to them on the flatlands. It was mundane, too much road and not enough path. I was restricted to tarmacked straight lines, navigating intersections of canals and ditches that were there to keep this land drained and dry enough to farm.

There were moments of beauty in the roadside dullness.

The swirl of dust in the wind of a passing lorry.

The sudden clatter of pigeons taking flight from a rooftop.

The topology of plantations and vineyards provided art for my eyes. I walked through a mathematician's delight as the regularly spaced plants aligned, now in corridors and now in confusion. Avenues shifted as my perspective point changed, crossing and recrossing, like an acid-fuelled, geometric visual alignment.

But mostly the plain felt unusual and strange. It was a blank, silent place without hedges or fences, no tree gatherings greater than a copse.

The wildlife I saw the most were herons, a siege of them haunting the ploughed fields, long legs picking carefully on the clods. I would come across gatherings of six or seven, hunched silent in the trees, shrouded in their wings like caped spies, gloomy and threatening in the dismal grey mists.

One new problem I faced in rural Italy was the lack of shops. I was firmly in car-orientated society now, where people drive to the big weekly shop and, with fewer village emporia of small things, I struggled to find places to stock up.

Instead of village shops, Italy had a proliferation of vending machines. I saw them selling bread, pastries, milk and cheeses, flowers, cigarettes. Those placed outside pharmacies were the most amusing; containing all the things I could imagine someone frantically searching for in the dead of night – baby formula, nappies, contact lens solution, painkillers, plasters, denture glue, antacids, tampons, vibrators, lube. The condom selection was extensive.

In my tiredness, I was drawn to spend too much time snuggled down in bars. They did sell food, of the snacking variety. *Tramezzini*, white bread sandwiches with the crusts cut off, wrapped around a spoonful of tuna and a scatter of cocktail onions, or some slimy mozzarella and lettuce. A small selection of buns with ham or salami flapping down from the edges. Croissants were available in glass display cases with small doors for you to open and help yourself. People ate their croissants like ice-cream cornets, holding them vertically wrapped in a napkin and consuming from the tip downwards.

Coffee and croissant and tuna sandwiches were nice but I needed good nutrition, so sometimes I went to a restaurant, thinking I would just get a single course, a cheap plate. It didn't work like that, there was a sense of occasion about going for a meal here. Even in a cheap canteen for customers in paint-spattered overalls there were still napkins on the table, glasses turned upside down waiting for wine, two sets of cutlery. A restaurant meal had a process that should be followed – pick your choice of still or sparking water, a first plate, a second plate, a small carafe of wine, perhaps a dessert and always coffee. It was unthinkable not to finish with coffee.

One day I called in at a riverside restaurant, a single isolated house built on the floodbank, with a straight road cut between fields to get there. On the step outside, there was a cat basking in the sunshine, inside, a dog lay sleeping and a small fire flickered.

There were six people eating, all professional men. I admired the smartness of their jumpers, fine wool sitting smooth over their crisp ironed shirts. I just wanted some quick food but didn't want to challenge the waitress's incomprehension that I would eat a single plate of food without drinking something, so I gave into the ceremony of the meal and ordered pumpkin and sage ravioli, which came soaked in butter and cheese, tasting sweet like marzipan. I took each mouthful slowly, mopping the plate with bites of crusty bread, taking sips of wine. I basked in the room, the sunshine dappling over the small plants on each table, the white tablecloth and napkins, so clean and crisp. I savoured my ice-cream meringue semifreddo, my coffee, my slightly fizzy red wine. The whole experience was as good for me as a languorous bath. As I finished, they were getting ready to close at 3pm. I wonder whether this place would exist in such a lonely location in the UK, serving ten people at lunchtime for €23 each.

Later that evening, making my camp in a secluded tree plantation, I ate the carton of heavy barley soup I'd been carrying for two days, chopping a mozzarella ball into it for extra protein. A hare rustled nearby – I caught sight of its ears bounding a hasty retreat when I turned to the noise.

Since descending from Slovenia, I'd spent six weeks on flat ground, less than 150m above sea level. It was a relief to climb hills again, heading into the Apennine Mountains, streetlights twinkling all the way over the plain behind me to where the Alps hovered, benevolent in the distance. A fleeting emotion hit me when I realised I was surrounded by trees for the first time in weeks; it was a calm and gentle sensation, an internal settling. I hadn't realised how fundamentally strange and artificial that wide open land felt to me.

The birds changed. The blank herons who waited silently at water edge had gone. So had the suspicious cormorants and the sarky seagulls, who fluttered behind ploughing tractors. I was back amongst the bright-eyed twig perchers and hedge hoppers, blackbirds bustling in the undergrowth, and they were all starting to sing again.

As the land changed, so did the way I crossed it; I was no longer walking in straight lines through quadrants of canal drainage but back to wriggling around the hills again, following the ancient paths that humans have made instinctively over centuries of working this land, feeling my body working and stretching differently. The tracks were mud or crushed stone, covered with blown oak leaves and they wound down to cross streams and then climb again, much more satisfying.

On the evening of Imbolc, the festival between the winter and spring equinox that celebrates the beginning of spring, I got lively whiffs of a warm wind and saw a few green shoots of bulbs poking up through the mulch. I'd managed to pass the worst of the winter down on the damp, misty plain.

The day I left Fidenza I had too much food, because people kept giving me sandwiches! Their eyes would widen when I said I was walking to Santiago de Compostela and they gestured to their arms to show me the goosebumps. They would ask me to say prayers for them as they handed me a couple of apples or a big ham sandwich. My prayers would be pebbles thrown into the sea at Finisterre as I thought of all the people I'd met, all the land I'd crossed to get there.

The day was mild enough that I could sit on the grass at the roadside and eat lunch, something I hadn't been able to do for months. It gave me a few moments where the worry lifted and it was only once I started to feel happy that I realised I was sad.

Without anxiety, I would have been completely happy and satisfied with where I was, my journey, my life. But this type of survival came with constant brain chatter that was hard to switch off. I had a mental ticker tape rolling in the background. *Hydration, leak in sleeping mat, budget, miles until next day off, how's the weather, do my shoes need replacing yet, how much food have I got, how high is the next mountain, what's that pain in my ankle?* The journey took a lot to maintain. Small details took on huge importance and, with so much solo thinking time, I fretted over each problem.

A few days into the heights, I was climbing a mountain, my first in weeks, treading my way steadily up towards the 1,300m peak. Someone told me there were wolves here and that's why I set up the tent that night, on the edge of cleared ground in the middle of the forest. It was a mistake. I awoke after a few hours realising that strong winds were bowing the tent down on top of me. Getting out in a fuzz of emergency adrenaline, I pegged the guy ropes out more firmly, but it didn't work. The wind was blasting off the river plain onto the mountain, slamming into the cleared area of trees and it wasn't long before the tent poles cracked and the tent collapsed on top of me.

I lay there, a dismal letter in a rippling plastic envelope, and rustled the phone out in front of my face. It showed 11pm. There is a certain black humour I experience when everything is truly fucked and all I can do is hold on until it passed. A huge rip in the tent fabric directly above my head allowed plenty of air in and the condensation to escape. All I could do was lie there in my useless tent, smiling grimly at how silly this was, try to get a semblance of sleep, and wait it out until morning.

I woke up again at 7am, still in the flat tent. A muscle had cramped deep in my glutes, sending spikes of pain around my hip bone when I lay on my right side. Despite this, I had managed some sleep and got out groggily to pee. No signs of wolves or boar, just a glorious golden sunrise and a clear blue sky, as if the overnight assault had never happened. I looked at the ruined tent and wanted to cry, but instead I crawled back into it and pulled the sleeping bag over my head for a few pathetic minutes before admitting that this was ridiculous behaviour and would not solve a single problem.

This journey was about so much more than the physical walking ability. It was about logistics and problem-solving. It was about maintenance and self-care. It was about stubbornness and stamina.

Now I had a new puzzle to fret over – whether to attempt to fix the ripped tent myself, buy a new one from limited options nearby, or buy the best one I could online. Each solution had drawbacks, time delays, inefficiency, potential equipment failure and there was no immediately obvious right answer.

Over the mountain and down to Bardi, the next town, where all the hotels I called were either closed or full and I sat in a bar, forlorn, trying to think through what to do next. By 4pm I was starting to feel desperate and after friendly conversation at the bar, a man said that I should come with him to the priest.

As I followed him through town, not knowing where this would lead me, I realised that he was drunk on a Sunday afternoon, kind eyes over a moustache that wriggled when he smiled and a faint booze reek that I hadn't noticed at first. He was gentle though, and Don Luigi, the priest, although a little nonplussed, listened to his explanation and then took me next door into an empty, functional building full of ice-cold air. We climbed four flights of stone stairs, trailing my hand on a dark wooden bannister that curved around each turn and at the top floor, the priest opened a door marked *Stanza dei pellegrini* showing me into a sparse room with bare walls, three single beds with thin blankets, a small kitchen unit in the corner and a central table and chairs. Don Luigi wasn't very talkative, just handed me the key, telling me to come down in the morning and tell him how long I wanted to stay – or so I thought.

I explored the kitchen for cooking supplies to complement my rucksack stores. A tin of peas, some pasta. Not much. I ate my packet of cheesy polenta, with the peas tipped on top, plus some dried sausage meat. The faded tinned peas felt despondent. It was a sad meal to eat alone, but it was all I had, and I needed the nutrition.

I felt like I could sink down to the ground and instantly fall asleep. I had shed no tears but my body felt as if I'd had a crying fit – that strange, empty calmness that comes after an extreme of emotion, where your chest is both hollow and heavy at the same time and everything feels brittle and unreal.

I wanted to be held but I felt delicate, as if I was liquid inside and if anyone took me in their arms I would burst open and disintegrate. My life was just one small, stupid existence, too tiny to matter, and I was using it to walk across the surface of the planet with a level of determination that was approaching madness.

This was the reality of my second winter of walking. I was deeply tired and experiencing strange swings of emotion that were difficult to balance.

I felt stuck, no idea what to do next. I had a huge rip in my tent, limited material available to fix it, and I wasn't even sure it was worth trying.

I had already claimed two replacement poles for this tent, the last one just a few weeks previously. I feared that the company would say this purchase had reached the end of its life, but decided it was worth a try and messaged them despairingly before going to bed. The blankets felt damp from lack of use, while the gas heater clicked on and off all night, slowly bringing the room to a liveable temperature.

The hollowness of deep exhaustion not only manifested in my body but in my actions. I ate at a pizza restaurant. I spent time in the back room of a café, spinning out a tiny coffee. I wandered around the town a little but fundamentally had very little to do. I felt limp, low energy – unwilling to wash, or mend my kit, or do anything wholesome. It made the room feel extra sparse: the dirt on the two electric hobs of the kitchen unit, the dingy thin metal cooking pots piled in the cupboard.

I already knew that I had a hard time being alone in hotel rooms. The utter solitariness of more than two days in the same place weighed heavily upon me and I didn't want to wait too long in this strange, blank room in the echoing, empty building. Despite my attempted explanation, the priest didn't understand why I was here, as I realised when he knocked loudly on the door of the room to ask when I was leaving. I did my best, showing him the ripped tent and the email I'd sent to the tent company, translating some simple phrases on my phone. He went, seeming to accept it, but I was left with the uneasy sensation of being unwanted. This room was for pilgrims on the Franciscan Way to stay one or two nights and I was pushing at the boundaries of propriety by staying longer.

After a couple of days nervously refreshing my email, eventually I had resolution. The company would replace the broken tent pieces, but warned me it was the last time! I just needed to wait another four days for a package from Ireland. I enlisted the help of a friendly woman I met in a yoga class to translate for me with the priest. The first thing he asked for was my name and what journey I was making, and I realised just how in the dark he'd been about this strange woman, brought to his doorstep by a drunk, unable to speak more than broken sentences of a common language.

Once the priest gave me proper permission and I knew the tent piece was en route, something settled inside me and I could relax into my enforced break in Bardi. It's very easy to get stuck in the pressure of constant forward motion and be unable to mentally release yourself. I cooked good carb-heavy food for energy replenishment – beans and rice, chickpeas and lentils, in thick tomatoey beefy stews.

Across a café, I started talking to people with Welsh accents and discovered the depth of migration history between Bardi and Wales. Many of the Italians who'd emigrated to Wales over the past century, setting up cafés and ice-cream parlours as ways to survive, originated from here. Romeo from Ebbw Vale had retired back to Bardi, his ancestral home, and brought his Welsh wife with him; they invited me for tea. This felt like an area of Italy without airs and graces. When I entered the country, I had been in awe of the meals, the pomp, the ritual, the classy clientele after the raw and rugged Balkan people. Liguria was relatively poorer, less showy than Veneto, mildly grubbier.

Finally, after the unexpected week's break, I received the tent and could set off again, receiving a grudging farewell from Don Luigi. I would climb again, taking a route up to 1,700m and joining a long distance path called the Alta Via dei Monti Liguri (High Route of the Ligurian Mountains), snaking its way along the watershed between the immense flat Po valley and the Mediterranean coast. Water that fell to my left would travel 20 miles to the Ligurian Sea while the water that fell to my right would go more than 300, popping out into the Adriatic Sea a few miles south of Venice.

The Alta Via was very remote, not designed to end neatly at evening accommodation, or pass near lunchtime restaurants. It didn't seem to route through any villages at all, for the full 300km length. I would have to make special detours down to shops for refuelling. I missed the lack of bars for coffee and sandwich stops but enjoyed planning for multiple days without shops, counting the number of meals left in the dwindling weight of my food bag.

I spent a night on the slopes between Bardi and Bedonia, tucked against a woodpile high on the hill while the wind blew all night. Then I plunged happily into the patient forests where deer barked and boar snuffled, to the depths of trees that stood silent in their winter bareness, waiting for the birds to sing again and the sun to show them spring. The leaves were thick on the ground, the bright orange of beech and oak blown into the grooves of the path that wound thin and twisting, up and ever up into white iced, rocky summits.

Navigating frozen snow patches on the shady sides of summits was sometimes a hairy experience and I was only at 1,700m. The frozen heights of the 2,000m Alp crossing into France loomed ahead, only a few weeks away.

I enjoyed these Ligurian mountains, walking felt right again, no longer a tired struggle. I didn't understand what had happened down there on the plain, whether it had been illness or landscape or the long dark nights of January 2020, but I had felt awful for a few weeks. Now, after the unexpected Bardi break and the passing of Imbolc, as the earth was turned towards spring and I was climbing in the free and open air of higher ground, I felt good again.

The sun turned from weedy to warm and started to blind me

in the afternoons, beginning its full golden summer brightness. I started to see flowers, clumps of primroses, solitary shafts of crocus and occasional violets, tiny and sheltered.

Torriglia was the next town for resupply, a tight little collection of tall houses, beautifully antique in the way that only Italy had managed on this journey so far. I came through an arch into the old town square, a sign on the wall casually stating that this had all been here since the 12th century.

I looked more closely at the sign and cheered: St Ursula was patron saint of the town!

Having an unusual name is wonderful. I love being the little she-bear, but one small downside is that I rarely meet other Ursulas and will search in vain every time there is a display of inscribed mugs or keyrings.

I made enquiries in a restaurant and the kind owner called the priest who called the library who called the local historian and so it was that I found myself standing in front of the church with Giuseppe the assistant priest and Mauro the historian, learning more about the life of Ursula and how she came to be associated with Torriglia.

I made a final visit to the carved doors of the church to take a photo with the legendary Ursula, and a woman rushed across the square to greet me. She was British Laura, and the village telegraph had called to tell her there was a countrywoman in town.

I walked with her down to the next village, where she found me a free pilgrim bed at the church. Then the next day she shuffled English lessons around to come and accompany me up over the mountains.

Laura was another intrepid woman, who had run her own thousand-mile journey from Rome to London, following the Franciscan Way.

It was refreshing to chat so easily to someone who understood so much of what I was going through. She didn't put any blank wall of uncrossable difference between us by calling me crazy or asking why. She knew how it was to sweat and grimace and collapse and after a short time on the ground feeling close to death, to get up and keep on going, just because you had an idea and you're determined to see it through.

After a couple more joyous days of gorgeous mountains, I dropped down to Genoa for a birthday weekend break. Ursula was 40!

Genoa was piss-soaked and grime-crusted. I wouldn't sit down in a single doorway. A port town, it had the faintly disinterested air of a city where thousands of new faces have been arriving and passing through for centuries.

Down at the harbour, I looked back from the water to this lego city, blocks of buildings jutting out from the steep mountains, built against and on top of each other. I walked through tiny narrow streets in the old town full of delightful shops, like garment repair or musical instruments, butchers and greengrocers, and wondered at the variety of human faces, the different shapes of bodies, the distortions of age.

It was a city of dogs. Dogs in shops, dogs in restaurants, dogs belonging to shops, standing in doorways, unfussed by crowds. Dogs pissing on antique carvings.

I floated through it, scattering leaves under café tables, eating divine cakes, twisting through crowds, struggling to absorb this labyrinth, distracted by the whirl of consumerism. Forests were simpler to exist in; I felt purposeful there, connected to the fundamentals of existence.

Aurelio, my Airbnb host, was calm and kind; we ate meals together, chatted in the kitchen. A few people were cancelling their bookings with him, citing the coronavirus. He felt foreign tourists didn't realise how big Italy was, that problems in one part of the country shouldn't affect another. A few people in the narrow streets were wearing masks, but life mostly proceeded as normal. There were no cases in the city.

During January 2020, as I had been crossing the flat land of central northern Italy, coronavirus came creeping around the world. The first few cases in Europe would have arrived as I was climbing into the Apennines. It didn't feel like a present danger to me, more like a strange news story centred on China, some kind of mystery new disease. I wasn't really interested, focused on actualities rather than abstract dangers.

I don't recall Covid being discussed by the pensioners of Bardi at the beginning of February, just days after the first cases were confirmed in Italy.

When I came down into Torriglia, eight days later, I learnt that a few towns up in provinces further north had been put into quarantine. I tried to remember whether I might have walked through them, counting dates on my fingers as if I'd missed a period. Laura, the bouncy Brit, was being asked not to travel to Milan by the mother of one of the children she taught. We discussed the paranoia that was clutching some people in a particularly intense grip. She needed to pass through the huge city to visit a friend and we discussed how unlikely it was she'd encounter someone who was ill.

For us two adventurers, who had trained ourselves not to be intimidated by risk, it seemed overcautious to be so scared. The online rumours all seemed so abstract. I stayed so far away from other people most of the time, camping in the wild, waving at cars from a distance. This didn't feel like something that should affect me.

On the 27th February 2020, I hugged Aurelio as I left his house to take the train back to the small village high above the valley and the busy roads down to Genoa. I didn't know that it would be the last time I'd touch anyone for almost five months.

I was a couple of weeks away from France and felt tired of Italy, ready for a new country, the feeling of progress as I crossed a border. I decided to walk a bit harder, take less time off. There were the Alps to cross and I wanted to go up high on a wild route.

After a week I called in at Carcare to dry my damp kit and charge my power bank. There was a restaurant – 'closed for cleaning' said the sign on the door. I'd seen the same in a few places recently, perhaps a code for sheltering themselves against the coronavirus, which was now thickly sweeping some parts of Italy. Not where I was, yet, only 24 cases in a regional population of 1.5 million, but maybe this was a good time of year for a restaurant to close, hope this would all be gone by summertime when the real wages were earned. The virus felt present in Italy now: there were posters telling people to keep their distances, pasted newspaper bills listing the latest deaths. I eyed people warily, as they watched me in return. Would anyone ask why I was travelling? Would anyone tell me I shouldn't? A woman was coughing behind the greengrocer's counter, pulling a scarf up around her face and trying to hide her sniffs as she worked the till. I washed my bananas when I got back to the hotel room, made sure I threw the bag away without touching the handle again. Was this how to keep safe? It felt clumsy and ineffective, a pantomime of precaution taking.

Overnight, Italy locked down entire provinces, putting regions to the north and east of me into lockdown. My hotel landlady and I had a quick chat in the morning. 'It's serious, isn't it?' We stood at the doorway in silence, acknowledging this weird situation before waving an awkward goodbye where we might have briefly touched each other's arms, maybe hugged.

The forest felt completely natural in contrast, far away from this strange infection. I sat to eat my lunch, comfy on a patch of sun-warmed pine needles, watching the light dapple through the trees, lolling in the dirt as if it was a dinner table. *There is no separation from this place for me, it's not somewhere I visit, I live here*, I thought.

And yet that was an illusion; I may have been living closer to wild nature than many people, but I was still firmly bonded to the human world.

I found myself estranged from both as I woke up to the news that the whole of Italy had gone into lockdown. I'd found a church in a forest clearing, the building locked up but with an arched opening into a cellar that I could shelter in. It had a long wooden table and benches, smoke-blackened walls from dozens of ineffectual fires in the crumbling corner fireplace. I'd slept cosy on the bench as winds crashed branches overnight and now I stared in disbelief at my phone screen, world news barging into my nature bubble.

The government had confined people to their homes.

I looked out through the archway to the forest, where water continued to gurgle from the spring, the trees swayed in the breeze, and the morning mist slowly dissolved in the heat of the sunshine.

Movement was restricted.

I wasn't supposed to go anywhere.

I had nowhere to go.

FLEEING

Hunkering down in Italy for an unknown length of time felt unnecessary when I was so close to the border and the freedom to continue walking in France. I hadn't touched another human being for twelve days, and I spent most of my time alone in nature; how could I be a risk?

A useful tweet caught my attention: 'In a troublesome situation you need just enough information to make a plan. Any more than that only feeds anxiety.'

So make a plan then, I thought, as I sat in the forest with no idea of the state of the country outside it, and I created three options:

Continue as planned on the Alta Via, which should take another week to get to the border, including the high mountains. Cons: potential snow on high ground and uncertain legality of my leaving the country on foot.

Find somewhere to lockdown in Italy. Cons: difficult to find somewhere to stay, either expensive or with a stranger, unknown length of delay to the journey.

Get out of the country as quickly as possible, by bus or train, doesn't matter. Cons: feels like giving up in the face of difficulty, compromises the integrity of the walk, I would lose the claim of walking every step.

Was public transport running? Were hotels open? I asked my Italian-speaking new friend Laura to find out. I read that police checkpoints had been introduced on major roads and train stations. If I went down to the city, would I be able to leave?

Laura came back with the news. The hotels she'd called weren't allowed to accept new business unless people were travelling on 'essential' journeys.

Without hotel access, I couldn't go down to the big city, so that left two options. Stay put or get out of Italy ASAP. People were contacting me to see if I needed help finding somewhere to stay, but it just didn't feel right. I wanted to keep moving. This was the only country in Europe to confine citizens to their homes and I wasn't resident here, or an Italian citizen. I had the right to leave, didn't I? This was all so new and uncertain.

Looking at the map, there were some low hills ahead, a couple of small towns, and then the huge mountains started, with a long, thin valley poking west into a surrounding semicircle of 2,000m peaks, the French border snaking along the highest points. I hunted around the map, trying to find paths that would cross into France without climbing too high into dangerous snowy conditions that I was unequipped for, and eventually fixed on a route at the head of the valley.

At this point, it didn't occur to me to break the journey and flee to the UK; a lockdown in a single country didn't feel like enough of an emergency yet. I thought I could get to France and be free to walk again; there were hardly the number of cases there that Italy had. Going home felt like giving up, and the effort involved in entering the transport system to cross borders, going to cities and putting myself into enclosed transport tubes, exchanging air with other humans, seemed like the worst way to catch infections. For ecological reasons I choose not to fly across Europe, so breaking the journey to go home would mean a complicated and stressful multi-day, multiple train or coach journey. Much better to keep walking alone in the fresh air.

The Italian news kept coming. 'No non-essential travel... Fines for those who do not comply... Police checkpoints.' Yet here I was, all alone on a track in a beautiful, quiet forest, crunching through drifts of fallen beech leaves, just as it had always been. What was happening out there in human society?

All this frantic phone checking had depleted my battery. I had 17% and nothing in the power pack. I needed to find a place to charge up, buy some food, then I could head straight for the border. At the first crossroads there was a bar, with a scrawled notice on the door, flapping in the breeze. 'Closed because of coronavirus until April 6th.' There were people inside and I knocked, standing back from the door.

'Are all the bars closed?'

'Yes, the government has shut us down,' said the small woman who answered me, black eyeliner crinkled in the corners of her wrinkled eyes. I stared in shock, not sure what to say, my terrible Italian limiting me to the basics.

'Please can I charge my phone?'

She let me in.

Inside I found six people milling around the bar, TV news blaring at full volume. I plugged in and we all sat in silence, the room thick with stressed plumes of cigarette smoke. They did not know what would happen to the business, only that they must close. They did not know if any government help would come, only that they must stay at home. The room looked so normal, just six other healthy people, but could one of them be harbouring a dangerous illness? This virus was starting to feel as if it could be everywhere.

I said goodbye, avoiding the well-meant handshake, and set off towards the town, already feeling like a fugitive.

It was an odd road, first passing through the tunnel entrance of a deserted Napoleonic fortress, then past a derelict restaurant before closing off to vehicles altogether. I clambered over the barriers, thick drifts of windblown leaves covering the unused road. A landslide had destroyed the road further down, winter water rushing underneath the tarmac and picking it away, pebble by pebble. I slept in the forest, under the bright moon, with deer crashing nearby.

As the first few houses started and I walked on cobbled streets, looking at shuttered windows and crumbling wood, I wondered if there was anyone there at all. In this sense of chaos, normal expectations had shifted, as if I might find smoking ruins or hear wailing from windows. I ducked away from a couple of policemen on a street corner, quickly checked my map for a back street detour. A cluster of people outside the pharmacist, hanging about at a safe distance from each other, eyed me in silence as I walked past, head down.

In the supermarket, it had all changed. There was tape on the floor to tell us the distances to keep while queuing, lots of people wearing masks. It felt tense, lots of sideways glances. I packed my bag with three days' worth of food and got the heck out of town. There was a side road in the valley ahead, then a few miles on a main road before I could cut away to escape onto a track that wound around the edge of the high mountains and down into France, seemingly unopposed.

I walked past sunset and realised I was on the edge of a village with no time to cross it before darkness. Finding a boarded-up house, I sat under the eaves to eat a carton of bean soup with a creamy mozzarella ball chopped into it. A man appeared, talking on his phone, cigarette hanging, bustling at the boot of his jeep. I froze, then sighed in resignation and kept eating until he finished his call, trying to at least get the messy food out of the way before he kicked me off the property. He was fine in the end, seemingly that kind of guy; busy, tough, able to cope with anything. I told him I was walking to France. 'But the coronavirus,' he said, and I told him I couldn't stay put with nowhere to live. 'There's police further up,' he said, referring to the border between Piedmont and Liguria, up at the head of this valley where my side track joined the main road.

I liked how he'd immediately accepted that I would go, without telling me I was wrong. The world had gone awry and everything felt strange and uncertain, but at least this man was not judging me.

'Can I sleep here?'

'Of course, I'm sorry I can't open the house for you.'

There was low mist in the morning and I could see snow on the mountains as swirls of the hanging cloud opened and closed. I was in contact with family but, once I knew everyone was ok, it only added to the sense of urgency and worry. Anxious people were pressuring me in every electronic communication, creating a background buzz of tension that it was difficult to disconnect from.

At about 11am, I had to walk in front of an industrial estate before entering forest track. A police car came slowly towards me. This was it. I was caught.

He rolled down the window, sharply gesturing me away as I bent down to hear him.

'You should be inside.'

I said nothing.

'What are you doing? Where have you walked from?'

I named the last town, trying to pretend that this was normal and I was just out for a stroll. 'Where am I going? Oh, just the next town.'

He stared at me, taking me in. This threadbare subterfuge obviously wasn't working. I took a deep breath.

'Actually I'm going to France.'

There it was, the exposed truth. The man asked where I was from, where did I live, how long had I been in Italy? As I told my story, he understood then – that there was no home for me to go to.

'You're supposed to stay still,' he said in English, 'the coronavirus.'

I looked at him, admitting quietly and with finality, 'I can't.'

We paused. He stared ahead, fingers moving to his radio mic. I was telling him openly that I could not follow the rules. He was realising that the only way to solve this problem would be to take me with him and find me a place to stay.

'Oh, go.' He flipped his hand in the air, sighing. I stammered out some words about living in the forest, about not being a danger, but he didn't want to hear them. The decision was made. I was a problem best avoided.

I was not jubilant as I walked on, but relieved. Was what I was doing illegal or did it just feel that way? I was a foreign citizen and Italy's borders were open. I had the right to leave the country; I just wasn't supposed to walk to the exit.

This seemed to be Schrödinger's exodus, simultaneously legal and illegal, and I felt a strong urge to remain unseen.

I walked upwards, tired, on the third day of lockdown stress, my tenth straight day of walking. Clouds misted around me as I climbed 500m and I walked in dripping wet white. The winding road had ragged edges, occasionally it had fallen away completely.

I looked ahead on the map to see the first houses, thinking I'd check there for water. They were summer cabins, shuttered and empty, but one had an outside tap. I slept in the porch to avoid putting my tent up in the mist.

I breakfasted on powdered oats and a banana, counting out my food rations for another day, the portions of protein and carbs. I hoped to cross into France that day, but didn't know how much snow I'd face. My route wound around the shoulder of the high Alpine peaks which had been gleaming white at me for weeks.

I started the day in mist, as I ended it, but occasional swirls of wind cleared the cloud and I got flashes of the view, incredible scenery, with edges of high mountains to my right and a long valley to the left. After 5 miles, I reached the final village before I turned off the track. It was empty. I laughed to myself – of course it was, in this newly apocalyptic Italy. Closed roads and shuttered villages, it was a coincidence that they'd all appeared on my route since the lockdown started but it added to the eerie feeling that the foundations of society were shaking. The shuttered ski lodges looked creepy in the mist; I saw no sign of life anywhere. I stood by the fountain and refilled my water bottles in the silent village.

The track that would take me across the border led away from the central crossroads, a long straight path that climbed to a shoulder swoop between two peaks and then doglegged back behind the mountains to my right.

It was tarmacked for a while but eventually landslides covered the road and the manmade path bubbled away to grass. It was a long steady ascent, easy enough. The mist started to wisp away, giving me glimpses of blue sky, then lifting completely so I could see the forest below, the hills ahead and the thick white snow drifts, steep above me.

Stressful messages crowded my phone; I tried to respond but wound up in tears. It all felt so awful out there, everyone on high alert, the internet buzzing with frenzied questions that nobody could answer.

I'm tired, I can't think, I've been walking for days, I'm trying to get out of the country, I'm climbing mountains. Leave me alone, this is really hard and takes all my focus just to keep going. I needed support, not to be warned how dangerous everything was or to be bombarded with stupid questions about travel insurance.

I put the phone away, blubbering. *Let society carry on imploding, far away from here.* In the beautiful, peaceful bubble of a day's solitary mountain walking, I had all I needed to survive. I didn't need to be weighted with the constant worry over Italian quarantine, I didn't need to carry the anxiety of other people; to get through this I just had to be present and focus on my steps. As I breathed in and out, and looked around me, the tension eased.

The track was mostly clear, but when it curved around the slopes there started to be snow patches in the shade. At first I could swerve around them but soon the track was thick with ice and I stopped to put on my ice spikes.

It's harder to walk on snow, each step takes more energy. I was in brilliant sunshine and away to my left there was a sea of cloud, which sometimes lapped over me in ethereal gusts of mist that glowed golden white with the sunlight outside them. At the shoulder of the mountain there was a strange tunnel, about 20 metres long, cutting through the earth to the other side of the mountain.

Ahead there was another view; more snowy mountain peaks nearby and another sea of mist, but now I was facing France. I lunched at the tunnel mouth on a tin of tuna, a tin of white beans for extra carbs and the usual instant potato with mayo and parmesan mixed through it.

As the mountains faced south there was no more snow on the track, just a bright, open path, and I could walk quickly down and around the basin of the valley where the final Italian village nestled. After another small climb I was finally standing on the border. All these weeks I'd been focused on France, wanting to finish Italy for the feeling of progress, the starting of a new country, but, for the first time on this journey, the border crossing was a complete anticlimax. The achievement meant nothing. I just wanted to descend to the first town, find a hotel and feel safe.

I'd had sore skin on my inner thighs since I left Genoa, having bought some unsuitable leggings that had stretched until the fabric bunched and rubbed the skin away. I'd been extensively bitten by unknown insects. Every morning there were two or three new red patches on my back or legs. My skin felt clammy with congealed sweat, I could rub black rolls of grime away under my fingers. I had tape on my chafed skin to stop it bleeding. I itched. I'd walked for ten days straight, wearing the same clothes. I was a stinky, blotchy, greasy, chafed, frazzled, nervous mess.

The downwards path descended into pine forest, winding around mossy boulders and fragrant trees. Up on the mountain was large and wild, the sense of untameable spirit that big mountain views always give me. Here the sensations were small and cute: streams crossed the path back and forth, sun dappled through the trees and there was the pleasant scent of pine.

Just before sunset I found a flat spot and settled down. I was in France. I made it. 'Bonjour,' I whispered, as I woke up, and giggled to myself.

Fear grew as I approached La Brigue, the first village with a hotel. World worries had got under my skin. As much as I'd tried to shake it, tension had me gripped. How could I ground myself when the earth had shifted?

I felt as if I had the word 'ITALY' stamped on my forehead. That if police spotted me they would force me into fourteen-day isolation. That the hotel would ask where I'd travelled from and refuse to take me. I imagined the plague bell ringing, the pressing of an under-desk alarm.

None of that happened. I went to a bar and ordered a coffee and pain au chocolat, listening while the other customers chatted about the coronavirus and the Italian lockdown. We were in a beautiful square in the centre of a very sweet village, with yellow stone houses, all very calm and picturesque. I called the hotel from the bar, 'It's 11am but can I come now?' They asked for my passport, processed the arrival, and took me to the room without any questions. I collapsed face down on the bed, the beautiful, smooth, clean bed, shaking and close to tears, finally feeling safe after a very tense and uncertain five days.

The Covid tension was here too, I hadn't left it behind in Italy. *I should look for a place in France,* I thought. *I'll get somewhere to stay while this feeling of international chaos blows over.* I'd only need a week, maybe two, I naively imagined. I don't think I wanted to believe how serious this could be.

Everyone was shouting on social media, broadcasting barks of fear but nobody seemed to be listening. Half of the newspaper articles were suppositions: 'Here's what could happen if...' and we were all swimming in a whirl of uncertainty, running out of breath, toes feeling for the bottom, panicked body jerks when there was nothing there.

FIRST LOCKDOWN

Have you ever swum so far out to sea that you can no longer see the shore? Have you ever been untethered there, the only object inside the circle of a thin straight horizon line, floating in endless blue?

The closest I ever came to it was in a kayak, as I paddled the length of the River Danube, most of it a mile wide, and then followed the edge of the Black Sea from the river mouth at Sfântu Gheorghe down to Mangalia, the last port town in Romania before the border with Bulgaria.

I realised many things on that journey; one was that I make bad choices of men. That time on the river, I did wildly dangerous things when my bad choice of man hurt me at my very core and I got the wrong kind of drunk to obliterate the pain. All of these things had happened to me before, but this time I could see the relationship between them clearly. I was hurt, I learnt, I got publicly shamed and I almost drowned in the Danube; and all of those details are a story for another time, that perhaps will never come.

Another thing I learnt back then was the elasticity of time when you are a tiny, slow-moving thing immersed in a very large space.

It's hard to sense progress when hardly anything around you seems to be moving; when you look at the land close by, it slips past slowly, tree by tree, but when you look ahead at the river nothing has changed and the tiny bridge in the distance remains exactly the same size. Minutes stretch on and the bridge comes infinitesimally closer until it looms large. Passing underneath it is an epic event; a dark line of shadow rushing over the kayak to bathe you in shade, as you lean back to marvel at the structure, and then it is gone in a cold gust of air and everything is the same again, just the wide river and the distant banks, as if the bridge was never there.

Once into the Black Sea, I spent hours kayaking in the hot sun, where the ripples shone like molten metal if you looked towards the light.

I kayaked beside a thin line of yellow beach, a dusty road that I could barely see and telegraph poles stretching away until they jangled into a fuzz of overlap.

Dip dip went the kayak paddle as I churned past, counting steadily the monotonous progression of poles to 5, then 10, then 20. Dip dip, paddle on; for hours the sun shone on me and the water, and the telegraph wires swooped and rose. Eventually, the last pole, number 84, came towards me and then there was nothing; they were never there, just the waterline and beach remained, a high row of sand dunes and me in the water, dipping my paddle endlessly.

Back on the Danube, when I turned the final bend, I had experienced the shock of the riverbanks ending and the water opening out to meet the sky, unbounded, for the first time in three months. Plunged into lockdown in Artignosc-sur-Verdon, Provence, the banks of the known world had receded.

This quarantine was like swimming in the ocean where I could not see the land. I was lucky, I had to keep remembering this. The water was calm for me; thanks to donations, there were no crashing waves of financial uncertainty. Instead I was becalmed. All I had was the slow, monotonous chop-chop of arms into water and the lapping, spitting and breathing, over and over again and no knowledge of when this would ever end and no land in sight and no way to mark progress and everything was the same every morning, another day alone just swimming, swimming to stay alive and not drown.

When the lockdown came to France, a day into my La Brigue hotel oasis, I put out a message to friends asking for help and through someone's sister came the message, 'Yes, we have an empty home

200km from you. Take a train, here is the code for the key box. Help yourself. Be welcome. Please water the fruit trees.'

I didn't think too far ahead, only glad to have a place to stay in a world that had suddenly become even more unwelcoming to a person without shelter. France had made it illegal for people to be outside for more than an hour and, having fled one country, without the energy to do it again, understanding that this awful situation could no longer be avoided, I needed somewhere safe and I gladly took the offer.

I didn't anticipate that I was plunging into a deep pool of solitude, leaving me floundering in loneliness that was sometimes choking.

Every day was the same. I had very little to do and I would see nobody unless I walked the few minutes to the small village shop to attempt conversation in a language I barely spoke. Neighbours politely waved but were uninterested in who I was. We had all withdrawn to our known circles, there was no safety in strangers, conversation had become contamination.

It was no good trying to talk to people anyway. I often felt tears welling as I tried to speak, unable to smother the strangeness of my situation in daily pleasantries.

Conversations on the phone kept me connected to UK friends and family but they only lasted a few hours and there were so many more to fill.

I knew that lurking depression was undermining my foundations like hidden rot and did what I could to guard against it with a schedule of healthy activities: a plan for dancing along to online exercise; a wrestling of the bramble shoots that infested the bottom of the garden; a regular stroll. But my body hurt, my mind fizzed with anxiety, and I couldn't settle to anything for longer than an hour.

I sank inevitably into a monotony of days, struggling to find the motivation to be healthy, knowing that I would suffer if I didn't, suffering anyway. My attention span crumbled to dust and I flitted between minutes with the breathless angst of a butterfly at a window.

The creeping sun came to heat the sofa space where I lay, staring at my phone in slothful monotony until I was sick and disgusted, fed to brimful with information that was all empty sugar and no nutrition.

The lack of comfort to be found online only intensified my isolation. Social media postings festered with fear and anger and nit-picking and conspiracy.

It felt like there was no firm definition to the world, that we had lost the certainty of prediction that gives humans their power over nature. The shape of the future was gone and emotions churned in the face of the blank, black maw that had opened instead.

Many people were vomiting fear-fuelled speculation online, frantically unfurling fragments of information, trying to twist thread, knit stories, desperate to lay down facts into paths that we could follow back into a known world and reclaim our future.

I felt scared by these slack days, this unproductivity, this infinity of time. I didn't feel strong enough to maintain a routine, not certain enough of who I was. All my confidence dissolved, I no longer believed in myself, I hated what I saw in the mirror.

I felt that I would unravel, cease to exist. I wavered at the edges of self. The sea would swallow me. There is no perspective from water level when we are swimming to survive, no sensing of the size of the ocean.

Part of this struggling was because I was unavoidably confronted with the state of my satisfaction with life. This quarantine had locked us all into cupboards and, for many, once we had spent time hammering at the door, there in the quietness after the commotion, we had to turn and face the bare bones behind us, waiting in the dark.

When the known world shifted under our feet, when I was vulnerable, when it had been almost three months since I touched anyone, without an exciting journey to distract me, loneliness came creeping like a softly lapping tide to overwhelm me with the fact that there was nobody in the whole world waiting to open their arms to me, to press the length of their body against mine, to lie down with me and let our skin slide softly against one another.

And there was nowhere to go to escape that feeling. Just a slow desiccating stasis in endless days of the same routine, the same place that I could not leave. And the knowledge that I made the choices that brought me to this.

Life confined didn't suit me at all; I felt like a zoo animal, confused, frightened and frustrated to madness at the abrupt restriction, these alien circumstances.

I missed the freshness of the forests, sitting in silence watching the dappled sunlight through leaves with no thought of time, no deadline to return home, no limit on how far I could walk. I missed spontaneity and freedom, of walking all day with no knowledge of where I would sleep that night, no decision needing to be made until a couple of hours before sunset.

I felt at my calmest when I was walking long distance, the motion of movement and new stimulation, the certainty of a destination point but no pressure to get there. The wondrous pleasure of wild camping, sleeping in the forest or field corner and waking up with rain or birdsong. It was when the essentials of life were the closest to meaning everything; the engrossing simplicity of food, water, shelter, pain, sensation, sweat, stink, appreciation, wonder.

The days lengthened while I waited on hiatus.
The distant forests grew leaves.
The frosts thinned and melted to vibrant heat.
The lawn became lush and thick.
The moon waxed and waned.
I had crossed from Italy in snow, but would return to bare stone.
Eggs had been laid and fledglings had flown.

I watched it all from behind glass, separated from the meaning of the seasons for the first time in two years.

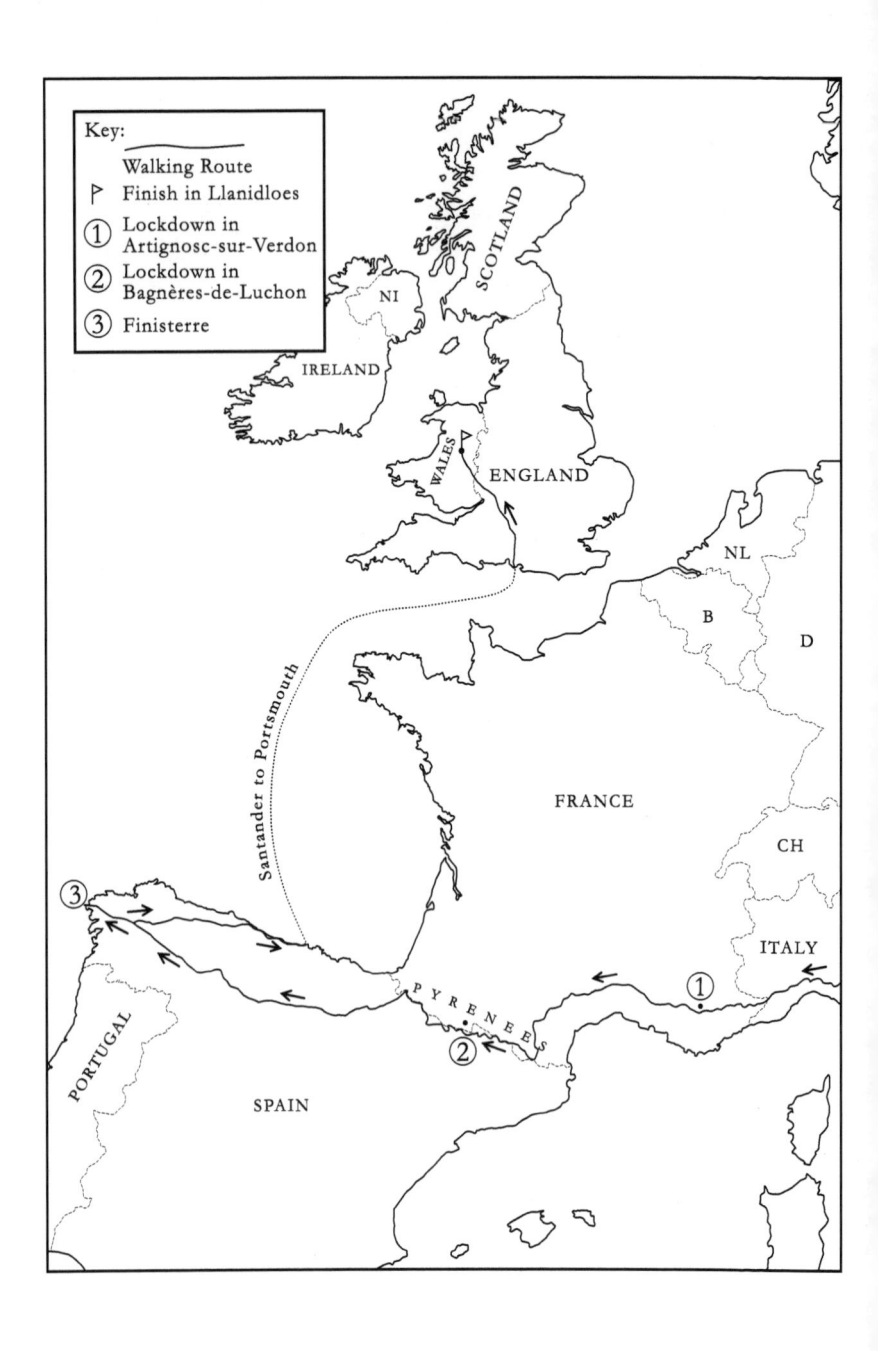

Key:
— Walking Route
⚐ Finish in Llanidloes
① Lockdown in Artignosc-sur-Verdon
② Lockdown in Bagnères-de-Luchon
③ Finisterre

FRANCE

By the end of June, infection rates had reduced, hospitals were no longer overwhelmed, economists were champing at the bit and Europe gradually regained its freedom.

Once French citizens were allowed more than 100km from their homes, after ninety-three days of waiting, I returned to the Alps and started walking west. The certainty of the journey had completely disappeared; the very acts of travelling, of mixing with strangers were freshly dangerous in a way they hadn't been five months previously. But I couldn't see any other way; this walk was my imperative and people were allowed to leave their homes. This journey was my everything, I had to do my utmost to finish it. While there was a chance to go ahead, while people around me had freedom of movement, I would continue.

As it came time to leave, I fretted my way through the final tasks, swallowing great gulps of fear that wanted to choke me as I scribbled frenzied lists. Part of me didn't want to leave; as much as I recognised the deep unhappiness and unsuitability of my situation, I still wanted to stay lying on a sofa watching Netflix forever, the eternal stasis of the ideal laze.

Starting again felt like plunging in as I closed the big wooden door to my lockdown home. Intrepid Elaine, the helpful neighbour, drove us 200km back east to the base of the peaks that marked the Italian/French border, as far up the stony mountain tracks as she could take the car. We paused, knowing we shouldn't, and hugged goodbye.

I set up camp in the grounds of a remote chapel. *This is it*, I thought, as I ate cold quiche and wiggled my toes, peering out of the tent flap every so often to check nobody had come to visit in the final hour before darkness. *I'm living on my wits again. I'm managing my life, carrying my own shelter, sourcing my own water, in charge of my movements.*

It was an immense satisfaction to sit in a tent that was not much bigger than my body, mesh roof brushing against my head, possessions tucked around my mattress, to look at my feet and know that they had made the journey today. That all I was achieving was coming from my own power.

That was what I had felt so intensely during lockdown: that my life was not under my own control.

The speed of time changed overnight. I sped up to striding again, measuring progress in steps not sunsets. The dreary limbo state of anxiety-induced purgatory was wiped away by the daily grind of mileage, nutrition, hydration and heat. I was immersed in the world, no longer trapped behind a screen. Like flicking a switch, my life became fluid again, wiping away the hopelessness of lockdown with a rush of enjoyment and appreciation of my surroundings.

As I trudged from the chapel up to the 2,200m peak of Monte Sacarello, seeing Italy brought a spurt of tears, remembering the rush and worry of my final days there, fleeing without a backwards glance. I could have restarted my route from La Brigue down in the valley but I had needed to climb this mountain and return to the border, to acknowledge Italy and say goodbye.

Retracing my steps, I descended through the green smell of growing things and the faint perfume of broom flower. Where sun came striking through shadowing pines, laburnum trees glistened in golden hollows. A return to nature meant a return to normality; there was no coronavirus in the kingdom of the lark.

A single chamois goat ran the long length of the downhill slope, frighteningly surefooted, before pausing at the tree line to stand and watch me. It gave a high-pitched alarm snort before disappearing and I wondered what it thought of the humans reappearing to invade the peace. How many more animals were free to mate this season without fear of the hunt?

Back in La Brigue, I spoke with the owner of a hotel. 'How is it for you? After the Covid?' I asked.

'This year will be hard,' he said. 'Normally we are full from May to September but last weekend we had half bookings and next week nothing at all. I will keep working, it's all I can do, and hope it will be better next year.'

'The hard part for me was being alone,' I said, 'that was my struggle of *le confinement*.'

'People in the village didn't help you?'

'Some did, but mostly they didn't know I was there. It felt like a time when people didn't want to reach out to strangers.'

'Here it was good. We helped each other a lot. It made us stronger, closer, as a community.' He smiled to himself as he wiped the milk from the coffee machine.

I'd returned to the summer heat of southern France, where I quickly learnt that it's best to get up as early as possible, 5am if you can. Watch the pink light of dawn come gently, then the strong yellow line of sunshine travel down from the mountain tops, get moving before the full heat blooms and the shadows are still cool.

Continuing west through the Maritime Alps, I made four huge climbs in the first ten days, each one more difficult than the last as my flaccid stamina slumped under pressure. My underused muscles had shrunk away and my legs felt hollow. The backs of my ankles hurt; once thick with springy muscle, they felt like overstretched plastic, flexed to splitting. I stuck to my targets, a rest and a swallow of water for every 10% altitude gain. The 60% glug, the 70% slug. Legs aching, hands pulling against walking poles, feet picking steps carefully, with a steep drop always to one side. Lizards flickered out of sight in the dry grasses, great lumbering beetles, occasional mosquitoes, that are not as sly as they think. The real ninjas were the sneaky tick and the invisible flea, unseen threats clinging to every grass blade.

I walked into small villages which clustered on protrusions and peaks, like barnacles moulded into sheltered crevices. I saw no animals, no agriculture; nobody was making cheese in their sheds or scything hay. The surrounding terraces, centuries old, so carefully carved and buttressed, were overgrown. Ripe cherries dangled glorious in the breeze. I would marvel at the beautiful architecture, peeling shutters, stone archways and perfectly placed plant pots, throw out some hopeful love towards a creeping cat, wash my face in the fountain, run my arms underneath the spout and feel the blood cooling under my skin.

When there were cafés to stop at, I watched the people of the village, as they kissed cheeks in greeting and clustered around tables. I saw waiters wearing masks, or with masks under their chins, or with no masks at all. Perhaps it was an intrinsic French disregard for rules, perhaps the slow slipping of pandemic precautions was happening everywhere. The brain's alert to danger in the mere brush of two hands together takes longer than mere months to establish.

As children ran playing, the village life I saw in rural France felt very far away from the fear and information overload of the pandemic news whirl. I was allowing online chatter over case numbers in New York to heighten my fear in France where, in this region of one million inhabitants, there was currently one diagnosis of Covid-19 per week.

I'd been alone on the footpaths for almost the entire fortnight, spotting a scattering of people on the weekends but mostly I saw no other walkers. I found myself covered in dozens of ticks, almost daily, and imagined them all waiting forlorn throughout the lockdown months, poised at the tip of grass blades, wondering where their next leggy dinner was.

I walked through the sawing screech of cicadas, which occasionally trailed to an apologetic halt as they sensed my approach, like a couple caught kissing in a quiet side street.

I walked along forestry tracks that trailed illogically in unexpected directions, splitting and turning for lorries on steep inclines. There were often no houses in the valleys, ancient shepherding traditions long decimated. Instead I stared out over pure, unbroken forest fuzzing the contours of the low mountain sides like body hair. I thought about all the deer with freedom to roam there, the wild boar, all the bears that would have been. People still warned me of wolves, but they were lone trekkers rather than an abundance of large packs and there was very little chance I'd encounter one. I imagined them as grizzled standouts against imposed development, locking themselves into their houses, peeking through curtains, burning compulsory purchase orders as golf courses and motorways are built around them.

In France, for the first time on this journey, I found more wild boar in the forests than deer; they were often heard foraging around my tent at night, lots of squeaking and snorting, pattering of feet. When I called out to let them know I was there, they didn't immediately leg it like the deer do, in a pell-mell crashing through trees. The boar would stay and make noise, rush to and fro, seeming to leave and then bustling back again in a cacophony of grunts and occasional deep, rumbling snorts that sounded terrifyingly monstrous. Over time, I realised they were creatures of habit and when their schedule was to eat at my camping spot that night, they would get agitated when they found me there. I was a squatter at their favourite lunch table, the one by the window, where they meet every week at 1pm, so all this noise was them gathering by the bar to stare and chat shit about me, just loudly enough to make me uncomfortable.

The walking became less solitary as I joined the GR4 footpath and came towards the tourist honeypot of the Verdon Gorge and Lac de Sainte-Croix.

Although entry from the UK was only permitted with proof of residency, summer holiday Schengen zone mixing was in full flow. I heard German and Dutch languages, overlapped for a few days with three Parisian boys. This mingling together, after so much considered separation, now felt wildly dangerous. We had all suffered, in different ways, and now, in those countries with reducing infection rates, we were emerging from restrictions, working out what had changed and how we needed to adjust ourselves, perhaps all in need of some small holiday joy.

My route west from the Alps through southern France took me close enough to my lockdown location that it was easy to detour and meet the owners, my benefactors, released from London and their intense medical jobs to flee to their beloved holiday home, denied to them for four months.

I had been their Covid-19 refugee, creeping in, pathetic and desperate, to shelter from a suddenly uncertain world. I had done what I could to ameliorate their longing (and my guilt at being there while they were denied) by sending daily photographs – tiles lit by the afternoon sunlight, the fresh flowering of the lily, an abundance of vine leaves, the view of the swimming pool. I tried to record the singing of the nightingales and orioles, told them when the poppies appeared in a gauze of red at field edges.

After months of online correspondence, they got out of the car in masks and we waved awkwardly from a distance. They'd come from a city with a much higher infection rate than here, and one was a doctor, so they were the danger to me and we had to forgo the welcome hugs.

I had arrived in the Artignosc house a couple of days before them and experienced a faint flickering of bad memories when I looked out from the sofa to the long wide view beyond the terrace, remembering all the days of staring at the same view, imprisoned in the frustration of endless time and not enough tasks, all the hopelessness of no escape.

The house was nicer with other people, especially those who were relaxed in their own home, unafraid to bring the table out to the terrace and use placemats and the good cutlery. We ate rabbit in mustard sauce, scalloped potatoes and a chicory salad, then a buttery rich apricot tarte tartin, as the sun set and the mosquito coils smoked thinly.

At a reunion lunch with Ruth and Elaine, the helpful neighbours, we drank champagne on an airy restaurant terrace overlooking the miles of flat plains towards Manosque and everything felt light and happy. We drove home through the thickly fragrant air of the full-bloom lavender fields, the deep thrumming of thousands of honey bees, hard at work on their harvest.

The sun was almost setting and I decided to swim in the fading light, sleepily buoyant with the remnants of lunchtime drinking. The light on the water matched the colours of the sunset sky, orange and pink, caught and framed in the dark pool edge, and I slipped into liquid warmth, enveloping me like velvet, like cream, like bliss.

I swam and floated and watched the light fade, feeling completely tranquil and realising I hadn't felt like this for months. Simple, beautiful moments of pleasure had gone missing, so agitated was I by the chaos of the pandemic, suffering in my lack of freedom, in my loneliness.

There weren't many moments that needed turning around in this journey; it was a mostly enjoyable experience, but in a passive way, obscured by muscle pain and insect bites. Joy is not the right emotion when you're gasping for breath, dripping with sweat, sitting on a faintly uncomfortable rock that is the only chance of shade, while mosquitoes hover greedily, even if you don't want to be anywhere else.

I so often talk about the grand feelings of this journey, the sweeping overviews of crossing mountains or sleeping under the stars. Sometimes though, my days were filled with a thousand small, beautiful details which made up a sense of awe and wonder that expanded to grandeur, but which feels impossible to capture.

The delicate conversation of a chime of barely glimpsed wrens, chittering from low pine branches early one morning, hopping and chatting as they watched me pass.

On one side of the hill, the grass was full of moths which circled away from my feet, making the ground seem to undulate with their flapping. In another place it was a host of baby grasshoppers in pastel yellow and green, who flicked themselves away from my passing in explosive group ecstasies.

Turning inwards on a curve of the path, I reached a stream and saw a deep pool. Unusually, it was crystal clear, just a tinge of blue in the deepness of the water, with no plants or algae growing, nothing lurking at the bottom but smooth rock. Slimy with sweat, I shrugged off my rucksack and lowered myself into the pool, fully clothed. The water boatmen jerked their way to the edges, away from this strange invader who was making ripples and loud noises. It was orgasmic, to feel the cool water against my skin; I sat panting, until I'd calmed down, watching greasy swirls of suncream and sweat spool out from me. A final ducking of my head under the water and I was out, to sit on a rock and drip from wet to dampness. I sat there and thought of everything and nothing, watching the sunlight, the leaves, the fine movements of insects passing. It was a moment of true mindfulness, something I couldn't grasp hold of back in lockdown, when my days were empty yet fretful.

As I moved towards the Luberon, France introduced a mandatory mask rule for enclosed spaces. I watched the half-adoption of these protection measures; waiters with masks under their chins, people pulling masks out of their grubby pockets to wear for five minutes before pulling them off again, hand sanitiser ready at the supermarket entrance but only used by about half the customers.

Cypress trees, tall and thin, dark lines of them, marked the scattered farmhouses in the dehydrated yellow hills. The Luberon national park was drier than the Verdon, fewer streams crossing my path. Rosemary and sage bushes covered the hills, their leaves curled by drought but still giving off bursts of familiar scent as I brushed past. As I headed towards the Languedoc region, the accent became more curlicued and I felt lumpy and thick-tongued in the attempting of it. The heat made it difficult to appreciate the Frenchness of the morning queues outside the bakeries, the women in flowing linen clothing, the men in neatly cuffed shorts and shirts, the effortless chic. It was hard to pay attention to the shaded village square, the Virginia creeper on the trellis, the yellow stone of the church, the smooth grey bark of the plane trees, the lion-head fountain, when my immediate urge was to plump down in a chair and ask for a Fanta with lots of ice, put my head on the table and wipe ineffectually at my streaming forehead.

Calling in for water at the last house before climbing out of the Golden Triangle into the Petit Luberon mountain range, I happened on the last permanent residents of the valley. Retired hippies, they'd built their house in the 70s, among the peasants and farmers, and then watched the valley change to holiday homes around them. Parisians and international migrants arrived in the 90s, clutching 'the book' (*A Year In Provence*). I expected them to passionately decry the change but they were quietly resigned, sitting on a sunny terrace sipping coffee from homemade terracotta cups, reminiscing about Mnsr. Dubois and his grand courgettes, the weekly trips to market with carts full of melons.

The people of the land were less apparent here, lost in a sea of gated holiday homes, peppered with privacy notices and security cameras. The countryside felt empty and quiet, full of large-scale crops that needed little maintenance; olive trees, sunflowers, lavender, vines.

I missed the rural fecundity of the previous summer, where Serbian villages felt bursting with life in comparison; gardens planted with lines of peppers, onions, potatoes, animals grazing, people everywhere.

The changes brought by the wealth of France felt similar to Britain; commuter villages, convenience foods; all the cars were modern and bland, the new builds suburbanly characterless. Security of wealth had replaced community trust and the whole country moved around, disconnected from roots to place.

***

The heat was the inescapable theme of this section, oppressive and never-ending, even at night. It felt like I was in an oven, when the supposed relief of moving air just puffed another enveloping huff of warmth to drape down, basting me, an unwilling roast piglet.

The stress on my system grew infinitesimally, sweat dripping into my eyes bead by bead. I mopped my cheeks and chin with the cloth wrapped at the head of my walking pole, breathing coming harder, faster, panting, pain in body increasing, until I looked at my arm to see the sheen on my skin and realised that every part of me was hot and sticky and overwhelmed and I had to get into the shade and stop.

I napped every afternoon, an exhausted fall into unconsciousness where I couldn't catch my breath and the water I was gulping seemed to have no effect. I would lie down on the ground and pass out within seconds, waking to a deep sense of cellular calm in my body where I hadn't realised there was agitation.

On the worst day, it was 29c by 9am. I'd walked 17 miles the previous day and set out late from my camp on a hill ridge, with a small river gorge to the left and a wide-open valley to my right. It was open, unsheltered ground, dry scrub and a yellow stone track to follow for 9 miles until I reached the next village. I had three litres of water until my next water point, a particular challenge in this heat, when I was drinking five litres a day and still hardly peeing.

The heat of the sunlight wasn't the problem, but the heat of the air, which took on a bloated presence, hot gusts bumping against me like bobbing balloons. I was laminated with heat, moving in soup, coated in gloop.

The map showed a wide river a few miles further on. *I'll rest there*, I thought to myself, *I'll swim in all my clothes. The dirt and grease will spool off me. I'll laze in the water until I am cool to my core and then I will lie in the shade until I am dry. It will be magnificent.*

At 1pm, approaching the full peak of the heat, it was very strange to breathe in air that was hotter than my body. Cars rushed past as I paced the road edge, careful to keep control of tired footsteps that wanted to waver and sway. Down a path to the river, I descended through trees, balancing on protruding roots in the eroded sandy slope, hopeful of rest, until I found that the river was missing and I faced a desiccated expanse of yellow boulders, a bridge straddling nothing but air and stone.

I surveyed the scene in disappointed silence. I couldn't walk on without a break, I'd expended too much effort to arrive there. The sandy, sloped riverbank provided an almost acceptable spot to lay out my tarp and lie down. The heat was impossible now, over 40c, and when I stuck my hand out from the shade it felt struck by the force of the sunlight. I tried to doze but the breeze puffed hot air against my back and even after some time lying there, I was sweating. Lying completely still, in the shade, sweating. This was impossible. I was dehydrating just staying still – I had to go and find more water.

The village of Vic was a few miles further, along a track between a bare, inhospitable hill and rows of dusty vines. I seemed to take an age over it, walking along wondering why I was hardly sweating and wondering if this was heatstroke. The heat set the pace. I was under the overwhelming pressure of a huge hand; there was no fighting this.

I sat down under a tree, panting, swallowed another few gulps of unpleasantly hot water and spoke to myself. *Quarter of a litre left. Come on. Up. The only way to do this is to do it*, a bland motivational phrase that, nevertheless, got me back to my feet.

There was no fountain in the main square and the shuttered village felt like it was sleeping, until I heard English being spoken from a cellar door and could ask for water, swallowing the momentary tears of relief at arriving at a source of help, hydration and friendly conversation all at once.

I was sweating, panting and unable to think or speak clearly, but a short sit down with a nice British couple, some friendly chat about travel adventures, and the quick gulping of a bellyful of water helped to calm me down again.

As thunder rumbled faintly in the distance, I joked about dancing in the rain and left the nice couple; walking through the quiet village and out again into the wooded hills. The path ran twisting and tiny through low woodland, scrubby oaks and spiky undergrowth. I slept on the edge of the trees, in the stubble of a harvested wheat field, soil baked so hard and dry that I could barely push in the tent pegs.

In the pink light of a flamingo dawn, I was woken by the rustle of an approaching family of wild pigs, crashing and squeaking in alarm as they realised there was something moving in the dark lump by the field edge. As I fumbled on my glasses to watch them, I saw one of the mothers whirl into a defensive stance, legs splayed and facing me while the others trotted on, a piglet coming back for her, running too far and having to swerve back as she left, stuck to her centre of gravity like a planet on a wildly elliptical orbit. I turned to the hazy dawn and admired the sky, the peace and promise of sunrise, happy and tired and damp and dirty.

A new day and I was alive and undamaged, able to walk my body in its sturdiness and strength through the forests and vineyards to villages where I would buy a slice of pizza in a bakery, speak Spanish to the owner and be given a strawberry tart for free; wash my tent in the fountain and dry it in the village square; drink coffee in the bar and fill my water bottles.

Sometimes I was flowing in unison with this journey, sometimes I was carried along by it and sometimes it bowled over me, leaving me paddling in its wake.

***

Covid cases were rising in western Europe once again. Well-meaning people messaged me stressful links containing irrelevant information: 'Are you going to Catalonia?' 'Do you know they've closed beaches in Brittany?'

Would governments go to the extent of a full lockdown again? It felt impossible to inflict such economic damage. But the attitude of newspapers and social media seemed to anticipate full lockdown over any number of cases.

What would I do if France locked down for a second time? My mindset had always been success at all costs, but that was when all the costs were to myself – financial, physical, emotional. What if my journey became a danger to others? How could I measure the possibility of being an asymptomatic carrier and continuing to walk from place to place? I may have been living a solitary life in a very distanced fashion, but I was still entering multiple public places, no matter how briefly.

I could focus on this walk to the bitter end, creeping around border closures, sneaking through local restrictions, waiting out national lockdowns. But was that ethical? When did it stop being worth it? I had to balance self-benefit with the greater good.

The challenge lay in accurately assessing each threat; as worried people shared fear all over social media, I had to keep remembering my baseline adventure knowledge, that just because I *felt* unsafe, didn't mean I actually was. It's the same as waking up to wild boar around your tent, their snorts and grunts and rustles amplified in the darkness to sound like fantastical beasts, then seeing them trotting and nosing in the daylight, reduced to about a third of their imagined proportions.

Humans are not wired to cope with uncertainty; any noise in the bushes could be a predator and, as our brains evolved, knowledge became power and those who remained uncertain were weaker, more vulnerable.

But the ramifications of this new global pandemic were too complex to immediately understand, so we all had to live in uncertainty for a while. Would we all be OK? Would I be able to complete this journey? I didn't know, and for the first time I could not power my way past the problem with stubborn self-will.

The walk continued, with big pandemic threats hovering in the background like the ever-present chirring of cicadas, and tiny problems that I became bogged down in: the sticky pine sap on my leggings, an impenetrable tin of tuna, the way my camping pillow was never quite fluffy enough.

I felt separated from the people of France, there were very few invitations for coffee, as had happened multiple times a week further east.

People felt more private here, wealth kept behind closed doors, many more tourists, pandemic-induced nerves. Community felt reduced to a tight group of locals and too many passersby to bother acknowledging. It was hard to tell the reason why, especially as I'd only experienced a post-pandemic France, but I could have a brief conversation on the street without any particular interest being shown by either party.

'Excuse me, where's the fountain?'

'You need water?'

'Yes.'

'There's one down the road by the parking place, there's a small bench where you can eat a picnic too.'

'Thanks.'

Same interaction in the Balkans a year before and it's unthinkable that there would have been no further questions about what I was doing, a funny little spark between two strangers, looking at each other with interest, drinking each other in.

It felt hard to sense France, like looking through a dirty bus window, I got bleary glimpses that disappeared before I could understand them.

Tiredness had me fragmented. I struggled to speak when I'd been walking for hours; focused thought required scraping back together senses that had been spread thin during exertion, squashed under a load of muscle noise.

There was a dreamlike quality to the walking; days floated past me in a sweat of steps. I felt like a patient horse, lathered, blinkered, plodding on.

When I laid down each night I struggled to remember what I did that day. It was walking, of course, but where, what happened?

Lying in the twilight, I felt the unrelenting stiffness of my body, too tense to allow me to pass out, my glutes twitching in a flutter of quick clenches. Sparkling threads of sensation ran through my back, glowing and shrivelling like burning grass stalks, blood returning to my rigid muscles. I breathed out, trying to relax. Where did I eat lunch? What did I see?

There was a puddle of golden sunlight on the mossy trunk of a tree that split into two, curved just right for me to sit and rest my back against one trunk with my feet high against the other. I let my breathing calm down, listening to the nearby stream as I massaged my calves and ankles to let the tension drain away.

There was a delicious bottle of drinking yoghurt, cold and thick. Sitting on a shop's shady concrete step, I drank slowly and watched people entering in the last minutes of Sunday opening, wondering when the patience of the shopkeeper would run out. He came outside to bring in the postcard racks, lighting a cigarette with slim insouciance, before bustling back inside to serve the stragglers.

Those were small moments of pause in long days of exertion. Most of it passed in a blur of calorie intake and movement. Palming a handful of nuts into my mouth, licking the salt from my fingers, gulping a litre of milk for extra protein, spooning in my evening mush of potato and lentils and tuna. This journey was a fuzzy, fluid thing and I best navigated it by never trying to cling too firmly to any particular expectations.

I'm reminded of an essay by David Foster Wallace, 'The B of the Bang'. He describes his frustration at athletes' dispassionate, mundane descriptions of their championship winning experiences. 'Well, I just kicked the ball to the left and it went in, pretty good goal.' David wants to sense the extreme emotion, how it feels to be at this pinnacle of personal achievement. But then he realises that the point of extreme athleticism is not to feel but to do; the necessary immersion in the immediacy of intense physical exertion is at direct odds with the psychological distance needed for assessment and analysis.

This was my life now, two years in, too mechanical for poetry after so many thousands of miles. I had been buzzed by insects too many times, said hello to countless deer. We find it easiest to romanticise the experiences that we only visit.

I found an abandoned cabin to shelter from an oncoming storm, two empty rooms with a cracked sink, a fireplace full of broken glass and a low metal bed frame. With no doors or windows to impede the fluttering bats, I watched them swoop soundless in and out of the dusk. There was a loud scuffling in the roof and small mice crawled a vertical ninja run down the stones of the fireplace; the first one scampered straight out of the door without pausing. The second was more fearful, perhaps sensing my watching eyes from the far corner. I stayed still for as long as the mouse did, holding my breath until eventually its courage broke and it moved towards the door, but then squeaked and scuttled underneath a stone. A hummingbird hawk moth came to inspect me and buzzed so close to my face that I got a full body shiver from the deep vibration. In the orchestra of flying creatures, this insect is a double bass.

And yet I felt no magic there, just sat and ate my meal, read a little, watched the bats and mice, turned over with the twilight and fell asleep in my cosy feather cocoon on a bouncing bed of rusty woven wire. This was my place. I'd come past the beginner's sense of wonder.

Was I, after thousands of miles, mindful or mind dulled? I couldn't tell the difference.

***

I was on the flat plain of the river Aude, walking around the city of Carcassonne through the satellite small towns.

I knew it would be a hard day, sticking to long, boring, straight, flat roads for maximum efficiency, where there was nothing to do but trudge along with a view that changed too slowly to be interesting. I got my earphones out and plugged into some music, which I only do when I'm facing many miles on tarmac. A dance mix, designed to induce euphoria, usually helped along by a stimulant of choice (mine being caffeine and croissants) gave my body a regular rhythm to move to, reduced my pain and kept my attention span satisfied.

Ahead of me were the Pyrenees, a great wall of mountains blurred soft blue in the distance, layered in hazy white mist. Beyond them lay Spain, where I would walk clear across the top of the country until I reached the Atlantic Ocean.

I imagined myself standing on a high peak up there, revelling in all the glory of the wind and the effort of attainment. I imagined myself meeting the ocean. The music lifted me, in elation and exultation, cresting on waves, swelling with glee. Tears came and I wept, sobbing in joy and awe at all the struggle, at the size of this journey, the smallness of me making such a mighty effort.

There was more behind me now than ahead; a chain of steps stretching two years back to the other edge of Europe, and I was beginning to appreciate the immensity of the achievement.

The distant strip of the Mediterranean Sea glowed gold in the morning sunshine as I traversed the sides of a few Pyrenean foothills in a final couple of days of walking before a break in Prades, a ratty little town.

I stumbled in, a sleepy walker seeking to collapse onto clean sheets in a piebald crumple of wet, grimy, chafed, bitten, scratched, crusty skin.

The first day of my break, I was almost entirely unable to get off the bed, lying there in a dream state, thinking that I would move at any minute but completely unable to manifest any actual activity. It took a few days for my muscles to truly relax and my feet to stop hurting when they pressed against the floor. I would lie on one side and reach behind me, twisting my whole spine and aching down every single part of my back.

I moisturised my whole body, the sunburnt arms, my dry feet, trying to massage out the pain from my tight ankles and calves.

Next up came the mountains. They were already many times bigger than me, even before I was fragmented by tiredness and scattered to the wind. There would be no conquering there; only the ecstatic joy of the wind blowing past a curled warm body; the glee of a twinkling mouthful of stream water, tangible and alive; the full satisfaction of a view that includes no houses or roads.

This would be the hardest section of the walk, the highest I had ever climbed and the most difficult thing I had ever done.

PYRENEES TRAVERSE

I entered the Pyrenees at Canigou, the highest mountain in the eastern section, to trace a line west through the peaks, crossing and recrossing the spiky border between France and Spain, all the way from the Mediterranean to the Atlantic. After almost 350 mountain miles, I would pop out at St-Jean-Pied-de-Port and begin the Camino de Santiago.

I was following the Haute Route Pyrenees guidebook, a combination route, not officially waymarked, that aimed to take the highest tracks along the central ridge. It was going to be a monster challenge, with huge daily ascents and descents, and I combed the guidebook for information, trying to get an awareness of what I needed to understand about the route – weather, water points, locations of refuges.

I was nervous and emotional as I left Prades to climb into the peaks, knowing I was entering a very challenging situation at a low energy pace. Online comments exacerbated my doubts, telling me this was too difficult for me to attempt. *What if this was too dangerous and I shouldn't be up here?*

When I asked at the first refuge about their services, it seemed there'd be many more options for hot meals than I'd experienced in other wild places. I also found a useful website that showed every shelter throughout the entire mountain range, from basic stone huts to large, manned hostels. As I walked into the mountainside, the doubt fell away. The challenge of this Pyrenees section would be the scale and intensity of it, I could handle the terrain and daily weather conditions. If I took this slowly, at my own pace, of course I could do it.

Documenting my walks online, while being fat, female and 40, meant I was often underestimated, receiving patronising comments and unnecessary, overcautious advice (as well as a great deal of admiration and support). I was used to the slow scan down and up my body when I told someone I was walking across Europe, glances resting in disbelief on my heavy tummy. I enjoyed the honesty of sharing my imperfections, especially in a social media world full of heavily curated images.

It's hard, accepting weakness, the sense that you are a finite individual with limited abilities. Comparisons pop up everywhere: 'You could have this body if you train hard enough,' 'You could look like this with just a little more effort.' I couldn't help holding up my 20-mile days as personal bests, but I accepted that occasional days were six milers. I've had to embrace the fact that I am incredibly strong in a particular way – put me in a sprint and I'll lumber, but set me to walk every day for a year and I'll succeed. This was my endurance specialism, using the body I have and managing its capabilities to achieve my best over such a long period of time that many others would never even begin.

I wasn't making a hero's journey. I wasn't trying to appear capable. I wanted to tell a journey story that was honest about weakness and strength, sometimes a difficult dichotomy.

I realised I might be selling myself short.

People were very quick to warn me of the dangers, to tell me that I shouldn't be afraid to change my plans.

Don't go to the mountains, they said.

Don't camp in the cold.

There are wolves, they said.

There are robbers and thieves.

If I listened to each warning, I would never leave home. I had to choose who to pay attention to, judge how their experiences informed their fear. Perhaps in my desire to appear fallibly human, I was failing to show my ability.

All I was doing was saying publicly that something was hard. Did other adventure writers not do that? Patrick Leigh Fermor skipped across Europe. Dervla Murphy always had a wry tale of yet another broken bone. Rosie Swale Pope is made of pure steel. Don't even get me started on the polar explorers or all those smug Victorians, conquerors all. Did they feel no self-doubt or did they just not make that part of their stories?

***

Autumn was almost here and I was doing this, walking up into high mountains. Rowan trees were in full fruit with bunches of pert red berries and leaves beginning to brown and shrivel. Dead, dried pine trunks scattered the mountainside like spines. My spirits brightened in this new place, treading on the bouncy pine needle strewn earth. The forest hummed with insect activity and a cow lowed down in the valley below me.

I was entranced by the green, mountainous glory of my surroundings. It was the first time the journey reminded me of Wales. A chill wind blew as I walked on wiry upland grass, bouncy underfoot, and I cried for home. The tears dried, though, as I spotted squat shuffling marmots in the meadows, shrieking high calls from boulder tops to echo down the valleys, disappearing into their burrows when humans came near. Herds of isards, Pyrenean chamois goats, pranced on the slopes, small and slender with dark stripes over their eyes and thin vertical horns. I spent a full afternoon climbing to 2,750m in strong wind then crawled into the squat igloo shape of a stone shepherd's shelter, shivering as I ate my cold meal, but too entranced by a herd of goats grazing around the hut entrance to rustle out my bedding and scare them away.

Each day I was making huge climbs and descents, first gaining sight of Spain, then more of the French Pyrenees to the west, dozens of peaks in view. The land has a voice up there, the glory of it, the wide-open power of it.

The hugeness of the view was awe inspiring – normally I didn't see three hours walking all at once. There I was trekking my way around a mile of slope with a high pass above that seemed impossible to reach; but steadily, over hours, I made my way over each small obstacle of tree root, unstable boulders, rocky scrambles until I got all the way there and saw it wasn't so impossible after all.

Descending brought a quietness, a miniature normality, shrunken down. Peaks became a silent panoramic backdrop again, their song to the sky unheard down in the valleys.

There was a violence to this mountain beauty, it was not a tame view. Walking here was like being too close to the speakers at a rave as the bass made your chest tremble. Like the excitement of getting high at the beginning of a party, exultation swelling within you. I would blow apart if I could let myself feel all the power of these mountains, and as it overwhelmed me I would not know if the sensation was laughter or tears.

The moments of natural magic came every single day. One morning, at dawn, I woke up alone in a sheltered bowl of mountains that held a small lake cupped between them; all was calm and still, the alpenglow of orange light fading from the tips of the peaks, dissolving into day. A few hundred house martins wheeled and dipped around the lake, appearing from nowhere. Birds were filling the air all around me, rising and falling, ruffling the surface of the lake as dozens swooped to take mouthfuls of water on the wing and I sat perfectly still, entranced. They circled a few times then the flock rose high again and headed over me to the south-east. This was a water stop on their great migration and I felt in awe of their communal urge, going together to warmer climes.

Small frogs scramble-jumped away from my steps, folding legs back under themselves from clumsy emergency landings, so perfectly suited to their cold, wet homeland.

On a still clear dawn, as I reached the top of a col, with just 8 miles downhill until I got to a village, I surprised a group of isards that bounced away from me. This time it was quiet enough that I could hear their alarm sniffs, the same sounds as their cousins, the chamois goats.

After a day of worrying about the scale of the Pyrenees trek, I relaxed as I knew I could do this. After a week of mountain walking, I stopped being able to look forward at all.

I couldn't handle the future, it only contained too much of the same thing: too much effort, too much danger, too much difficulty, too much pain. I closed the guidebook that detailed kilometres per section, metres of ascent and descent.

It was simple to read printed numbers, but in reality they meant hours of effort, looking at a thin track at your feet that wound upwards into a jumble of boulders. It was too much to think about all the days of rucksack rations, all the gaps between village amenities, all the high peaks and precarious descents still ahead.

I could only do *this*. The *this* right in front of me. Here, now, this moment.

The *this* which is a night camped by a lake, faintly damp from the showers that hit me in the final hour of walking, peeking out of the tent door to watch lightning flashing in the faraway sky, admiring the perfect stillness of the lake surface as the light fades.

The *this* of each laboured step on an extremely steep slope, placing my feet into cups of bare earth worn into the slippery wiry grass. Carefully choosing each foothold, I push weight on my walking poles, like a human tripod, these wooden crutches are extensions of my body now. *Don't look ahead or I'll get dizzy at the steep drop, put off by how much more there is to go, at how slowly I'm inching my way down this unbelievably steep path. Back and forth, back and forth, winding my way down. Concentrate on each step, don't mind the rain, don't mind the time, don't pay attention to the tiny voice of fear that will shout loudly if I let it, releasing a rush of trembling nervous energy through my body. This has to be everything, this step, this rock. Will it wobble or will it stay put? Can I balance on it, or should I shuffle and twist to allow the other foot forward? Focus. Falling is serious injury. Focus.*

***

There was a vulture feather pushed behind a map on the wall of a quiet refuge, no more than two sheets of metal hammered into a triangular shelter for six people. When I pulled it out, it was longer than my forearm, the quill as thick as my little finger. I imagined the glory of this bird, swooping and spying all day, turning slow circles of surveillance above miles of mountain.

My sleep that night was in the comfortable dark nest of my sleeping bag on a plastic-covered gym mat. There were mice in the cabin, first I heard them scuffling in the hollows they'd nibbled out of the insulated walls, then they were all over the kitchen area where a battered biscuit tin contained grimy playing cards and someone had left an incongruous bottle of pink Lambrusco. They didn't find my food bag hanging from the rafters or visit my corner, and so I slept sweetly. Outside, fresh mountain spring water ran from a plastic pipe into a hollowed wooden trough. The mist gathered and a deer barked in the far distance, come to the plateau for a midnight bilberry harvest.

The world outside the mountains had receded into something

very far away. Global news came to me at a remove, as if I was a cave dweller, where the taletellers of Twitter came in from strange lands and shared ghost stories, their exaggerated gestures flickering in firelight shadows on the wall, telling of boogeymen and danger and awful things out there. The news blurred – pandemic statistics that had become meaningless; ecological crumblings, such as wildfires in California or polluted rivers in the UK, floated past my attention like small pieces of ice falling from a glacier. I cowered a little, in my comforting safe space of mountain life, not wanting to burst this lovely bubble.

Because lovely it was, for all the hardship. The pure joy and exhilaration of life outside, up there in the places where the marks of man are faint and few. The peaks were blaring into the sky, each one an organ pipe delivering the vibrations of deep earth up and outwards to the air, where the breeze blew it into me, this soul food I didn't know I was hungry for.

I was nourished, at the same time as I struggled for nourishment. My spirit filled as my legs were emptying. I had never been so tired.

Seven days had passed since my last proper food shop and I had been living on absolute minimal rations in order to carry enough. Oats and powdered milk, dried potato and meat, with peanuts and chocolate. It was good enough, keeping me at the bare minimum of nutrition, although I could feel a deeper hunger creeping in; each day the length of time between a meal, and hunger for the next one grew shorter.

As my energy depleted, it was hard not to groan when I saw yet another huge climb in front of me. What was this struggle for? Why was I putting myself through this? Yet somehow there was no question that I would try.

The weather had turned. At first I'd experienced intense

thunderstorms punctuating mostly sunny days, but now grey clouds hovered around me, wreathing the surrounding peaks and constantly threatening rain. I was lucky enough, for this final section before the halfway break, to be walking between regular refuges. Strange little cabins in the wilderness, built with great effort so people can have emergency shelter. Two of my favourites had been the size of horse boxes, wood-lined, with up to nine bunks crammed inside. Probably helicoptered into place and secured on their plinths, high above lakes of dark water held cupped in raw rock.

There was a great excitement in arriving at the long-anticipated shelter, seeing the shape, opening the door – sometimes a heavy metal catch and sometimes a piece of string wrapped around a protruding nail – and discovering the interior. Would there be beds? Or just a sleeping platform? What kind of things had people left there? Packets of soup, tins of sardines, emergency survival blankets, matches, salt. All in varying stages of age and disrepair. Would there be other people inside? Hikers to share route information with, maybe compare kit recommendations.

It was really fun to meet other long-distance walkers on this section, something that had been conspicuously absent from the rest of my journey, unless I detoured to join other people's routes. There was a particular understanding between us that overlooked the grime, the aches, the suffering, the terrible food and the danger that stops most people in their tracks; that knew that this was totally worth it, up here wild and free, to sleep outside and breathe the good air, to be surrounded by rocks and trees and the spirit of a living earth. The dirty hiker suffering-yet-fuck-it-let's-carry-on spirit.

I was lucky enough to be offered a rest day roughly in the centre of the Pyrenees, by a British couple running a guesthouse out there. I descended a boulder field and a steep drop to get picked up from a snowless ski resort, very ready for a rest.

'Big snowstorm in the Pyrenees,' said the forecast, 'unusual weather for this time of year.' I waited an extra day down in the safe haven of the luxurious house, but felt impatient to continue.

The next day I would gently ascend 800m from the valley bottom up to a refuge at 2,150m, nice and simple. The second day I was less certain of, climbing up to a mountain pass at 2,550m and descending to another refuge. There would be snow, but how much?

The gentle ascent went well, winding up from road to stone trackway, horses pawing at the few centimetres of snow to munch stoically at the grass underneath. It only got tough in the final kilometre, leaving the trackway for a thin path up through rocks and then a muddy pathway around a lake. The snow was thick but manageable until the final lake where I was clambering through thigh-high drifts, a little shocked by the depth.

Mountains circled the lake, covered in white, mottled with dark rock.

The first refuge was cold and a little mechanical. It was their final night of the season and the staff were obviously very ready to pack up and go home. I hung up wet clothing, put my socks and boots to dry by the fire, and asked about the path to *refugio* Restanca, the next shelter on my route. 'Has anyone else passed that way?' The receptionist made a face: she didn't think so, but called some other visitors over and we came together, faces masked. There was a group of three who were walking some of the same route as me, climbing up to the big pass and then descending to a different refuge. Even if I couldn't keep up with them, I could follow their footsteps.

We had to vacate our rooms by 7.30am and were all nervous, going outside to look at the snow and the frozen lake, admire the sky. It was going to be a beautiful clear day, but windy. Feeling my heart beating fast, I sat on a bench and waited for the others to be ready, closed my eyes and tried to keep calm.

The problem was not the depth of the snow, it was the way it gathered on the land, hiding crevices between boulders until all presented a smooth and perfectly formed surface and you wouldn't know how far down your foot would sink until you'd probed ahead with walking poles. Even then it wasn't certain; perhaps you'd hit upon a large rock and your foot wouldn't sink at all, no energy wasted. Perhaps though, once you put full weight onto the next step, the snow would give way and you'd slide into a gap between rocks, into the snow up to your thigh. All the muscles of your body jerked and tensed as you fell, trying to keep you upright, and now you were floundering, trying to push down on a soft surface to extricate yourself and get back to ground level again.

I fell multiple times that day, stuck like an upturned turtle and having to slowly roll and press my knees into the snow, clumsy under my pack, trying to keep a larger surface area so I wouldn't sink any deeper in the effort to right myself.

It was frightening at first, struggling with every footstep, panicking, which only sucked more energy. It took a great deal of effort to travel even a few steps and there were many more ahead.

I lost the protective foot from one of my walking poles. My waterproof trousers flapped open at the bottom, meaning the snow filled the top of my boots every time I plunged in over my ankles. I felt myself getting angry, cursing at my crappy trousers until I took a breath and realised that my anger was fear.

I was scared here, in this white valley, facing a huge climb in difficult conditions. I felt alone in the face of huge danger and the impossibility of rescue.

All I could do was tell myself to be calm, keep walking and focus on each step. I moved on, trying to think of a few positive things to change my mood.

It took a few hours for me to properly calm down but, after a long while, I realised I had stopped thinking about how and whether I would do this, and was simply doing it.

The three people ahead had long since disappeared. I'd had glimpses as they began the steep climb at the valley head, admiring the synchronisation of their footsteps, the determination of the tiny line of humans trudging slowly up the steep snow slope. Only huge boulders broke the sheer whiteness, each one sculpted with a skirt of blown powder.

All I had to do was follow in their footsteps, all the way up, winding as they switched left and right to find the places where rocks showed through the snow or the faintest signs of grass blades, where we could be more certain that there weren't deep invisible clefts. I saw the places where they'd fallen and flailed, I saw the places where they'd slipped deep. It was easier to place my foot into their steps, to be more certain that there'd be solid packed snow to press weight upon, even though there were always surprises. Every single step was uncertain – it was exhausting.

All the while the sun shone bright and clear ahead, the wind wisped small whirlwinds of snow crystals around me and the clouds feathered in thin streams of moisture high above. Knowing that there was bad weather coming later, I regularly glanced towards the horizon as fresh pieces of skyline came into view, watching for the gathering of darker clouds.

It took me until 3.30pm to reach the top of the col and I gasped in amazement. There was an incredible view ahead, dozens of harshly pointed peaks, every single one covered in snow, the stark splendour of utterly inhospitable land. Fine powder crystals blew against my face, gently exfoliating me to redness. My eyes were dry and crusty; I had broken my sunglasses and was at risk of snow blindness without them.

I remember feeling pessimistic the previous year, as the wet weather began in a Croatian October, and I faced the hard facts of a winter to come with nowhere to retreat to, nothing to do but walk through it. I felt uncovered again in the Pyrenees, going against the ancient human response of slowing down, spending time inside in the warmth, knitting and weaving and mending, hoarding food and waiting for the warm months to come again.

On the way up that difficult snowy climb, I felt intimidated by all the hardship still ahead in the Pyrenees, thinking bleakly of all the many mountains still to come, peering timidly at the weather forecast, seeing challenging snowfall again later that week after only a meagre few days of easy sunshine.

While climbing, I considered the decision to abandon this route and walk lower down until the snow cleared. It was immediately clear that this was not failure. Walking alone in this territory, in these conditions, was very dangerous. I could have injured myself in any single one of those slips, if my leg became trapped between rocks and I had to struggle to get out. I'd just be stuck there, my safety whistle echoing pathetically around empty mountains, while the snow melted slowly into the gaps in my waterproof clothing. Looking ahead from the col, to get to my planned refuge I had to descend 150m to a small lake, and then climb again 100m to another pass before descending a few kilometres to the refuge. Absolutely nobody had passed that way, I would be completely alone with no markings to guide me. It had taken me seven hours to climb 430m and I only had four hours of daylight left.

To my left ran the line of footsteps of the other three walkers, who had turned south to descend to a different refuge, much closer.

Interesting isn't it, we torture ourselves with the 'what ifs', agonising over imagined possibilities, but when the absolute dangers come, they're easy to deal with. It wasn't a difficult choice. I turned away from my route and followed the marks in the snow. *Stay safe, Ursula, you've done enough today.*

The worst bit came first, following the contour of a slope, a steep drop to my right. I pushed my heel into the snow with each step to break the frozen crust and make sure that I wasn't going to slip and slide to injury. Once I came off the icy slope and back to boulders again, the rest of the descent was easier. Feet could slide deep down into the snow as it was all downhill, whether controlled or a slip. I could even sit down on my bum and let myself slide down the steepest sections. I'm not sure if I saved myself any time as I had to sit and giggle for a while every time I did it.

My feet were long past soaked, but fortunately I had kept up enough effort that my blood circulated well and warmed the wet inside of my boots. I trudged onwards, groaning now in the bodily shock of every bad slip, the horrid sharp jolt where one leg disappeared thigh high into the snow. It was so much effort to drag myself out again, I found myself sitting back against the drifts, wanting to pause. My body may have been ready for rest but it wasn't safe to stop there; I had to dig deep and push on for the final couple of hours to the refuge, down past frozen lakes and streams running under snow. Up high on the surrounding peaks the wind blew a steady stream of snow into the air, so each mountain seemed to smoke like a set of factory chimneys. Yet more snow came trickling out of the sky in tiny flakes.

Finally, in the last half hour before darkness, I knocked at the door to the refuge and fell into the warmth within. The three other adventurers had been thawing themselves by the fire for a full four hours already and we exchanged excited stories about what an awful day it had been. When I'd seen them pacing their way up the steep slope, they'd been ready to turn back, almost overcome by the difficulty of the climb. 'A little further, then we'll see if we should stop,' they'd been telling themselves.

I ate a hot meal of chicken soup, omelette and pasta then went to bed by 9pm, knees and back aching.

I was really happy that I'd pushed myself to achieve that climb but was in no rush to repeat the experience. My assessment of failure had changed from abandoning my route, to stubbornly continuing on it and dying. I decided to descend south from the highest route, and walk parallel for a day or two, until the worst of the snow had melted, and then ascend and try again.

A few hours down from the snowy refuge, I entered a beech wood, tall slender trunks fuzzing out to bare twigs, the ground a dull orange carpet of shed summer hair. I breathed differently there, something let go, a release of tension deep in my chest. The calmness of trees is my most nourishing place to walk. The mountains may give you glories of wild exultation, but it's clinging, scratched survival. Forests are the nurturers, the places of comfort and peace.

Apparently, these heavy snowstorms were unusual for this time of year. What bad luck for me. My path ahead, through the central section, the highest part of the route, with the option to climb Aneto, the tallest mountain in the Pyrenees, if I was brave enough, became a detour to the lower-level variant, and then in the face of further storms, I had to descend again to 1,200m, well below the snowline.

The constant threat of snow changed everything. If I could just keep focused on small distances ahead – the 700m I needed to climb that day on what would be a snow-covered pass that I knew nobody else had walked through recently – then that was fine. I could do that day, probably. It would be wet and cold and dangerous and tiring but I could do it. It was the day after that, then another and another and another. Each one with the potential to be wet and cold and dangerous and painful and tiring. For another twenty days of this mountain route. That's where pessimism crept in, and I'd get intimidated, think about creeping away and quitting.

This snowy territory meant climbing up and up and up, from where the trees gathered in the dip of land, to where the forests stopped growing, where it was just short, spiky grass and occasional flowers, where the streams grew small and thin, where water trickled and pooled. There were small scraps of snow at first, wet soggy crystals caught in flattened grass, water dripping from icy slush. But they grew, these scraps, became patches in dips of path, lines of white wavering with the contours of the dark ground, turning the valley zebra striped. Climbing further, the patches joined together until most of the land was white. It was slow, taking me a few hours to climb to the top of the col. Then came a huge drop down the other side, clouds misting around me and a treacherous slippery path with an inch of snow on top of wet grass and mud. I was exhausted in bed that night, once I reached the bottom of the valley and found a small patch of pine with a beautiful, sheltered place to camp on a blanket of bouncy pine needles.

Tucked up in my tent, I struggled to eat. I had tried to eat three meals that day, sometimes I only managed two. But the evening meal was difficult, feeling as if my stomach didn't want to accept the food. The mystery was solved when I went for a wee before sleep and my body got rid of everything I'd eaten at lunchtime. Not a proper stomach upset, but close to one, and I lay down feeling queasy, hoping I wouldn't vomit out the latest meal before I'd had a chance to absorb some nutrition.

In the morning I woke at dawn for another unpleasant digestive episode. Back in bed, trying to doze and think about what this meant for the day ahead, I coughed suddenly, after lying still for a long time, and so startled a nearby deer that it spent a long time shrieking indignantly in the trees that bordered the track. It reached a pitch so shrill and incandescent, unlike the usual barking cough, that I wondered whether a passing fox had decided to join in. I started packing away in the gloom, wiping the night's condensation off the tent before rolling it up. The sunrise illuminated the peaks at the end of the valley in a bright pink alpenglow.

Those peaks were where I needed to go that day, another tough climb, with tricky, steep, snow-covered, rocky slopes; 'one of the harder days,' said the guidebook.

And my mood did one of those 'turn on a sixpence' things again, where suddenly I was utterly unsure whether I wanted to attempt anything difficult at all.

As I headed downhill, vacillating, uncertain; one moment I thought I should just try it, the next I felt like I couldn't possibly.

I passed a thick pine tree, here before the existence of the track which had curved to avoid it and, while pausing in admiration, was moved to put my hand on the trunk. I received a tiny sensation of the deep vibration of this giant being, that swelled in my chest and brought me to tears. I said thank you to the tree and became aware of how starved of loving interaction I was, how easily my mind could be set whirling, untethered. There was nobody to bounce ideas off or give support when I was feeling weak. I felt like a mad little ant that had left the colony, trying to find a new way of life. The peril! The danger! The rushing water! The dark deeps!

I think the thing that people didn't see when I was publicly agonising over whether to tackle a very hard bit was that this entire journey only existed because I said so. Once I decided that I didn't have to do part of it, the illusion dropped and, like the emperor's clothes, it became clear that the whole thing was imaginary. If I didn't have to do the *very* hard bit, why did I have to do the hard bit? Why did I have to do any of it?

***

These mountains were breaking me.

I was coming to strongly dislike the pain in my knees when I had to put weight on one leg, not knowing if the frozen snow crust would give way and my body weight jerk downwards. I strongly disliked the way that every step was more effort, every step more dangerous and every step took more time. I strongly disliked looking down a steep slope, a glissade of sparkling white, and knowing that a fall would not be a simple one of a few seconds with a bruise, but a slide of dozens of metres at increasing speed with a potentially severe injury.

I was tired, emotional, in pain.

My back and shoulders were stiff and sore.

I kept crying at TV programmes.

I was having bad dreams about abusive people from my past.

I accepted this as part of the journey that I wanted to make; a journey that takes you out of your normal self and shows you your limits, your definitions, shows you who you are.

Beaten down, I decided to walk on low ground for a couple of days before trying the snow again, enjoying the autumnal feeling that came as I descended from bare rock and snow into the multicolour of woods in transition, the fire orange of beech and rowan. The calmness of the forest didn't last long before I was forced to retreat in a hostel, avoiding the 150mph winds of Storm Barbara and preparing to cross the mountains again from south to north, Spain back to France.

Waking up in the wild morning of the oncoming storm, I packed away my tent at 6.30am, fumbling in the darkness. Starting on the road that was nothing more than a mild silver shining in the faintness of the hour before dawn, I checked the news and learnt that Navarra, the region of Spain I was due to enter next, had closed in a local Covid lockdown. Nobody could enter or leave the region unless for emergencies; bars, hotels and restaurants were closed.

It meant I couldn't exit the Pyrenees at the planned point to start the French route of the Camino or get to the town where I had planned to take my rest days and receive an important supply package.

All the stress of being a 'fugitive' in Italy came rushing back. It's all very well to make yourself deliberately vulnerable, letting go of support systems in order to feel liberated, but when the shit hits the fan it becomes a nightmare.

The pressure of Covid homelessness mirrored my cancer experience eight years previously, when I innocently went to a friend's doctor and suddenly faced major abdominal surgery while sleeping on their sofa. The visceral vulnerability was profoundly unsettling.

So my first response to the Spanish route closure was to melt into traumatised, worst-case scenario thinking. *I can't do this. I shouldn't do this.* It immediately felt as if my remaining journey was a selfish intrusion into places that were suffering under a pandemic and should be left alone to heal. I was facing a ghost Camino – only 18% of the usual numbers of pilgrims had passed through Roncesvalles that year. Winter weather, closed hostels, hardly any other walkers, and restricted cities where pilgrims were told to take buses around the edges. It was nothing like normal, so was it worth it? Why not just cut out this 1,000-mile hairpin bend across the top of Spain and turn north right now, head through France and towards Britain.

Slowly, through the following hours, I started to consider how I could continue. The Navarra lockdown was due to end in two weeks, only a brief restriction. Small hopeful sprouts of *Well, how about...?* began to grow. There were options; I didn't have to make an immediate decision.

I could continue walking in the mountains, all the way until the west coast, rather than coming out at Roncesvalles.

I could walk a lower route in France to avoid the ridgeline border of the closed region.

I could take some planned rest days which would take me almost until November 4th when I'd find out if Navarra would open again.

If Navarra did open, I'd definitely continue walking into Spain – so why couldn't I do that now in the currently unrestricted Basque regions?

Every morning I checked the restrictions, anxiously looking for how many more Spanish municipalities had locked down, or set curfews, or closed hotels and bars. The number rose daily, same as the Covid cases, a 52% increase in the last fortnight. 1% of the population in Navarra had it in that moment.

I felt a conflict between personal gain and public good – but maybe that was true of all our actions, pandemic or otherwise, especially when you factor in ecological concerns and the living standards of the first world. The most genuine public good – to go back to Wales, find a place to live and stay indoors – wasn't even on my list of options. I wasn't prepared to give up the whole walk and I couldn't financially anyway; living on £100 of savings each week was only possible when sleeping in a tent, and there were no jobs waiting for me in pandemic-stricken rural Wales.

It was late October 2020; Covid cases were rising everywhere once again, financial insecurity was hitting. This wasn't a situation I could retreat from, so perhaps the immediate challenge was to learn how to live with the fear and uncertainty. I decided to cross into France and keep walking west as planned. Perhaps in another week or two, by the time it came to enter Spain, the circumstances would be better.

Five days later, however, the difficulty just wasn't easing.

I lay on my air mattress in the corner of a whitewashed room, bare apart from a sink unit with no taps and a worn wooden bench. The wind roared outside, so strong it had almost knocked me over a few times on the descent to shelter. I had seen this building from up high, as I came around the corner into this new valley, fresh from climbing alongside a long green ridge, red shale paths snaking through it, grass trodden through by sheep and walkers. The wind had started blowing strongly just as I came to the most difficult bit, a thin path trodden into fallen rock and scree that zipped along the side of a tall triangular peak. The mist came at me fast, clouds barrelling over the ridge and pouring down into the valley. I could see straight north, further into France where the flat lands lay. How strange to see flat land; for there to be no more intrusions of ridges and peaks, just an absence in the sky and a long sense of distance, like the ocean.

I trod carefully along the steep slope, not letting my gait swing fast and free, wary of a sudden gust of wind coming to topple me. Rain hit as I started the main descent, rocks changed to grey granite, eons of ageing underfoot. The shepherd's hut was 300m below, in the valley bottom; it looked to be in use, a sheep fold there with bare trodden earth, a neat, low building with grass roof, fresh paint on metal shutters and a low stone table outside. *It won't be open, don't get excited*, I thought to myself, but I tried a door handle in hope and lo, it opened to an empty room left for winter walkers, the rest of the building kept behind locked doors. I tucked up in bed and stared out of the half open stable door at sheets of grey rain misting, listening to the booms and roars of the wind.

I was tired, in a visceral way that would not be assuaged by a single night's sleep, even if I did finally fuss the pillow into the right position on top of my bundled fleece, on top of my food bag, on top of my empty rucksack.

I was tired in a way that needed days to make up for, taking time for my muscles to release and allow me to sink into drowsiness. The tiredness wouldn't stop until I finished the mountains. I was so tired it was taking me ages to finish the mountains.

Thereby the whirlpool whipped, and I was sinking under the weight of my own task.

***

I'd been able to ignore the world's problems while I was in the mountains; issues like weather and food access thrust themselves so completely into my consciousness that the rolling ticker tape of rising infection numbers became a background scrolling that was easy to look past.

But this pandemic was the toothache that glowed quietly and steadily in the night; it was the dank mould under the kitchen sink, the heavy tree branch hanging over the garage, the persistent ache in ageing joints. It was a problem we could ignore, trying to carry on as usual while it gnawed away at us invisibly, until suddenly, explosively, we couldn't continue, we very much couldn't.

This pandemic was the underlying stress that made small disasters catastrophic. It was the reason why decision making was difficult. It was the reason I felt close to tears whenever I met someone who was kind to me.

I remembered these feelings from cancer; the sense of

vulnerability to an immutable force, of having my world shaken, the rules being overturned, of everything, including physical health and bodily autonomy, suddenly in question. But now it wasn't just my world, it was everyone's.

At 6.30am the following morning, when I wriggled out of my sleeping bag, and opened the door of the shepherd's hut, everything was white outside. It had snowed! I laughed in shock as I stepped out into wet, crunching snow and tiny flakes tinkled against my face. In the grey, faint, early dawn I could just see the clouds hanging low on the surrounding mountain, the complete white covering on the nearby fields.

I prepared breakfast, still giggling to myself. Normally I would have walked a couple of hours before eating but the snow meant that I wouldn't be stopping much that day, certainly not to unpack my bag and eat a full meal. I left the door open to watch snow TV while I filled my belly. The flakes came thicker and thicker as I watched, entranced, until the air was completely white, a mist of fat flakes now, slowly, silently falling.

Down in the village I was shocked by the news that French bars must close, another tightening of the Covid net restricting my liberty. I restocked with food, spent a night in a hotel, and quickly got out of town the next morning, back to the safety of the mountains.

'Just keep taking small steps and don't stop.' It's the phrase I chose to sign my last book with, told to me by a man I met on the Offa's Dyke Path as I was struggling up a hill.

Keeping on going felt like all I could do, despite the looming awfulness of the world, the fear that I was following a fool's journey, sidestepping between Covid restrictions like they were swinging blades.

Leaving Lescun, I climbed slowly from the autumnal valley bottom, up into frozen snow billows and a view north into the green sea of flat France. A single chamois mountain goat watched me from the top of the cliff. All felt very quiet and still. After a night in a cabin and a walk on a frozen plateau, climbing in and out of clefts, I reached the northern cliff edge and went into phone signal for the first time in thirty hours, where I found out that France was entering a second full lockdown.

Being up there on the mountain top, straddling the border between two countries, gave me the luxury of choice. Did I descend into Spain and fight to keep walking through a variety of regional restrictions, or did I give in to the full clampdown of France? To submit to an enforced rest was a relief and I gladly chose France. I could try to recover from the Pyrenees without having to think about immediately moving on.

Maybe Spain would have opened up by the time France regained freedom. I was always hoping this was temporary, in a blinkered fantasy that did not want to accept how serious this was, that my plans might be permanently thwarted.

I decided to keep walking for a few more days and stop at St-Jean-Pied-de-Port, rather than retracing my steps to a closer train station. I had a full food bag and would follow a remote border ridge without passing through any villages.

It was pretty eerie, striding alone on a ridge between France and Spain, looking down over both countries and imagining the people confined to their houses. All the fear down there, all the irritation, all the stress. I floated free in the breeze for a couple of days longer, up in the mountain dream-world where Covid restrictions couldn't be easily enforced. It was very nice, clear, open ridge walking on gentle rounded grassy mountains now. I'd left the rocky rawness behind.

I camped in a grassy hollow just off the ridge, disturbingly near a grim sheep skeleton, but it was the only place to avoid the rushing wind. An orange sunset on dried grasses was replaced by a bright full moon which illuminated each night clearly as I made my way down into the foothills, through beech and oak forest, plenty of trees tumbled down by recent storms. Pillowy drifts of leaves filled the crevices of the path and the earth underneath was sodden and muddy. I trod slowly and carefully but even so, with boots that were losing their grip after almost two months of abrasion on sharp granite, I slipped and fell several times.

For my final night of camping out, I bivvied down on a flat promontory above Larra valley, looking back to the snowy caps of Pic d'Anie, full moon rising above the snow and into bare branches. The trees had lost their leaves while I was up in the heights and I hadn't even noticed.

I awoke early with a cold nose to the glory of pale pink dawn clouds, the rich earth brown and copper tones of bracken and beech leaves resonating in the strengthening light. The moon was misty now, indistinct. To the south was a bonfire of an autumn morning, the hillside silhouetted against bright orange glowing clouds. The onset of lockdown matched the end of my mountain route and I finished happy and proud to have pushed myself so hard to complete the Pyrenees.

SECOND LOCKDOWN

My walking life halted again as the second wave of Covid crashed across Europe and individual lives swirled, like grains of sand in the swash, leaving us all scrabbling for solid, familiar ground.

Having begged a safe haven with the couple who'd offered me a rest day during my Pyrenees traverse, I returned to Bagnères-de-Luchon, a resort town nestled in a thin valley poking south into the mountain heights. A snowy peak stood at the head of the glacier-carved gap that dropped down from the high border with Spain. There was a long, straight main street, classical music playing through tiny speakers on every lamp-post, soothing tunes for the spa customers, frail or limping, who were the backbone of the town's custom. You could get a state-sponsored stay in one of the multiple hospitals, prescribed by French doctors, a chit allowing you to come and take the waters. There was ski tourism in winter, walking and cycling tourism in summer, including the draft of high excitement as the Tour de France blew past, and hot springs all year round.

The streets were empty through the gloomy, damp days at the end of autumn. Shops were dark and locked, signs inviting people, with a faintly plaintive air, to 'click and collect' a sheepskin hat or velvet pillow. Some had websites and some had just phone numbers, unused to appealing to anything more than foot traffic.

The ending of this second lockdown was more ragged than the first as, across Europe, governments experimented with different styles of restriction, trying to portion out the discomfort while maintaining economic activity. Infection rates didn't seem to be dropping after weeks of movement restrictions and the great Christmas festival was looming, when we all wanted to be hugging and eating together, beating back the winter darkness with cosy celebration.

I felt chipper at first, ready to stretch, exercise and get through this imposed immobility with my strength intact, but was quickly overcome by an intense, hopeless lethargy. Life was stuck under a thick grey fog and I was peering through to try and see what was ahead.

There was extra pain through my back and shoulders after they'd taken more than usual work levering myself up and down the steep steps and scrambles of the Pyrenees. My knees were crunching on the stairs; if I twisted carelessly with weight on my left knee, it spiked pain through me.

At first, a four-week French lockdown was mandated, and we awaited further news from President Macron. Where France had gone for a total lockdown, each region of Spain was deciding their own regulations, with travel not permitted between them and differing dates for their regulations to end. It was a longer, slower confinement, life reduced but not completely restricted. As a result, infection rates were taking longer to slow down but life was more enjoyable, the economy still productive. Bars and restaurants were open at semi-capacity. People were free to leave their homes, to work and travel wherever they wanted within their regional boundaries. In Navarra, the first Spanish region on my route, restrictions were set to end on December 18th. Maybe they would be extended again, but I wouldn't find out until at least the 14th.

I was caught on the edge of action, either ready to plunge in over the mountains to Spain or give up and turn north through France, and I wouldn't know which was possible until a few days beforehand.

President Macron sat in a very well-lit studio that gently smoothed away any wrinkle on his handsome face and explained that we were all doing really well and that he was thankful for all the efforts of everyone working together to beat the coronavirus menace. Geoff had made chilli and we put the fire on in the living room to watch the announcement together, trying not to let the crunch of tortilla chips obscure any important point. I strongly wanted to ask how old Macron was but stayed quiet as he explained that shops were going to open, we were going to be allowed to exercise further away from home. But no travel yet, not until the 15th of December, and then only if infection rates fell lower than 5,000 a day.

Bars and restaurants would stay closed until mid-January, ski resorts were an unknown detail. Geoff and Vic talked quietly to themselves about government assistance, whether it might increase, whether they'd be classed as a place where large groups of people meet, which would definitely not be able to open at Christmas.

My problem was an afterthought and I stayed quiet as they talked over the future of their business. They'd been shut down twice, suffered during the meagre late summer with many fewer international visitors. They were surviving, but only just. Losing Christmas and New Year would be a blow; losing a second full ski season would be fatal. Government help was designed to keep people alive, not to keep them comfortable or pay business bills.

Vic got up to tend to the fire and silence fell.

'So is it OK for me to stay a bit longer?' I said jokingly.

'Well, we're not going to put you out in the cold,' Geoff joked back.

The Spanish regional closures also extended and so I stayed another few weeks, waiting it out. Nothing was known about future infection rates, safety of public movement, and all we could do was to sit and wait while decisions were made that we had no control over.

Could I walk through Spain despite the restrictions? As a traveller when tourism had been pushed aside, I was falling through the cracks. The rules governed average behaviour but I was an anomaly; homeless in a time when we were all supposed to stay at home. What was in place to prevent a person walking alone through fields and sleeping in a tent? Almost nothing but the fear of being caught. Fear was being used to rule behaviour for the national good. 'Stay indoors, don't touch strangers, wear masks, track your own movements.' For the national good. Did my personal goal usurp the national good? No. Did I want to do it anyway? Yes. The ethical valuation of my behaviour was for me to decide. All around me, people were doing all kinds of things to bend the lockdown rules – swift hugs with friends they met on the street, illicit walks in the mountains, driving to Barnard Castle. Others were overcautious through fear or, living with reduced immunity, restricting themselves to only moments outside the house, strictly masking their faces, or carefully washing every piece of shopping before they put it away. How could I know the right thing to do?

Information came in either tiny portions that formed an incomplete picture, or great dollops that were impossible to make meaning of. Total number of cases in France since the pandemic began: 2.44 million. Statistics crowded the news: number of cases yesterday, number of cases in a particular region, number of cases in hospital, number of cases in intensive care, number of cases per 100,000 people, R rate, yearly death rates. Tier 2, tier 3, regional restrictions, curfews.

So many indicators to tell us whether the current situation was 'good/bad', but it all still depended on the successful behaviour change of the writhing mass of contrary humans that form society. It was worse once you realised that no matter how hard you tried to interpret an objective picture of public health from the confusing statistics, government actions were subject to other imperatives anyway – economic and popular. No politician wanted to be seen to cancel Christmas.

I was ravaged by fear but unable to give up on my goal. It was the enforced stillness that frustrated me, not the walking. Nothing would be better if I returned home. I might as well struggle on in the place I wanted to be.

Once France lifted movement restrictions on the 20th December, my hosts needed me to graciously make way for paying guests. I could give up on Spain and turn north for Calais; drain my savings on French accommodation while I waited for Spain to open fully, stuck in the listlessness of a paused project; or continue the journey as planned, into a country I wasn't supposed to enter. When it finally came to it, I wriggled my way around restrictions, using a Christmas loophole to carry on with the original plan, as my heart desired.

On the 23rd of December, Spain's closed regional borders became porous – visits allowed between family and friends during Christmas and New Year. With permission from an old friend in Burgos, if stopped and questioned, I would say I was on my way to visit them ... on foot.

It was a tenuous excuse, whose acceptance would depend on the attitude of the questioner. I frantically researched the rules for each region; under Spain's semi-autonomous style of government, all had their own. Like Italy, Spain is a group of very different regions that outsiders call a country. A friend advised me to know less, play dumb. I hated all of it, the restrictions and the subterfuge. Fixed on achieving my goal, I just wanted to walk, but I couldn't stop worrying what would be ahead. For a person without a safe place to retreat to, this was a lonely and vulnerable time to exist.

ENTERING SPAIN

I travelled to St-Jean-Pied-de-Port to spend a few fretful days waiting to cross into Spain. My brain was dulled with the stress of hundreds of days of *What's going to happen?*, overwhelmed by jittery nervous energy or extinguished by boredom-induced social media scrolling. This was my first Camino town, where pilgrims have gathered to cross into Spain for hundreds of years. It's a beautiful place, white houses with painted wooden beams spread out over a wide valley and the old town clustered on the slopes of a hill, with a ruined fortress at the top. The houses date from the 1700s, family names and dates carved into stone lintels above each doorway. Many of them were pilgrim hostels now and I imagined the excited bustling there would be in normal times, everyone gathered to start their adventure, comparing kit and blister techniques, anticipating the exertion and achievement that lay ahead. It was an empty place for me, many buildings shuttered, no walking poles tick-tacing on the cobbled streets. Pedestrians passed, masked and shifting away from one another as if buffeted. I had never felt less capable of connection with strangers. Eye contact was a rarity and it was hard to smile behind a mask.

That first day was a very long tarmac plod, the valley of St-Jean-Pied-de-Port opening out below me to show the hill fort and the town patterned around its base. I was slow, coated with a thick, gooey sweat as I surprised my body with intense exertion after fifty slothful days on lockdown. I started at 11am after a late breakfast in my hostel and a nice chat with an Englishman called Mark, who'd just walked the length of the Pyrenees – on the French side, through the French lockdown, defying all restrictions. He'd done exactly what I feared to and I quizzed him about his experience. People had been friendly, he'd had no problems with police, although he had stashed his pack at the town edge every time he went to buy food supplies.

'Did you feel comfortable feeling like a fugitive?' I asked.

'I didn't mind it, no.'

This is where we differed – the feeling of being an outsider, rejected, completely reliant on the generosity of others, had been too intense for me. I had hated that feeling in Italy and had no desire to experience it again. But I could see how far apart our attitudes had drifted; he was friendly, relaxed and open, where I had sunk into my own miserable vulnerability, shying away from interaction and eye contact.

My fears were making spectres of sideways glances and police interrogations, but I had to look past the nerves. I was heading onto a route famed for its generosity and transcendental experiences. The Camino has always given space for the muddled pilgrim to find purpose, clarity and meaning about themselves and the world. Could I share anything close to that on a lonely winter Camino in a pandemic?

A friend told me there was a shelter high up on the mountain, and I thought I'd aim to sleep there. The sun set over Spain as I walked upwards, diffusing a gentle pastel light over the cold mountain, pale orange on the land and violet in the sky. My feet were incredibly painful now, the full intensity of beginning a journey where blood thuds in shocked feet, but I kept going as daylight dwindled into darkness, using my torch for the last mile as I left the road and walked on buoyant turf towards a ridge of jagged rock. Here at last was the shelter, but I swore as I saw a tumbled pile of stones with a dark open doorway.

I'd been shown a photo of a concrete building with a wide bench to sleep on, but had obviously identified the wrong mark on the map. This was an ancient shepherd's hut with a doorway I had to crawl through and a roof I could only kneel under, the bare earth floor just big enough for a single body. Laughing to myself at the sparse conditions – so challenging and yet so normal – I laid out my bed on the hard ground and began to make dinner. Looking around me at the piled stone walls, I saw a small scrap of paper wedged into a crevice; drawing it out I read a poem:

> Far from home
> But home is all around us.
> We breathe the same wind
> And kiss the same sky.
> Turn the same earth
> Live the same lives.
> Home is all around us.
> Home is within us.
> Keep going...

Someone in the web of pilgrims past had left this note in kindness and inspiration for a stranger who might see it and feel comforted. Cheesy as it may read now, the sense of the passage of other people was exactly what I needed as I lay there alone, to remember that I was only the most recent of millions to walk this route, in suffering and in hope.

Twisted to a semi-comfortable position on the sloping earth, spare clothes bundled under my head to make a better pillow, I drifted off to sleep, waking after a couple of hours to the sound of animals around the hut, contentedly grunting and chatting. Boar! Springing to instant awareness, I flung a piece of wire mesh into the doorway, sending the pigs pelting back down into the woods. As I slept, a strong, cold wind had started blowing, whistling in through the gaps in the piled rock walls to snatch my body heat. Lying back down, I laughed at these terrible sleeping conditions, resigned to an awful night's rest, and wry at my own contrariness; that this adventurer's endurance, the peculiar familiarity of lying on bare earth and making the best of it, was what I had been so desperate to exchange for lockdown's lethargy and comfort.

Descending from snow patches in strong winds, through the calmness of beech forest, I walked into my first village of Spain. There was a bar on the outskirts, advertising breakfasts for pilgrims leaving the monastery of Roncesvalles, which provided hundreds of beds at the foot of the mountain pass. Both were closed now, as I'd find along most of the Camino.

I was setting out to walk a route that, for the last few years, had been inundated with walkers. In the high season, it's a huge conveyor belt of people moving across northern Spain, a multimillion-euro income for mostly small local businesses. The only living creature I saw on that first day was a cat padding towards me with a mouthful of mouse, before it jumped away to dine undisturbed.

If it was a normal year, at every turn of the path I would have seen people ahead, padding along under heavy packs, panting, sweating, all of us fixed on the same distant point of Santiago de Compostela, 750km further west. But there was no one there but a cold wind blowing through pilgrim ghosts of past years, past the closed stone houses, the bare fields in winter's fallow sleep. Christmas lights twinkled in doorways, but hardly anyone was walking the streets; I'd come out wandering during a time to be hunkered down inside.

I was a ball of nerves on those first few days, so scared when I walked into my first bar that I forgot how to order coffee. The waitress raised her eyebrows as I sweated and stuttered, leaving me unsure of whether she was surprised by the presence of any pilgrim or merely my own awkwardness. I sat with my coffee and watched the people, masked or not, how they greeted each other, the clear distances between them, how often the waitress cleaned tables. All of it was different to France; there was a great deal more respect paid to Covid precautions here.

People walked their dogs in a quiet village, saying good morning as I sat by the fountain mixing water into breakfast oats and milk powder. Nobody was challenging me, but the guilt and worry hung over me and it came to a head at 2pm on Christmas Eve, sitting on wet moss on the side of a forest track and sobbing over my rucksack.

Pamplona was the problem; a big city that I would arrive into on Christmas Day. I'd imagined I'd spend Christmas walking and camping, a lonely but beautiful experience. But I was almost out of food and had to navigate the shops' holiday closures. Camping on urban edges can sometimes feel desperate, finding yourself a hidden spot in factory wastelands or the grimy litter strewn grasses of the fields beside ring roads. There was a hostel in the city centre for only €15 a night and, in a phone call, I was told there were plenty of vacancies and I could just turn up.

I slept above the Arga river valley that led into the city, wild boar snorting in the nearby hollow and rain pattering on the tent through the night. Only three days of walking after a six-week break meant that my body was not ready for the 18-mile day necessary to reach the city, my body feeling bruised wherever I pressed it, especially in my legs and back.

At about 2pm, I called the hostel again to confirm and had a rude shock. There were no rooms available and I should have reserved; the man had no idea who I'd spoken to the previous day. I put the phone down and burst into tears. It all overwhelmed me: the frustrating second French lockdown, the unwelcome feeling in my lockdown house, the fear of walking into Spain, the question of whether I should walk at all, the Covid contagion risk of staying in a shared hostel, the worry about my budget, nerves about approaching a city on Christmas Eve with nowhere to stay, being alone on Christmas Day, everybody being so worried and stressed, a pandemic that was killing people. I sobbed, big, deep, moaning tears. *This is so difficult. Fuck.*

And when I breathed deeply again and stopped crying, I was still there on the side of a track, my bum getting wet on the damp ground, my food bag still empty and still without a place to sleep that night. I had to fix the immediate problems, had to. There was nobody to save me; I could not wilt under the pressure of my overwhelming misery.

Six hours later, with bruised feet, after a rush through the twilight city suburbs, a desperate flick through the late night corner shop food offerings, and finally a frustrated wrestle with a broken hotel check-in machine, I slumped onto a clean bed with a glass of Bailey's and a takeaway pizza, biscuits, a carton of vegetable soup and another pizza to eat cold the next day. Being comfortable and clean and safe was the best I could hope for and I was grateful for it.

My second solitary Christmas Day was easier to bear. UK lockdowns had started again on 20th December; Boris had indeed cancelled Christmas. We were all suffering and it made my Christmas dinner of cold pizza, eaten alone in a blank, bland hotel room, much less painful.

I set off through the Boxing Day streets of Pamplona, very clearly a pilgrim with my huge rucksack and walking poles, battered boots and muddy leggings.

I hadn't seen a single police officer yet. In France, during the Luchon lockdown, police cars had patrolled the streets and once, as I took my daily stroll, two uniformed officers silently watched the congregation filing into a town centre church. Although the Spanish were taking more Covid precautions and people wore masks at all times, even outdoors, there had been a feeling of being under scrutiny in France that I didn't feel in Spain.

On the way out of Pamplona, people went out of their way to say, 'Buen Camino' – the classic pilgrim salutation, that literally means 'good way' but also says good luck. One woman pulled down her mask to mouth the words, making sure I saw her and received the blessing. These Spaniards saw me, the pilgrim in a pandemic, and they supported my decision. The relief was incredible and I realised just how starved of positivity I was, like a parched traveller drinking from a rare mountain stream.

Coming into Puente La Reina a day later, after camping in a barn, I had a shock when I saw an *albergue*, run by the Priests of the Sacred Heart of Jesus and connected to a seminary. I'd been passing many pilgrim hostels, all closed, chained gates and notices in the windows. This one, though, said 'Open. Call this number.'

I stopped and stared. It was only 4pm and I'd been planning to walk through the town and camp a few kilometres further on. It was only a night past my Christmas rest day, I didn't need a bed but felt drawn to sleep there. Perhaps I could have my first conversation about whether I was doing the right thing.

Fifteen minutes after I called, Juan Carlos arrived to open the door, a stocky round man with a wonderfully bright air about him; he faked a shocked jump against the wall when I told him I'd arrived from Kyiv. I asked how many other pilgrims he'd seen? 'Almost none, but there are others, one or two every fortnight.' Someone had passed through the *albergue* on the 21st of December, six days previously.

I gathered courage to ask, 'What do you think about the people who are walking now?'

'The best,' he replied unexpectedly. 'People who are walking through this awful time, through the pandemic and the winter have the strongest reasons, the deepest connections to their motives, whether it's religious or spiritual or whatever.'

'But what about the pandemic? How do you feel about me walking now?'

'If you wear your mask, use the hand sanitiser and keep your distance, then it's fine with me.' His certainty was reassuring.

He showed me a photograph of a pilgrim who had passed through the *albergue* on the 19th of November and messaged the priest of his arrival in Santiago a month later, having walked through three closed regional borders and the closed city limits of Santiago itself, where nobody was supposed to enter or leave. 'Through and into the city,' he said with a sideways glance to tell me it was possible, '*sin problemas*. If you relax, go calmly, then you'll be fine.'

We giggled together, this priest and I. He sang me an old folk song with my name in it and gifted me a credential – the booklet for me to collect stamps and prove myself a pilgrim. He was exactly the person I needed to meet, to tell me that he didn't judge me, lifting me out of the deep rut of self-condemnation.

Heading south-west towards La Rioja, I walked through growing numbers of vines and olive groves. I sat in a café in the town of Los Arcos, having slept with my tent tied to an olive tree to keep it unbroken during the winds that battered the fields day and night.

The café was like many in Spain: a thin room with a long bar, a line of seating on the opposite wall, very compressed. Usually people would stand companionably clustered at the bar, eating *pinchos* (morsels of food: small sandwiches or plates of olives, anchovies, tortilla, potato salad or fried meat). Now, with no standing at the bar allowed, a supposed restriction to 30% of usual capacity (although I had not seen that in any bar I'd entered, nor had I seen it policed).

A very frail looking old man came in, blotched skin that made me think he was around 80, mask floating over his nose. He stopped at the entrance to sanitise his hands, fumbling at the dispenser. Two younger guys entered just after him, mid 20s. They had their masks on properly but didn't sanitise their hands. They sat for coffee and the old man bought a loaf of bread before leaving again. Once we were sitting at our tables, we were all allowed to remove our masks and breathe unrestricted into the unventilated room. The boys left, giving good wishes to the owner, telling her to 'take care'. And this was where my doubt came in: the vulnerable old man doing his best to stay safe and any other person might be carrying the infection that could kill him, myself included. Despite all the time I spent alone, walking solitary stone paths and seeing nobody, I was still part of the risk, going into a new bar almost every day. I had to take responsibility for being here and all the justifications, calculations and mental gymnastics I made could not nullify that entirely.

A large part of the stress of my Covid experience was the social and legal pressure to follow all these quickly invented, wildly varying rules and some of my mental conflict came from the fact that the rules were so malleable, so clearly manipulated for economic reasons, for public happiness as well as public health. I was always a person who had reacted strongly to the constriction of unfair rules and manipulative pressure used to enforce them, having experienced so much of it as a child.

I arrived at the border between the two regions of Navarra and La Rioja, a line I wasn't supposed to cross. On either side of the line, people were free to move and mingle. They could get together in groups of six, from any household, at bars and restaurants.

They couldn't cross this border. Except they could for work. And emergencies. And for this Christmas and New Year period they were allowed to cross the line to visit family and friends. It was just me that couldn't, who had nobody to visit, who was walking outside all day and sleeping alone, keeping every interaction at a safe distance. Me, who had woken up in a tent that morning, who hadn't hugged anyone since France, who had to clear her throat every time she spoke, after spending hours in silence. I stood on the gravel path, completely alone in the fuzzy green field, a busy road nearby. Me who lived almost completely outdoors. I was not supposed to cross this border, a large stone marking the change from Navarra to La Rioja.

I crossed the border.

In the end, as I walked into La Rioja on New Year's Eve, the reality was a complete anticlimax. I followed the dusty pavement alongside a busy road where cars whooshed unrestricted. There was a huge sign welcoming me to the region, a picture of grapes. Nothing happened, nobody was watching.

I was so unsure that I was doing the right thing, but it felt safe, even if it was technically illegal. I was fed up of everything and just wanted to walk.

As I advanced further into Spain without interrogation, the ethics of my decision retreated back into ethereal abstraction, and along came the wind, days of it, sweeping across the open farmlands and hitting me right in the legs.

Snow arrived, coming down from the Pyrenees and the Picos to ice the lower lands, blowing a fine sugar dusting into the wrinkles of the earth, highlighting the labyrinth curves of ploughed fields, creating mini drifts in the corners of road junctions, where bare seed heads poked through to wave in the wind.

It snowed in fine particles that accumulated like blown grit on my tent sides. I would wake in the night to shake the structure and hear the trickle tinkle of a million flakes rustling off my roof.

Fresh snow lay on bare vineyards, the sprouts of last years' growth trimmed back to leave stumps writhing from the earth like zombie fists, tortured fingers stark against the white blanket.

Getting into the tent was a relief from the wind, plunging into a tingling hollowness of quiet. While the temperatures lay just under freezing, snowy camping wasn't so hard but once nights dropped to below minus 6 or 7c, it became much more difficult. Winter camping requires precision, where tiredness must be put aside and action prioritised. Bare fingers turn numb within minutes, condensation from breath gathers cold on clothing, water bottles freeze, electronics turn off or charge more slowly. My sleeping bag clunked with everything I had to keep warm inside it.

Camping in winter means an eon of time before it will become light again, your part of the Earth is in its deepest lean away from the sun and the sunrise only comes earlier by one minute each day. Night-time is about patience; fourteen hours to lie there in the darkness, in the deep sleeping silence of a hibernating land. Listen to the wind that gently rustles the olive trees, imagine the ripples of the grass. Curl your legs up, shift your hips against the ever-present pain. Wake to the gentle pattering of yet more snowfall, hoping it hasn't blown inside the porch and covered your boots.

The usual pilgrim hostels were rarely open and I camped for a few consecutive nights in the snow, separating the frosty outer layer of my tent each morning to stuff it into the side of my rucksack where it could melt in peace. Taking down the tent was the worst part of getting up; my fingers needed to be in thin gloves for the fastenings and fixings and they inevitably went numb, as did my toes when freshly plunged into ice-cold boots. It took a while of walking before my circulation warmed the extremities again.

It was a shock, one afternoon, as I pulled the tent sausage from the side of my rucksack, to find it was still frozen solid. The cold winds had blown against me all day until my legs were red and tingling, penetrating the layers of insulation with icy needles and tattooing my skin with an Arctic treasure map, only visible to blind, white, marble eyes. My inner furnace was roaring from the exertion but, like an open fire in a grand hall, the heat only reached a few inches. In the shadow of the looming hillside, the blank cold pressed like a flat palm against my face, with the unrelenting sadism of frozen metal.

Storm Filomena hit the country and the whirling skirts of this ice queen flung a swathe of snow across the centre of Spain. I was on the northern edge, arriving in Burgos while snowstorms flicked flurries of small flakes over me. 'Minus 5c' said the display on the roadside monument. Minus 5 at only 2pm. The snow gathered on slippery pavements and I was glad to reach the hotel sanctuary, letting out an appreciative 'ooh' as the bedroom door swung open to reveal the calm white interior, making the owner giggle.

As I rested an extra day in the city, waiting to replace a popped sleeping mat, the snow stopped falling and then froze down hard.

I was shocked at the way people clustered in the city bars, masks around their chins. There were supposed to be 50% capacity limits in place, people weren't supposed to eat or drink while standing at the bar. None of it was being respected and it made my skin crawl, so unused to this 'dangerous proximity'.

Overnight the regional government changed the rules and I was barred from a café on the morning I left the city, my way blocked by the waiter. 'You can't come in, you have to sit outside.'

'¿Since when?'

'Since last night.'

To lose access to warm spaces and phone charging was a particular vulnerability while I had no home, but infection rates had risen dramatically since Christmas and it made sense. Having had time to relax, I felt the tension rising again. When the number of daily infections had quadrupled, surely the government would announce another full lockdown; when that happened, what would I do? Where would I go?

I obsessively checked the news twice a day, on multiple sites. The regional governments were asking for tighter regulations and the national government was resisting. I wondered who paid the bills when the economy went into enforced hibernation.

Castilla y León, the region I was walking through, brought the curfew forward to 8pm. The national government said it was only legislated until 10pm and began a court process to force the regional government to rescind the decision. Governing Spain meant keeping the independent identities of seventeen autonomous communities and two autonomous cities under the umbrella of one country. Allowing individual regions to break centrally enforced rules would be a crack in the force that holds the country together, a weakness that could end with Catalunya or the Basque Country breaking away to declare themselves a sovereign nation.

A few miles out of the city, I came towards someone pulling a trolley loaded with a rucksack and the obvious round disc of a popup tent. Another pilgrim? Another pilgrim! I was overjoyed at the chance to talk to someone. We overlapped a couple of times and finally sat for a smoke and a chat on a village bench. Neil had walked from Luxembourg pulling a small trolley behind him that contained 35kg of his possessions. He'd been laid off from his bar job in October when, unable to weather the repeated Covid closures, the bar shut for good. 'I couldn't stay at home with nothing to do. I'm

28 and I've worked since I was 16. It's now or never. I'll never get this chance to go travelling again.' So with his mum's help he had packed 10kg of rice, a kilo of tobacco, fifty disposable masks and set off to walk to Portugal. He'd given his phone away, carried a small plastic clock to tell the time and a laptop for occasional internet connection. I admired his bravery; even my nomadic life felt very safe in comparison, with my few thousand pounds of savings and my small monthly income. He had truly thrown himself open to the road and its winding ways, bouncing from gift to gift, trusting he would be safe.

It was only a little further out of the village before we camped up. Neil had walked 37km that day, from the other side of Burgos and was tired. He built a small fire from wet wood which took a long time to catch, and we messed around feeding it with damp scraps of dead weeds, intermittently eating and chatting about camping styles, comparing maps or knives or favourite foods. He'd found Spain much friendlier than France, as I had. Back there the police had kicked his tent in the night and told him he couldn't stay.

I wondered if this pandemic would create more space for adventures; if people who had lost jobs would go and follow opportunity, pursuing a parallel experience, unseen on hypercritical social media, disappearing into their personal wildernesses.

We squatted over the fire, agreeing how nice it was to have company, and a woman came along with her dog, exclaimed how cold it was for camping, and asked if we needed anything. I was the Spanish speaker, not Neil, and followed my usual instinct to say, 'No, thanks, we're happy and have everything that we need.'

I realised that Neil might have given a different answer and asked him what he says in these situations. 'Water, then I just take whatever they offer.' When she came back and asked again, I said yes this time, and she disappeared back to the village, returning past sunset with bottles of water plus a thermos of hot water, teabags, sugar and biscuits. It was a lovely caring gesture and we exchanged some kind words.

'When you ask for water, people always give you something extra,' said Neil.

Perhaps I'm too proud, too rigidly self-sufficient, too ashamed to allow myself to be so conspicuously in need. There's something impressive about the trust implicit in opening yourself to absolute vulnerability, so close to having nothing.

It was a very cold night, minus 8c, and in the morning the sun rose unseen behind a thick mist. Water coated us in frost, each spiky teasel, each bulrush head. Neil had got up at dawn, too cold to keep sleeping in his inadequate kit and had paced the length of the camp, waiting for the light.

I lent him a pair of gloves and thought I'd see him further on but his trolley was slower than me and once we got off the road and up to a countryside track, I must have completely outpaced him. The snow had drifted across the vehicle-gouged path between fields, and then frozen hard. I could awkwardly crunch across it, sometimes resorting to the soft ploughed earth when it got too much but I imagined how he'd struggle with his unwieldy luggage.

Following Burgos on the Camino de Santiago comes the famed *meseta*, the section of trials, where in the summer the flat open farmland offers high heat and almost no shade. Small villages nestle in billows, church spires peeking up, and pilgrims must walk for hours in the beating sun, through golden seas of waving wheat. It's talked about as the place of suffering, and the place of questioning.

For me it was a place of mist and mystery. The hoar frost didn't melt but thickened each night until every twig, every branch, every blade of grass was encrusted in feathery crystals that would shatter at the slightest vibration but, in the still mist, coated every growing thing in an inch-thick armour of delicate spikes. I spent days shrouded in frozen fog, unable to see more than 100 metres on all sides. Unless I was able to distract myself into daydreams, I'd suffer the infinity of a hundred minutes of the same view. Ploughed fields were swallowed in white, undergrowth loomed, indistinct. The track became a travelator, scrolling underneath me without any sense of progress. I walked from tree to tree, with no perspective; as one disappeared behind me, the identical tree would appear again from the mist ahead.

The frost added personality; it gave trees hairstyles and weeds a coat of armour. Hoar frost grows when the air is cold but wet, and condensation freezes on everything it touches. Every loose waving thread on my jacket became white, my breath froze on my hat, my shoelaces became coated.

After six days of walking and sleeping in the mist and frost, I reached Moratinos and the house of Rebekah and Patrick. I'd contacted Rebekah to ask if we could meet for a socially distanced chat about pilgrimage and to my surprise, she'd invited me to stay. Rebakah was an American journalist who first came to the Camino on a press junket promotional tour, in the Holy Year of 1993 when modern Camino popularity was just beginning. By the time she walked it in 2001, it had already changed, but was still inviting enough for her and her husband to emigrate a few years later and become immersed in hostel volunteering and Camino service.

In 1992, less than 10,000 pilgrims walked.

In 2001, 61,418 pilgrims walked.

2010 was the last Jacobean Holy Year, celebrated every time Saint James's Day falls on a Sunday and a special door in the cathedral is opened. Walking through it grants plenary indulgence (forgiveness of sins) and that year 272,412 pilgrims walked. That dropped to approx 180,000 in 2011 and then climbed steadily over the last decade until, in 2019, 347,578 pilgrims walked.

The supporting businesses have grown alongside the pilgrim numbers; every farming village has an *albergue* or two, restaurants, cafés, bag transfer services. In the height of summer you can expect hundreds of people arriving each night, all in need of rest and nutrition. Popularity has changed the Camino, as has modern capitalism and expectations of luxury.

I asked Rebekah whether the Camino had reached saturation. 'This year was going to be the test.' 2021 was the first Holy Year since 2010 and they were expecting the highest number of pilgrims in modern times, stretching what the Camino infrastructure could withstand, in terms of sewage systems, food provision, numbers of available beds. Instead the pandemic had closed borders and shuttered businesses.

Rebekah helps run a *donativo albergue* and spoke of her worries about the lack of space for those who walk without money. In the circular relationship between increasing standards and increasing expectations, where first hot water becomes standard, then comfortable beds, then private rooms rather than fifty squeaking bunkbeds in a barely heated dorm. The older hostels, which have provided only basic facilities in return for donations, could no longer survive without major investment.

Where *donativo albergues* exist, they offer a space of kindness and generosity, making it possible for the poor to walk, for the lost or disadvantaged who inevitably form a percentage of pilgrims to actually survive on the Camino.

Is the suffering that could arguably be called a necessary ingredient in the transformational potential of pilgrimage still present when each weathered traveller has not only daily hot showers and a bed but a little light to read by, a curtain to pull for privacy, Wi-Fi everywhere and shiny clean surfaces, the security of an online reservation ready for them at the end of every day?

Rebekah said suffering was seen as an outdated concept of Catholic Christianity, but to her, the suffering of the Camino, the struggle with challenge, is an essential tool for learning. When your life is so comfortable you don't need to think or question, there's no need to invite change.

She reassured me when I asked about whether the Camino was irrevocably changed, its essence become mythologised. 'You can't destroy the Camino and it will outlast this era of popularity.'

The struggle of walking 500 miles cannot be entirely ameliorated by hot showers and soft beds. Attempting a long journey on foot presents an immutable challenge and so the raw essence of pilgrimage, the possibility for spiritual transcendence and transformation, whether Christian God related or otherwise, will continue to exist, even if, in the 21st century, it has become tame, smothered under a weighted blanket of guidebooks, online reservations and baggage transfers.

There's a thousand years gone into the spirit of this path and it will continue to exist, no matter how many adverts line the way. Millions of footsteps have made this route what it is: a ribbon of hopes pressed into the ground, which cannot be dissolved.

'I love hosting pilgrims,' said Rebekah, as I made excited squeaks at the offer of roast chicken. 'They're always so thankful for the bare minimum.'

An unexpected benefit of meeting her, apart from the chance to discuss the intangible ideals of pilgrimage, was being connected into a web of helpers.

As we discussed the recent increase in infections and my worry of being caught in another lockdown with nowhere to go, Rebekah kindly made me a list of people who might help in an emergency and sent them an introductory email. Rebekah and Patrick welcomed pilgrims into their home unofficially, as a place where people could sleep without paying. They were the third option in the village, after two larger *albergues*, and so they received the overflow, those who might ask for grace at the other two doors and be turned away. She was used to telling her contacts further along the route to look out for a particular pilgrim in need.

She spoke clearly, 'I think you should go until you are stopped,' and told me how the police had treated pilgrims throughout the pandemic year. In March 2020 as Spain fully locked down, hundreds of confused, frightened pilgrims had to stop their pilgrimage and be repatriated, some spending weeks trapped in *albergues* waiting for repeatedly cancelled flights. Then came the numbers who returned in the summer as soon as they were able and through into the winter, defying the regional closures, pilgrims in decreasing numbers but still a trickle. It was luck really, whether I'd be stopped from continuing. 'The police don't want the bother, they're much more likely to take you to the edge of their jurisdiction, get you out of their hair.'

I said goodbye to Patrick and the cats, who were draped silently around the room – one had purred contentedly on my lap for a few hours – and we walked out of the village together towards the west, their three rescue dogs running ahead, an extra one tagging along for the fun.

We knocked elbows as a farewell salute then exchanged the warmth of smiling eyes, which can reach where touch is forbidden. I was just another pilgrim in the stories of thousands that she holds, but she gave to me as she does to all who need it, and I turned away reinvigorated, bolstered by the protection of the human web ahead.

The next day, the temperature climbed just a few degrees, the mist dissolved into a clear blue sky and the frost could no longer sustain its structure. Within hours, the imposing magnificence slid from the branches, reduced to small heaps of white on the newly revealed ground.

SPAIN: THE ARRIVAL AND THE FIRST ENDING

Covid infections were skyrocketing across the country. I thought I'd only stop for full lockdowns but it seemed the national government was reluctant to actually impose them. Galicia, my next region, only a week ahead, mandated the closure of bars, hotels and restaurants, but without the legal capacity to keep humans inside they could only request their residents to stay at home. If I continued on regardless, I would face nothing but closed doors, but I didn't want to wash up in Finisterre like flotsam, scared, unrested, unwashed, ungrounded.

Turning to Rebekah's list of helpful people, Ponferrada seemed like a good point to pause, a large town about four days' walk ahead, only 50km before the Galician border. Their severe closure was only supposed to be for three weeks; maybe I could wait that out and reassess.

I sat in a small picnic spot by the side of the path, a cluster of trees shading several benches, and made the call. The sky was blue that day and I could see the mountains; after all the flat land of central León, the barrier wall ahead came as a surprise, snow patches tracing the dips of the highest points. The Ponferrada hostel said yes, I just had to walk another four days to get there.

Before Ponferrada came Astorga, where people were incredibly nice to me. I walked into the pilgrim hostel and was treated in awe by the *hospitalero*. 'You've walked from where?'

Alberto was spending three months volunteering, most of it with absolutely nothing to do. 'It's the end of January and you are the third pilgrim this whole month.' Normally a mountain guide, he hadn't worked since 2019. He gave up his rented flat in Seville, bought a live-in van and arrived as a volunteer with a free bed and a small stipend for food. Spanish government provision for self-employed people in the pandemic was shockingly bad – they received 70% of minimum wage for four months of 2020, and then nothing until February 2021. We laughed together, morosely, at the sense of, 'Well, there's nothing else to do, no money to be earned, everything is awful, no point in going home to stew, might as well walk, or volunteer.'

When I told him that I lived on donations to get me through this journey, he got out his wallet and gave me €10. I wanted to cry. I didn't know what to say. How could I deserve such generosity and gentleness? Just because I decided to give up comfort and security in pursuit of a barely attainable goal?

I was brought to tears again the next morning; Alfredo gave me directions to a café called Sonrisas (Smiles) and it lived up to its name when the two friendly women with brightly dyed hair exclaimed over a pilgrim turning up. 'I've missed you all,' said the owner, and she came out to take a photo of my rucksack as I sat peacefully in the narrow street, watching a scatter of pigeons circle the main square. I told her I'd walked from Kyiv, we chatted a little and, as I turned to leave, a few people started to clap and cheer. I cried at having my effort appreciated; it was a time when I often felt like an outcast, slinking on the edge of society, possessed of a strange obsession.

It was twelve months since the pandemic began and I had woken up in the Italian forest, suddenly more vulnerable. During the tumultuous year that followed, I had spent six months on lockdown; stuck in place and waiting for freedom.

I was never far from tears in that time. The difficulties of the journey filled me, as did its glory. When you are stretched so thin, it doesn't take much more emotion to bring a hot flood of tears. I was full of misery and satisfaction, of throbbing feet and blue sky, flowers and loneliness equally. I was both terrible and brilliant all at once.

Along a long, straight road climbing gently towards the mountain wall, a man called out. 'Hey, are you a pilgrim? Where are you going to stop tonight?'

'Between Rabanal and Foncebadón.'

'I have a friend in Foncebadón. Do you want to stay there?'

The friend was an Italian man who owned a pizzeria up in the once abandoned village, now half rebuilt and revitalised by the pilgrim trade. I imagined a few beers in front of an open fire. It fired me up to push on that day, all the way up to Foncebadón, almost to the top of the mountain pass. I loved this entry into hills again, such entertainment for my eyes after the few weeks of flat land and mist. I tickled my vision with the pleasure of mountains, of forest, of scrub; this was home territory again.

It was past sunset and into darkness by the time I entered Foncebadón, carcasses of collapsed houses lining the main street, before a central cluster of refurbished buildings. I knocked and waited at the pizzeria, then called a number written on a piece of slate. A man came down to the street, wrapped and muffled against the cold wind. We didn't talk much – he led me around a building, through a ruin, between some caravans and to a low shed with a heavy wooden door. Inside were a couple of beds piled with blankets of uncertain age and filthiness, a cracked stove which had blown ash across the floor and a pile of sticks in the corner. It was not exactly what I was expecting but the forecast predicted wind and rain coming in around midnight and I was really glad to have shelter.

My feet throbbed; I'd walked a few big days in a row, and pulses in the big toe joints shot bright violent flashes of pain up my legs throughout the night. I was too tired to eat and ended up spooning a tin of peas directly into my mouth, smearing peanut butter onto thin slices of dried meat, needing to ingest nutrition in whatever form I could.

It rained heavily through the night, winds gusting against the cabin roof, and the morning sky was a whirl of grey clouds, with a shimmering veil of rain falling between me and the faraway sunrise. I packed up and closed the cabin door behind me, grateful for this strange bed and the generosity that delivered me there. As I walked up and out of the village, past the remains of a church tower, the raindrops started to hurt and I realised they had turned to ice. White gusts of hail showered onto the mountain; one minute I had a view, the next it was gone, rubbed out. I suited up properly, gloves on, hood up, and set out to cross the mountain into the El Bierzo region where the city of Ponferrada awaited.

Before then came the Cruz de Ferro – an iron cross set high in a heap of rocks – it was the highest point of the French route, 50m higher than my snowy Pyrenees crossing. It's a pilgrim tradition to leave a stone here in symbolic spiritual renewal, calling it the laying down of a burden. Another tradition of unknown origin, maybe fifty years old, maybe five hundred, in a place where traditions are hallowed as a way for pilgrims to belong.

The Camino de Santiago is very neatly parcelled, in the way of a tale told many times over. 'Here is where you will suffer.' 'Here is where you will experience enlightenment.' 'Here is where you will lay your burdens down.' Squeezing a set of enlightening experiences into a mere month of walking feels like too short a time to me, seeing as my own learning has come so gradually through years of walking and suffering.

The Camino is a church-sanctioned break from ordinary life which will allow you to return neatly, with barely a ripple in the pattern, back to work, back to family, back to familiarity. For those whose idea of suffering and edgy living is sleeping on bunkbeds in a shared dormitory for a month; it's escape for beginners.

But that's not very generous of me, is it, and perhaps I should learn to be more humble. That's my own personal failing, ever since I was the clever one in primary school. Part of the judgemental pilgrim hierarchy is believing that you're the best because you've walked the furthest and carried your own bag. Perhaps I had to walk further than everyone else because I have so much more to learn.

For most people who would not dream of packing up their possessions and setting out to cross a continent on foot, this was the closest they came to the edge of a normal life's rhythm, where they could step out of their usual pattern and look back to see it from a fresh perspective.

So I thought to myself: *Go on then, play the game. It's all prescribed here. Believe in this power of transformation, on the path where so many millions of questing footsteps have trodden, layering the energy of centuries of prayer, hope, generosity and belief.*

I'd picked a stone off the path, a pretty piece of pink quartz. I wanted to join in, to be part of this pilgrimage. I wanted to stop being alone, I wanted to learn how to stop excluding myself.

As I approached the cross, it was snowing again. There was a huge car park on the other side of the road, a picnic area, a small chapel, and it was all deserted in the January mist.

It was a pretty underwhelming place to be honest, just a little metal cross on the top of a tall, thin pole, like someone drunk climbed up a BT telephone pole and stuck it there for a joke. It sat on a weird heap of earth, just all kind of plonked there for no apparent reason.

Join in though, Ursula, access the power of this. It only exists because people believe in it so that's all you have to do too. So I got out the piece of quartz and held it in my hand and thought about what I needed to leave there. The rock in my hand became a piece of me, a little lump of ego, my value, and as I felt it hard and warm in my fist, it was as if a corresponding hollow in my chest became filled.

I got a flash of vision that showed me clearly just how much I am harming myself by not believing I am a worthy person, just how badly I think of myself and how awful and artificial that is. How can I hold so much compassion for others and none for myself?

The introspection didn't last long though, there was walking to do. Over the lip of the hill and as I headed downwards on the long curving road towards Molinaseca, I had to keep my head bowed and stay moving; as the snow blew steadily into my face, it was too cold and miserable to stop for long.

A car stopped and a woman called out, friendly. It was Kim, one of the nice people from Rebekah's list, she'd been waiting to meet me but I'd passed her village on my way to the shed in Foncebadón. She wanted to give me a lift off the mountain but I couldn't accept that kind of help and we agreed to meet once I was settled in Ponferrada.

There was an entire welcome committee down at the Ponferrada *albergue*, a few locals and a few retired Americans, all dedicated to helping the Camino. Bodies kept appearing and introducing themselves – Spanish Rafael, American Cathy, Priest Miguel Angel, who had given the ultimate permission for me to stay there until Galicia opened doors again. They weren't expecting pilgrims, but had posted a number on the door for anyone who happened to turn up. I felt nervous about asking for so much and not going home. Would they judge me? Would they turn me away? No, they brought me orange juice, a bag of books, a roast chicken and a spare pair of leggings.

Back in southern Romania, in the early spring sunshine, I

remember walking past a roadside rubbish dump festering with stinking heaps of food, nappies, garden clippings and torn plastic. There were a few dogs there, slinking shadows of animals, mostly disappearing quickly out of arm's reach. One waited for me, lips shrinking back to bare teeth as it contorted its body to present its tail. A bony young thing, I could feel every lump of its spine underneath the scruffy wild fur. There were enough scraps there to maintain plenty of animals but this one was ill, probably covered in parasites inside and out. I felt its desperation, the need to capitulate to me, a bigger beast of great strength. I stroked it a little, but really didn't want to touch this dog too much, covered in garbage dirt, grease and goo. It didn't beg or follow me when I walked away, just turned away lethargically, a sick, unlucky animal that had run out of hope that life could be different.

Some of the way I felt in Ponferrada reminded me of that cringing cur. Part of me felt worn out and thin and insufficient, desperate to be held and loved.

I tried to stammer out my reasons for walking, to explain why I couldn't go home and there was no point in doing that anyway – I'd be returning to a Wales in lockdown, with no house and no job.

'Relax,' says Rennie.

'This is your home for as long as you need it,' says Rafael.

Perhaps because I struggle with self-worth, I didn't fully comprehend the acceptance of pilgrims and their varied, sometimes unexpected behaviour, by those who support the Camino. Perhaps because I had only been a walker, not a helper, I could not understand what it is to receive so many people in their time of need and for it not to be necessary to know or understand their drive, only respect that it exists. The people of the Camino understand the quest. I didn't have to justify my need to receive help. I was worthy of it simply by existing.

I settled into a routine of good food and daily yoga, trying to stave off the inevitable depression that came from having nothing to do for an entire month, rattling around in a cold, empty building designed to house one hundred pilgrims.

Kim came to visit, a gentle benevolent soul, and we talked about the Camino, the different senses of pilgrimage.

I needed to listen to these people who knew so much more of compassion than me, who had seen so many pilgrims pass in all their many manifestations – who know that there are those who leave the shower dirty and those who clean up after others, and are able to hold a welcome for each of those people, every arrival.

Kim was getting ready to change her focus again; she had walked, she had helped others and now another change was coming, to retreat to a mountain village away from the Camino. Our urges don't have to stay the same, do they? We are not fixed beings, and letting go of one form of what we thought our life was is not failure. I could feel it coming for myself – the end of this walk might not be followed by the immediate urge to find another journey. I'd been itinerant for thirteen years and this journey was close to breaking me. I hadn't felt so vulnerable since my cancer.

I was less than 200 miles from the Atlantic Ocean, hanging onto the journey by a thread. I wanted the comfort of staying still and equally couldn't bear it. I knew that I was incredibly strong and incredibly weak. I wanted this journey to last forever, I wanted to reach home; the place I both longed for and was scared of reaching. The end of change and the beginning of it.

As Galicia reopened, I was free again after a month's pause and hopped over a mountain border, finding myself in a lush green paradise. Cows grazed underneath the tall towers of concrete that held up the motorway in the sky. Down on the rural roads, older cars puttered and ancient tractors trundled, dust speckled, driven by wrinkled faces benign behind masks.

The villages here were old farming places, half broken down and derelict, mostly populated by slow-moving, squat figures, grandparents all, wrapped in the fashions of their forefathers, aprons and crocs, corduroy trousers or thick blue overalls. I saw washing flapping on wooden balconies that I would not expect to hold weight. I saw two cows driven home at lunchtime, udders swinging awkwardly between their legs like overstuffed shopping bags, a woman with a thin switch, barking at their slow-moving backsides. It reminded me of Ukraine's small farming structure, pensioners growing food because they can't otherwise afford to eat. There was a market one morning in Melide, and at the edges, beyond the big tables vibrant with varieties direct from the wholesalers, were smaller offerings, where people with white hair unpacked bags of greens, spring onions, walnuts, white beans. A man sold eggs from his car boot. Individual smallholders bringing their cornucopia of small wares to market was another thing I hadn't seen in a long while west.

Occasionally I heard people of the small towns calling out in amazement. '¡Mira! ¡Peregrina!' (Look! A pilgrim!) It felt as if I was the first returning swallow of the year, a heralding of seasonal change. Imagine a life filled with a string of passersby until suddenly the path is empty, like a noise you've tuned out until your ears pop in the silence and you realise it's disappeared. Looking up the road expecting movement but it's just the birds in the trees. I was the first sign of beginning again, the dripping of the thaw, tap-tap-tapping along the road.

The flowers were coming out. Tiny daffodils waved at the sides of the path, triumphant trumpets calling out to me, singing the tune of growth, of new hope, of warmth and light to come. The birds were jubilant, shouting excitedly in the rush to partner up. I wonder how their bodies feel, what gives them these urges, the itch to mate, females in need of eggs, their bodies ready to become heavy, searching for a way but not even knowing it, wanting that swelling, comfortable weight.

Eventually I met the eucalyptus plantations, a cash crop valued for their paper pulp, the long, white trunks so impossibly tall I had to lean back to look at the tops where the leaves washed against the sky. There are few branches on a eucalyptus, it sheds them as it grows, the bark too, which hangs and sways in long strips, curled like cinnamon quills. The smell was rich and comforting, coming from the leaves which littered the path, seeds scattered like a spilt button box to roll underfoot.

Galicia could feel faintly hostile sometimes. I had the unsettling sensation of residents peering at me from windows, stepping back out of view when I looked up. I wondered how it is to live with so many visitors streaming past your front door, a flow of hundreds every single day of the summer. I wondered how many photos were taken of the 'quaint peasants' against their will; standing at their front door, which is also the front door of their forefathers, daydreaming for a peaceful moment before going to see to the pigs was intruded upon by the pilgrim paparazzi.

One day I walked a winding road through a damp valley. A cluster of buildings either side of the path seemed to be two great farms, each with stained and crumbling outbuildings. A row of towering plants stood in the garden, *grelos*, something like spring greens, where people pick the leaves as the trunk grows, leaving a tall thick stem with a bunch of leaves at the top. They were in every vegetable patch; to be eaten in Galician stew, a warming mixture of greens, potatoes and white beans, historic poverty food. The cobbled road went over a small bridge then narrowed and twisted between the buildings of the second farm, a wooden balcony hanging over the road and water dribbling over the stones, green and slimy.

The next building was a chapel; low white plaster and stone, a single wooden door with a rusted lock, spun further shut with cobweb lacing, only a small, barred window open to the inside. I walked up to the dark opening, where the light dimly filtered in. There was a tableau inside, carved figures looking down into the room, chipped and disfigured by the passage of two hundred years. The altar was a rabble of fallen vases and desiccated flower stems, burnt out candles grey with decades of dust.

In Galicia, all the layers of life upon life are still visible, the dust of generations lies thickly in every corner.

After a glorious fortnight of springtime walking, I reached Santiago, the long-fabled religious destination where I could get my sins forgiven. Millions of people have trekked here during a span of a thousand years, in two epochs of high popularity, the Middle Ages and the last thirty years. In each era pilgrims arrivals have numbered in the hundreds of thousands, annually.

I had seen other pilgrims in Galicia, even overlapped with some for a few days, but I was walking into the city alone. You don't actually see the city from afar, there's a hill in the way – Monte de Gozo, 7km from the cathedral and lapped at by the outstretched waves of city development. I ascended in countryside and, at the peak, found a huge development of low cabins; pilgrim accommodation for thousands, overlooking the city sprawl and the tiny cathedral spires showing in the centre.

I imagined people everywhere, sitting on the battlements of stone block benches that lined the pavement, drinking water, restless, waiting for a friend, tying shoelaces. Someone has forgotten the socks they put to dry at the foot of the bed last night and they're debating whether to go back for them and risk missing the midday pilgrim mass.

I imagined them singing, jubilant, a parade of excited people in various stages of footsore exhaustion from fresh blisters to inflamed joints, all gripped by this wave of movement, buoyed up, babbling, bringing each other along, moving through the city, choking the pavements, waving at buses, pointing at pigeons, until they reached the huge cathedral square of Plaza del Obradoiro and fanned out into the melee, to plonk bags down, check plasters, hug, shout, take pictures, see people they lost along the way, jostle through crowds for more hugs, more pictures, tears of joy. That's it, they're there, they did it. And more come in and more come in and more come in.

But I was walking alone into the almost empty square, the only pilgrim in an acreage of flat grey stone. It felt horribly normal, just like walking into any other city.

I felt the absence of other pilgrims very deeply. There was a faint sense of madness in the fact that I had battled so hard to get there, when the world had been kept at home. For what? For what? Faith that exists alone, without the corroboration of others, is delusion, isn't it?

Then it was to the cathedral, the gigantic building that the city clusters around in a maze of thin paved streets, arches, pillars and corridors, ornate fountains and unexpected flower gardens.

It was a sobering moment to walk into the gigantic, echoing building and turn to face the full, long, stately view down the entire length of the aisle to the golden glory of the altar, that inner sanctum, covered in symbols that transmitted the story of the higher power.

I thought of the medieval pilgrims for whom God was absolute and unquestionable. The power of this golden altar, these unimaginable riches thundered the statement that the glory of heaven is here: this is the portal. Oversized cherubs, bigger than basketball players, held up the gleaming ceiling. Imagine all the journeys the medieval pilgrims made, without guidebooks, showers, Gore-Tex or baggage-carrying service, to sit dazed, stupefied, exalted in front of the representation of heaven that their efforts had secured their own access to.

It was only at the pilgrim office that a wave of emotion overwhelmed me, waiting to get my Compostela certificate behind a pilgrim couple I'd met a few days previously. I paced back and forth trying to hold it in, until Luis put his arm around me and I sobbed into his chest. I didn't know what emotion was filling me, only that I could hold no more, that I wanted to collapse under all this. It was the proving of it, I think, to stand in front of an official record keeper and say, 'I arrived here from Kyiv.' I was part of this history now, I had joined this pilgrim community. I who was so often alone, who had always been faintly awkward in groups, who had a problem with unquestioning obedience to authority.

The woman behind the counter quelled my tears by being brutally literal, as she had to. I passed over the credential, thinly filled with irregularly accessed stamps, about one per week. I only got it in Puente La Reina, a day's walk after Pamplona. 'So you started in Puente La Reina?'

'Yes,' I said glumly, knowing that I didn't have substantial proof of anything else (the church does not accept an Instagram feed as evidence; it's dated stamps from official bodies marked on approved paper, or nothing).

'She started in Kyiv!' Luis tried for me.

She ignored the interjection and filled out my official pilgrim record, rightly so as unverified hearsay is fake news and will not grant you forgiveness of sins. According to the pilgrim office, on this pilgrimage, in this year, I will forever have started in Puente La Reina, 330 miles away.

I spent another couple of days in the city, enjoying wandering through the winding streets that I knew would be choked with tourists at any other time. There were innumerable souvenir shops, pilgrim symbology running riot now the triumphant finishers could splurge on all the heavy presents they'd craved while travelling light. Yellow arrows, shells, km markers, cathedral towers, boots. The buildings were fronted with stone archways where pedestrians can walk and merchants can display wares with greater protection from the rain that falls here a full 50% of the year. The city is designed for it, with sloping, well-paved streets and gurgling drains. Water seemed to disappear invisibly, never leaving more than glistening grey stone.

All the grace and elegance of the city was revealed in the lack of tourist crowds; tables and chairs set out in the street, under carved archways or near to little flower gardens deliberately planted with blooms that smell strongly after rain, tulips, hyacinths, snap dragons. It's an ordinary place, not conspicuously fashionable, where students are free to find their favourite cafés and sit for hours, while the elders read newspapers in different corners. I had hated to arrive as a solitary pilgrim, but loved to experience a silent Santiago.

Eventually it was time to leave; I had another four days to walk, aiming for another ending. I heard the sharp klaxon shrieks of seagulls in Santiago, simultaneously so familiar and so strange, a foretelling of how close I was to the end of the land. Finisterre, so named by the Romans, with its own, pre-Christian pilgrimage tradition, where a peninsula pokes out and flops south, surrounded by sea on three sides. It was the last point to see the sunset, the place where I could walk no further west.

Everything felt normal for a few days; the rain clouds that had glistened the grey stone streets of Santiago receded and I walked in warmth and easy times. Relaxed hills and plenty of open fields and forests for me to camp in. The route was more remote, minimal villages and fewer bars or *albergues*, everything closed outside the small towns. I even struggled to find water and had to ration it a little, in a throwback to good times in the Balkans.

I was scared of how I might feel, or might not. 'Will I cry?' I said to my sister on the phone. 'I feel like I'm going to collapse. But what if I can't let go when it comes to it? What if it doesn't come out?' This was such a pinnacle of the journey – I had been headed west for more than two years, an arrow flying in the direction of the Atlantic Ocean, always walking into the sunset.

I came to a hill far away from Finisterre, where for the first time I saw the peninsula sticking out into the ocean, and nothing but blue water beyond. The town itself covers the lowest part of the land, where the curve of the inner bay straightens out into the peninsula, just before the rise of rock that forms the cape. It looked like a hippo, a large lump of land for the body and then a smaller one to make the head, the lighthouse buildings at the end forming a prickle of ears.

I made a bed against the concrete wall of a closed *albergue*, and watched the wind blowing the trees in the nearby woods, trying to think about the importance of this moment, but mostly just drifting with tiredness and unable to concentrate.

After a 6-mile walk around the final bay, I arrived in Finisterre, where I had a reservation in one of the few open hotels. Stopping on a street corner to check directions, I realised I was standing opposite the municipal *albergue*, which had the door ajar. When I poked my head inside, there was a nice lady called Begonia who was overjoyed to see a pilgrim. The *albergue* was closed but she asked if I wanted a certificate. 'Really? But I don't have any stamps, all the *albergues* were closed and I've camped all the way here from Santiago.'

'You're here, aren't you? Of course I'll give you a certificate.'

I started crying and she clucked at me from behind the counter, sorry she couldn't give me a hug. She sat in front of a heavy pilgrim register, a sticker marking the line where the 2021 arrivals began, less than twenty names ahead of mine. Begonia told me that the last pilgrim had arrived at the beginning of March when normally there'd be a dozen or so each day. He'd walked from the Czech Republic with his dog. 'Now, where did you start walking?'

'From Kyiv,' I replied, with tears streaming down my face.

'Ah, only the crazy ones are walking now,' said Begonia, which made me laugh. It was true, no matter how much I wished it wasn't.

We took a couple of photos together, exchanged a hug with our eyes alone and I walked to the hotel, a little dazed, clutching my Finisterre Camino certificate. There were a couple more miles out to the tip of the peninsula and I dumped my rucksack in the room, only bringing a few goodies with me to the next end point of my journey.

A long road trailed along the spit of land and when I reached its tip, the view opened out. Suddenly there it was, open water on all sides of me, wide and infinite. I was here, I'd made it, I could walk no further west. A painful swell of tears rose to stop my breath, then fell away inside me, unbreached, like a nascent wave far out from shore.

With steep cliffs on all sides of the lighthouse, I climbed carefully onto the west-facing rocks and sat down to arrange myself. I popped the cork and poured Cava and peach juice into my silicone dinner bowl, sipping a cheap Bellini from my makeshift cup.

The nerves, the anticipation, were gone. I was there now, with the sea. It was a clear blue day and the setting sun gilded a golden path across the water. I was calm, the waves of emotion had stopped crashing and instead I sailed there, high above the water; I breathed slowly in and out and I was at peace.

All that way, all that way.

From Kyiv to Finisterre, Dnieper to Atlantic, east to west, Slavic to Latin, colonised to colonisers.

Through mountains and snow, ferns and forests, rain and drought.

The apples in Ukraine, the snow in Romania, the butterflies in Serbia, the bullet holes in Bosnia, the herons in Italy. Salamanders, tortoises, bears, jackals, boar, deer. Woodpeckers, curlews, nightingales, vultures.

It had been years now, years of this. Of sleeping in unlikely places, of incredibly dirty clothes, of muscles worked to concrete solidity, of joint aches and insect bites and sunburn and chapped skin.

Of always getting up again, of always trudging on, no matter how slowly; of never giving up.

What could possibly be a good enough reason to do this?

Was it really just that I had a fun idea and decided to stick with it?

Perhaps I didn't need a reason why. Perhaps this is just how I have decided to exist in this life and that decision is enough.

I had walked here alone but that was illusory. I was never separate from the air, I had brought the forests with me, I was the wind and the birds and the rock. I was Cava, I was peach juice.

I toasted myself, and I toasted the setting sun.

TURNING FOR HOME

Thinking I'd rest for three days in Finisterre, I wound up staying for ten; there's something about the place that sucks you in. It's the end of the Camino, the end of the land; with nowhere further to go, you can stop, drop and rest. I remembered that feeling from eleven years before, when I had passed through here as a wandering hippie, carrying a blue painted suitcase full of jewellery beads. I remember a strange calmness back then, that I didn't understand; going to the beach and seeing rows of people sitting contentedly, staring at the sea. I hadn't walked here then, I didn't understand the release of journey energy that bursts out with the definitive setting down of the bag and how the infinity of the ocean could absorb that energy. It's a hippie kind of place, faintly ragged, with tent communities at the beach that are regularly cleared out by police, a few souvenir shops with screen prints of mermaids and moons on handmade paper, shell and Celtic shaped jewellery.

There are chapel remains at the top of the end point, built against a much older site, the Goddess Cave, a place of pagan worship associated with fertility. I climbed there, sat with my head against the great rock that faces east to Monte Pindo across the bay, and felt the tickle of energy flow into my crown.

Celtic traditions abounded; I went out to celebrate the equinox with an assorted group of open-hearted humans who brought ukuleles, drums and bells to chant and sing and bless the four directions of the wind. There was also a Galician *gaita* – their form of bagpipes. People got up and danced in a light-footed circle, tripping backwards and forwards in a way that felt Irish and Scottish all at once. The echoes of Celtic civilisation on my island were mirrored here a thousand miles away.

The place where people can walk no further west is not always happy. The end of the line means some people land here and have nowhere else to go. If you have to retrace your steps to leave, as soon as you turn around you're facing all you've left behind. Perhaps it's less threatening to stay here, staring out to sea.

During those rest days, as the intensity of my arrival point reduced, I could consider the return journey. Infections were rising sharply in France yet again, with individual regions restricted this time, rather than a full national crackdown. I'd expended so much effort to reach Finisterre that my appetite for further suffering through France was entirely absent. I just wanted to get home and was finally willing to take a shortcut.

I decided to walk slowly towards Santander where I could catch a ferry straight back to the UK, wondering if I'd feel strange about walking in the wrong direction, away from the sunset. The sun had been setting at the same time every day as I walked across Spain, going backwards across the time zone as the days lengthened.

A battalion of pale grey slugs spread out on the wet road as I left Finisterre, like steam ships chuffing out across the open sea.

I had half a day of happy walking through the gentle coconut scent of warm gorse flowers, and then my calf muscles cramped up, leaving the joints and tendons around them screaming in pain, and slowing the following five days to Santiago down to a stumpy struggle. Back at Finisterre, I'd had a few massages in celebration, which brought on some days of deep exhaustion. Trying to relax my body only showed how much I was holding; my soleus muscle was stiff and every day it manifested differently, sometimes pain in the lump of muscle underneath my knee, sometimes in the tendons on the top of my foot, sometimes in the heel. My glutes were impossibly stiff, the pain of rolling from side to side in bed, trying to do yoga in the mornings inside a too small tent.

Now that I can talk about it, it means it's receded, and unfortunately that means I can't remember it properly. That's the saving grace of pain, isn't it, that it dissolves from memory once it's over, the intensity flickering away from neural pathways like a fish escaping grasping fingers, leaving us fools ready to go out into the world and gamble with the possibility of experiencing it all over again.

Pain turned me into a lumbering zombie with wooden legs and stones for feet.

It takes all your focus, when your body feels like a heavy weight that you're dragging around, when your rucksack fuses your shoulder blades together into an awkward block, when there are occasional sharp slashes of sciatic pain through the base of your back. I could lie down for a while, let the rucksack drop with a great sigh, press my back against the grass and feel my spine relax in a gentle breath against the cool ground, but it was never enough. Each break could only ever be a short pause in the onward grind, a small piece of relief in this daily plod. Enough to catch my breath and then resume. I must always resume.

I was holding focus that would not truly release until I reached the top of Great Oak Street, Llanidloes. There was a breath tight in my chest that would not let go.

A year previously, entering the mountains of Serbia, I would have considered this Camino route simple and straightforward. The terrain was easy, the paths were wide and well walked, the weather was fine; there were shops every day or two, I spoke the language, there were no bears in the forest. Yet I felt worn out and hollow, like a rusted climbing frame ready to bend and collapse in a tangle of jagged edges. I was barely interested in the sun shining on a mossy branch, gave the new apple blossoms a cursory glance, blinked at the sunrise and went back to sleep. It felt close enough to the end that I was finally able to make plans for the future, the return home, the time beyond the walk. Once I allowed myself to think of a time when I would not have to make a great physical effort daily, then I started to see how taxing that effort was. The scales were falling from my eyes, the journey was no longer absolute.

I had a day off in an *albergue* in Melide at the point where the Camino Primitivo joins the French route and I would branch off, to walk it in reverse all the way to the sea up at Villaviciosa. The owner gave me a bottle of rosemary-infused alcohol to reduce inflammation and I spent a few hours up in the dormitory, intermittently stretching and massaging my legs. On the way downstairs to return the bottle, instead of hobbling like usual, I felt much lighter, and tried walking normally instead of awkwardly taking the stairs one step at a time. My calves went into spasm. All that good work undone and for the next few days I could feel the cramp hovering there, a faint puckering and pulsing, like the beginning of a sneeze.

***

I met David and Celia, hosts of the Albergue de Bodenaya, a well-known *donativo* hostel since 2005. They offered an evening meal, showers, laundry, a bed, and breakfast, all with a genuinely warm welcome and no expectation of renumeration. There was a box high up on the wall marked 'donations' and they weren't paying attention to whether people put anything into it.

We ate and laughed together; it was easy with them, they were full of warmth and happiness and ready to share it with each new arrival. I arrived incredibly tired after a mere 8 miles of walking, ready to fall asleep at three in the afternoon.

It's easy to be happy in Spanish, the rhythm of the language creates lightness and energy. The tone of the exclamations change, they come more often, are more excited, more agreeable. I lost my voice in all the talking, feeling myself growing hoarse with so many more words than usual.

'You don't seem very motivated,' said Celia.

'I'm not, really. It's the end of the journey. It all feels very mundane.' I managed to turn it into a joke. 'Just another day at the office.'

She was shocked into laughing again when I couldn't remember what I did the previous day – I had no imprint of the sights she was so familiar with. Being used to pilgrims who are full of the energy and exhilaration of an unusual journey, for whom every coincidence is a sign of the magic of the universe, every flower exclaimed over, every view entrancing, every joke hilarious, I must have looked like a morose lump in comparison, head down, uninterested in life, the donkey plodding along at the end of the circus parade.

'You're not living in the present moment,' chided David gently the next morning, as I readied myself to leave.

'Yes,' I sighed, 'I'm so tired I'm only half here, half of me is looking ahead, anticipating the end of the journey. I'll have to come back again another time for a different Camino experience.'

'No, just change how you experience the Camino now.' He laughed at me, and I smirked ruefully, as the realisation of my lack of mindfulness had lasted mere seconds before I was thinking of future Caminos, jumping ahead again to anywhere but here.

To avoid a heavy rainstorm, I took a sneaky two days of rest in Oviedo, walking into streets of grimy apartment blocks overshadowing the tarmac, Spanish lives lived crammed on top of one another. Ordinary anonymous city life took over, people hidden beneath overcoats and umbrellas, stepping quickly between lines of traffic; a shared room in the cheapest hostel in the city gave me a view of twenty apartment windows, washing lines clinging to the dirty walls under each one and rats running in the alleyway down below.

Something in my energy changed when I left the city. I'd arrived feeling achy and tired after a 13-mile day, sharp pain shooting from the bones of my ankles and calves down into my feet, yet on the day I left, I walked 15 miles without feeling too bad. And the next day, and the day after that.

In fact, I walked 15 miles for six days in a row, something I hadn't managed since the *meseta*. It felt good to be powerful. I still had all the same aches in all the same places but they were no longer overwhelming and I didn't feel drained anymore, overcome by pain and wilting by 3pm.

The coastal route wasn't actually all that coastal. There was a lot of inland walking, a mile or two away from the beaches, swooping in and out of sea views. The mountains were close to the coast there, sometimes a towering wall of rock fuzzed with forest, climbing 1,000m, a mere 4 miles from sea level and sometimes a faraway lick of snow on jagged peaks, hovering in the distance like a mirage over the hazy humidity of lemon and orange trees in well-kept gardens, palm fronds waving. The motorway ran in this space too, built up on high concrete pillars. I swung from apple orchards deep below the rumbling road, quiet places where farmers come to trim the grass beneath the trees but otherwise let the cider crop grow in peace, up to windy hill tops, and bridges across the motorway. There was lots of tarmac on this route so I put music on, a rare treat saved for when I had many road miles ahead of me, and needed to pick up my rhythm, legs working and muscles pumping. The reaction to the music is stronger when you hardly ever hear it, and I felt like a mighty beast, an unstoppable force.

I had a schedule ahead of me; a countdown to the ferry, a countdown to release from quarantine and then a countdown to the end of the journey.

Individual days mattered little, I just wanted to get to Santander and rest. I ate bananas for breakfast, I bought more again. I stopped in the evening and spooned the usual camping mush of tuna, peas and potato into my stomach. I slept on a concrete porch outside the Chapel of Welcome, I slept beside a river with curious cows on the opposite bank and I slept in *albergues* with uncomfortable plastic mattresses to guard against bedbugs.

Each day felt like just another stretch of steps before I could collapse, sleep, and wake up to do it all again, groaning as I stretched my calves and felt that familiar yawn of a solid, deep ache. I was 95% of the way through this walk and had no room for new memories.

In what I hoped would be the final pandemic twist to this curly journey, my ferry ticket was cancelled when I was less than a week away from Santander – 'Foot passengers not accepted' – leaving me potentially stranded in Spain for at least another four weeks. For twenty-four hours I walked with no plan for what I'd do in Santander. Get a plane? A bus? Wait for them to allow foot passengers again? Try and hitch-hike onto the boat?

It wasn't just the immediate problem of how to get to the UK, it was the finish line date I'd set for myself, the friends who had it in their diaries, the people who were coming out to walk with me as I passed through their towns. If I delayed one thing, all the other dates would fall like dominoes.

I knew there was nothing I could do, so I tried not to worry about it, just plug in music and keep on walking. I felt like a bear, stomping along the side of the road.

Solve the problems when you get to Santander, I thought to myself, *you've got enough on your plate, there's no need to focus on it now*, trying not to check my phone too often for nonexistent solutions.

But in came a message from a friend. They were travelling home from Portugal and had a space in their van, did I want to come with them? YEAH! And four days before my original ticket, meaning less time to rest in Santander but more time to complete the final distance in the UK. We spent an hour messaging and then I waited nervously for them to confirm I was on their ticket. We did it. Problem solved, leaving me trembling and emotional. Yet another hurdle, yet another trap that I'd dealt with, through patience, steadfastness ... and a whole lot of help from other people.

Shaky, with the end of the day approaching, I needed to find a bed quickly, and when I saw an empty shed above the road, perfectly hidden from passing traffic, I thought I'd hit the jackpot. But as I climbed the bank I saw a younger guy sitting under the porch roof, bike leaning against the padlocked door and pannier possessions scattered around. After a moment of hesitation he invited me to join him and we settled down for the night. His name was Jakob, but he introduced himself as Kuba. Only 20, and taking his 'first big travel' as he called it, before he returned to Poland for a second try at university. He'd quit a philosophy degree, thinking he could learn it from books while he got a job, but soon realised that work takes all your time and energy, and he'd never have a better chance to study than before adult life sucked him in completely.

There's something particularly exciting to meet another true voyager, not just in a hostel or bar but really out in the wild, free. We were two tramps making easy connections between their equally unconstrained lives. He cooked eggs on his little campfire, boiling extra for the following days as the pleasant smell of eucalyptus smoke washed over me. He tended his fire and I stretched, teaching him a few words of Spanish as I did so, both of us laughing at his mistakes.

His face brightened when I said I had bananas, he had Nutella, and we made chocolate and peanut butter soup as the grand finale of the evening, loosening it with a little water then scooping the bananas through it, hunched over, heads together, eating straight from the tiny saucepan.

Being a philosophy student meant we'd plunged into the wide-ranging issues of life but I struggled to answer any of his personal questions – it all felt too big to explain.

As a child in primary school, I remember sitting on the floor as we were told about Tiddalik the frog, the Aboriginal creation story where he drank all the water in the world and had to be induced to laugh and pour it all out from his mouth so the other animals could drink again. I remember the storyteller miming a frog full of water, swaying their body in a waterbed motion and I felt the same; full of memories, bulging and wobbling with them and if someone asked me to truly unburden myself, I would word vomit all over them, in a splashing uncontained mess.

I held my arms open to mime for Kuba the amount of time I'd walked then pinched my fingers together to show how much of the journey was left. But the problem was that everything felt present, I was holding all of it at once, and I couldn't begin to process it until this journey was finally over.

I felt like an onion chopped in half, oozing pain, very aware of all the layers of this experience. I was returning after almost three years away, blowing the dust off valued friendships, finding a home again, preparing to re-enter the routines of living with no idea whether I'd find them comforting or asphyxiating. I wasn't planning another journey but I didn't know if I had what it took to stay in one place. I was sad and lonely and tired and happy and satisfied and proud of myself for what I'd achieved. I was incredibly strong and I was at the end of my reserves.

'Are you happy?' he asked me, and I didn't know what to say. Happiness is the last five minutes as much as the last fifty years; informed by both the stone in my shoe and the chocolate soup, just as much as my lack of partner and children, or climate anxiety and rampant cold-hearted capitalism. I was feeling more weary than happy, but I also knew that I would look back at all of this as one of the most wonderful things I'd ever done.

I had known loneliness during this journey like never before in my life. I had thirsted for connection like cupped hands under a dry tap, desperate for drips of comfort. Equally, I had seen how I created my own separateness in the way I broke eye contact, in the way I shielded myself from imagined rejections, in the ways I did not believe I was worthy. I was utterly alone and I didn't know how to stop. I didn't know how to create a life that included intimate relationships but I had finally understood that if I wanted to find happiness, I had to open myself to the possibility of hurt.

I mulled over how to say that to Kuba.

'I'm not sure if I'm happy, but I'm the best version of myself I've ever been.'

We talked into the darkness, feeding twigs to the fire until the metal holder was full of glowing embers.

In the morning I left early, said goodbye as the sun was rising. I was just a few days' walk from Santander and eager to push those final miles out. 'That was a really nice night,' said Kuba, sitting up, tousle headed, when I gently called his name.

'Yeah, it was. Enjoy yourself,' I said, and we gently smiled at each other, turning away in different directions.

The end of my journey and the beginning of his. The night the novice met the sage.

THE FINAL STRETCH

Standing at the back of the boat, chimneys streaming merrily above me, wind whipping hair into my face, there was nothing behind me but sea, a churned white path fading away into a blue horizon.

I finished the walk as an illegal overstayer. Brexit was done; past the broken deadlines, the extensions, the squabbles and the vitriol, Britain had left and I was no longer a valid citizen of the EU.

I was crossing the water back to Britain, my lonely island that doesn't know how to make friends, the bully child that doesn't play nice, stuck in the power struggle politics of its forefathers. It seemed like my country had had a horrible pandemic as I read the UK news from abroad, masked only by the quick adoption of the Covid vaccine, which meant that politicians could now spread the word about what a success it had all been and put the lies, corruption, delayed lockdowns and inadequate border closures, and hundreds of thousands of deaths behind them.

Before I could walk out of Portsmouth, I had to endure quarantine; my final movement restriction of the journey. I waited for five nervous days, fretting at the schedule of test dates and postage times. I had paid extra for fast-tracked Covid tests and an early quarantine release, as if money was security against this illness.

No rest could be adequate until this was over. Every abrupt stop-start affected my walking energy, and losing rhythm then having to gain it back again was hard on me every time. My body seized up, becoming intensely painful as I started walking from Portsmouth.

I saw the shock on my first hosts' faces after they'd picked me up on a roundabout and I struggled to get out of the car at their house, shuffling and wincing. It was my Achilles tendons that day, spikes of pain exploding from the back of my ankles. Then overnight in their comfy bed, thoughtfully provided with hot water bottles and a bath, pain bunched at the base of my back and a sharp spike hammered underneath my shoulder blade. I couldn't twist, I couldn't bend, I couldn't reach for my breakfast.

My stretches were ineffectual; I was a block of wood, wire wrapped, there was no releasing this rigidity. All I could do was jerkily heave my pack up onto my shoulders, buckle in and stump away like an awkward troll.

Less than 200 miles to go.

***

I had picked the most direct walking route between Portsmouth and Llanidloes, like a mole wriggling and scraping, on winding footpaths that took me through ancient forest, past Wolf Hall, to the source of the Thames and across the Severn.

I couldn't get over how English everything felt. The red brick, the thatched cottages, the village halls, Victoria sponge in the tearooms, muddy paths. Lots of things felt weird for a second and then totally normal. Plastic money. Salad cream.

My body pain incrementally eased into movement and I could walk, stiffly but steadily. 17 miles, 15 miles, 16 miles, day after day. The finish date was decided and I must reach it.

The woodlands were wonderful to walk into, a deep feeling of familiarity and comfort. The smell of the hedgerows, a blue haze of bluebells, wild garlic in the woods.

There were mice and buzzards and pheasants and badger setts. I saw two foxes slinking, a deer bounced away into the centre of a yellow rapeseed field, stopping with only a V of twitching ears in sight, turning this way and that.

One night, I camped on the edge of a bluebell wood, careful not to crush any plants. There were shotgun cartridges scattered around and deer barking nearby, providing percussion for a song thrush lullaby. I should have heeded the cartridges as along came a gamekeeper at 8am to tell me to move on. He wasn't mean or aggressive, he just very clearly stated that I should leave immediately and should never come back. It was very far from the cup of tea and nice chat I'd experienced when discovered camping in other countries. I know we're a densely packed island, but returning to the culture of aggressively protecting and policing private land was very off-putting. I saw more 'private, keep out' signs in a single day than I would have done in any given week before re-entering the UK. Add in neighbourhood watch and huge amounts of surveillance cameras, and, well, no wonder British people say sorry all the time. We're not relaxed.

Away from humans, the land cradled me and I slipped into Britain's nature like a favourite old jumper, swaying with tired happiness.

I was feeling really exhausted now, after almost two weeks of daily UK mileage; stuck in a general haze of grogginess when I woke up, no matter how much sleep I'd managed.

My adventure buddy Hannah came to walk alongside me for the final four days, a great burst of positive support.

Close to the end, we settled down for the night behind a disused chapel; the sunset was glistening through a meadow full of floating seeds and we were content after a happy busy day, having crossed over Radnor Forest, the hill behind New Radnor where I was granted my first sight of Wales laid out ahead.

Unfortunately I didn't sleep all that well; it was a cold damp night and the hollow in the grass that I thought would cradle me ended up giving me backache. I was achy and bleary in the morning; Hannah too.

'You're really hardcore,' she said, out of nowhere.

'In what way?'

'Well, here we are, tired and damp and not slept enough, long intense day yesterday, feeling a bit slow and unwilling to get up, but you're going to get up and you're going to walk some more and that's what you've been doing this whole time, keeping yourself going for thousands of miles.'

And that's it, I thought, that's what the core of this challenge has all been about. Never giving up. I had been at this for over two and a half years, there was nothing left of me but force.

I felt as if I was in another realm to most other people I met in those final weeks, peering from beyond a haze of exhaustion, in constant pain. I was entirely focused on achieving this, brute stubborn willpower the only thing driving me on.

I was both a jerking, wide-eyed marionette and my own puppeteer. Compelling myself forward on stiff legs, rolling over as if all one piece, animated by my own tenacity.

The final day arrived. 10 more miles and it would be over. Hannah and I ate breakfast on the bench near the chapel at Bwlch-y-Sarnau and slowly friends gathered. A happy group of fourteen turned up for the final day's walk, with more trickling in to join as we got closer to Llanidloes.

I felt like anything could happen at the final celebration, this huge climax to my journey. I might break down, start speaking in tongues. We circled around the edge of the town, coming underneath the market hall so I could have the finale I'd been imagining for months; to walk up the main street of the town and finish outside the arts centre.

I started hyperventilating, bent over, suddenly shaking.

The emotion took me over and I became a vibrating whoosh of celebration, aflame.

All of the journey was there with me, all the force of will, all the effort, all the sacrifice.

A great roar came from my very depths. A roar that contained all I had achieved, all I had endured, and all it had cost me.

I did it. I had finished.

I had walked across Europe.

I was home.

I walked the length of Great Oak Street towards a cheering crowd.

JOURNEY END

I look around at a living room full of boxes.

It's a year later. I have spent twelve months moving from temporary home to temporary home, spending four seasons with a sequence of kind friends who opened their spare corners for me to creep in and shelter.

First a shed, surrounded by birdsong and swaying leaves, with enough space for a bed and a small gas cooker where I could make herbal teas and sit in the doorway dreaming, watching the evolution of the buff-tip moth caterpillars steadfastly munching their way up and down each branch of a young oak tree outside my door.

I crept from a shed, to an annex, to a converted chicken barn; generous friends helping me from their settled largesse.

I needed these places as shelter, as sanctuary, as retreat and healing. Somewhere I could shut the door and sleep, knowing I would not have to leave imminently. But they were always temporary, unheated, uninsured, too damp, there were other guests coming. There was always a reason I had to move on, until now.

I have been offered a whole house to myself, the owner living abroad. I am going to pay rent for the first time in eight years. I am going to have my name on a council tax bill for the first time in nineteen years. I am going to stop being a voter 'of no fixed abode'.

There is a feeling of calm in this place. The sliding doors open onto a green riot of unkempt garden. There are fully grown house plants, carefully collected vintage furniture. The light shines across a wooden floor. This empty house is peaceful; soft carpet under my feet when I go upstairs into sun-warmed rooms that look out over fields.

Downstairs the living room is cluttered, full of dozens of boxes, suitcases, trunks. I brought my walking supply dump from my friend's art room, where I was sending kit and souvenirs back and requesting fresh kit regularly. I pulled the big container from deep in the back of another friend's barn, taped up and full of treasure. I went to my mum's attic and did a full excavation.

For the first time in twenty-three years, since I left home at 19, I have all my possessions together in one place, in a house that I have the keys to, that is mine for the foreseeable future.

After twenty-three fragmented years, it's time to coalesce.

It was time to open boxes. I picked them at random, the contents long forgotten. A bulbous congregation of newspaper-wrapped lumps were revealed to be the vase my great aunt bought me the year she took me to Glyndebourne, the fishbowl goblet I stole from a TGI Fridays on a work night out, and the mug a friend painted in celebration of my Welsh walk. I unearth layers of life; the telegram my grandparents sent me for my fifth birthday, a yellowed sheet of dot matrix printed paper, hand-delivered, stacked with the Rainbow Brite and My Little Pony cards, tender wishes from aunties for my eighth, tenth, twelfth birthdays. A sequence of carefully folded notes from school friends that have been squirrelled away for so long they've ossified into significant historical documents, the bones at the centre of my sense of self.

It's cringeworthy and it's hard, looking back at all the messy unformed past versions of me; the bleak memories of growing up in a household full of fear and sadness and anger come flooding to the fore. I must face again all the fiery impulses of a wild, unhappy teenage girlhood that led to so many painful mistakes.

I, who have deliberately unplaced myself time and time again, removed my supporting structures and identities to go out into the world and meet my truest, most vulnerable self, am returning to belonging. Each placing of an ornament upon a shelf is a return, a covering, a defining decoration.

I left behind labels, rejected definitions. Failure, mean, bad, selfish, ugly, manipulative, bossy. I packed those words into boxes and went away, fully and completely into the unknown where I could explore myself without the old boundaries imposed by others, without fear of running onto the hidden sharp spikes of parental judgement.

Walking across Europe stretched me beyond breaking and I arrived home stressed, injured and in pain. I was mentally and physically exhausted beyond anything I had ever experienced but also more certain of myself, bolstered with the knowledge of my achievement.

Walking calms me. It shows me my strengths and weaknesses, it shows me who I am. When I become exhausted and vulnerable, I'm the one who has to recognise my boundaries and then defend them. I have taken myself to my edges so I can look back and see my whole self. I am a stronger person for this journey.

But the deep vulnerability of homelessness during a pandemic, on top of the battle to complete a gigantic endurance challenge, took me far beyond any level of intensity that I would ever choose to experience again.

Finding a permanent home feels healing; after so much wild transience, the time has come to coalesce, to re-inhabit all my selves, all my history and all that I am.

This isn't a completed story, there is no happy ending. I haven't ended up with all I could ever want in life, like a happy, pretty, protected princess. But finally, in my 40s, I have learnt to identify and reject what doesn't work for me, to be more at peace with who I am, in heartfelt integrity.

It is time for a new era, a different type of test. It is time to take root.

ABOUT HONNO

Honno Welsh Women's Press was set up in 1986 by a group of women who felt strongly that women in Wales needed wider opportunities to see their writing in print and to become involved in the publishing process. Our aim is to develop the writing talents of women in Wales, give them new and exciting opportunities to see their work published and often to give them their first 'break' as a writer.

Honno is registered as a community co-operative. Any profit that Honno makes is invested in the publishing programme. Women from Wales and around the world have expressed their support for Honno. Each supporter has a vote at the Annual General Meeting. For more information and to buy our publications, please visit our website www.honno.co.uk or email us on post@honno.co.uk.

Honno
D41, Hugh Owen Building,
Aberystwyth University,
Aberystwyth,
Ceredigion,
SY23 3DY.

We are very grateful for the support of all our Honno Friends.